Hamlin Garland:
A Bibliography, with a
Checklist of Unpublished
Letters

Hamlin Garland:
A Bibliography, with a
Checklist of Unpublished
Letters

Keith Newlin

The Whitston Publishing Company
Troy, New York
1998

Table of Contents

Hamlin Garland, about 1900.
Courtesy Walter Havighurst Special Collections, Miami University.

Introduction

Hamlin Garland has long been praised for his relentless campaign to foster a distinctively American literature through the realistic depiction of the middle west in the stories gathered into *Main-Travelled Roads* (1891) and *Prairie Folks* (1893). He began his career in 1885 as an earnest and somewhat dilettantish poet, book reviewer, and essay writer; by 1891 he had matured into a compelling fiction writer. Five decades later, he published his last book, a curious work of psychic investigation entitled *The Mystery of the Buried Crosses* (1939), in which he sought to record the voices of spirits in an effort to prove the continued survival of the soul. In the years between Garland amassed an impressive and varied publication record of some 53 books and pamphlets, as well as hundreds of stories, essays, poems, and other ephemera of the professional writer. During a long and active life (1860-1940), Garland was intimately involved with the major literary, social, and artistic movements in American culture, responding as a zealous reformer to issues that still engage us today, such as agrarian populism, the inequities of the tax system, a concern for the preservation of the land, and the necessity for a more humane treatment of Native Americans. Pulitzer prize-winning author, proponent of local-color, regionalism, and realism in literature, unabashed advocate of literary and cultural elitism, dabbler in research on psychic phenomena: Garland's interests encompass nearly all aspects of American literary culture.

Scholars have been unable to adequately measure Garland's literary career because no complete list of his works existed. To aid investigation of Garland's publications and his rich correspondence, herewith is a bibliography of his published writings as well as a checklist of his unpublished letters, which I prepared in conjunction with the *Selected Letters of Hamlin Gar-*

land, co-edited with Joseph B. McCullough, and which is forth-
coming from the University of Nebraska Press.

Bibliography

To aid in gauging the shape of his career, Garland's publications are listed in chronological order. Section A records his
book and pamphlet publications; only those reprintings which
alter the original through revision, change of publisher or pagi-
nation, or through the addition or deletion of illustrations are
included. I have provided a list of contents for collections of fiction, poetry, and essays. Section B lists Garland's extensive contributions to periodicals, his many forewords to books, and essays included in various collections. During the 1890s Garland
offered an array of articles and stories to newspaper syndicates; in
some cases manuscript records indicate only the syndicate and
date; in other cases I have been able to provide a citation to a spe-
cific newspaper. Items which Garland later reprinted in book
form (many times under a new title) are cross-referenced by title
and year, but I have not included subsequent reprintings of fiction or poems in anthologies edited by others after his death.
Finally, section C notes articles about Garland which quote him
extensively and verbatim.

Checklist of Letters

On 31 August 1939 a disconsolate Hamlin Garland wrote
to Van Wyck Brooks, proposing to burn all his papers. "I have
gone beyond any illusions about my career," he noted. "Few are
interested in me now and no one will be interested in me to-
morrow" (U Penn). Fortunately for scholars, Garland did not
burn his papers, and a magnificent collection of them exists at
the Doheny Library of the University of Southern California.
But scholars have been hampered in their efforts to explore Garland's prolific and varied correspondence because of the diffi-
culty of locating and reading his letters, which amount to more
than 5,342 in number and are scattered in some 88 locations.
Garland was a prolific correspondent who made a habit of seek-

ing out and corresponding with the leading cultural figures of his day; his letters to these people have therefore been preserved with their papers in various archives throughout the country.

Scope

The form of this checklist reflects its initial purpose: to identify, date, locate, and select from all of Garland's letters those to be included in the *Selected Letters*. Accordingly, while most of the items listed here include a very brief annotation about content, not every letter is annotated, and in the interests of space annotation is limited by the amount that can fit on a line. A letter generally is not annotated if its content is similar to that of other letters to the recipient (e.g., letters to lecture agents William C. Glass and James B. Pond are typically about arranging speaking engagements), or if its content is trivial (e.g., arranging a dinner party). Virtually all letters to "significant" correspondents, however, have been individually annotated.

The sheer number of Garland's correspondents and variety of his interests make any assurance of a complete list impossible, and letters continue to turn up. For example, in 1995 Miami University (Oxford, Ohio) acquired the papers of Eldon Hill, Garland's first biographer, which included some 220 letters not previously available to researchers. While I have visited the major archives in search of Garland's letters, for other archives I have relied upon the helpful and courteous assistance of manuscript curators to supply me with copies of letters in their holdings. Depending upon the indexing method used, some letters may have escaped their awareness. Nevertheless, despite this caveat, this inventory of 4,370 letters (out of a total of 5,342) will enable researchers to locate Garland's letters and glean a thumbnail description of their contents.

For two libraries, this list is selective. Of the 688 letters held by the Huntington Library, the vast majority are to members of Garland's immediate family and concern personal matters, and most are dated only by the day of the week. Listing every letter would therefore offer comparative little useful information. This inventory does, however, list some 169 of the more interesting letters, including all letters to non-family members. The American Academy and National Institute of

Arts and Letters holds some 515 letters, most concerning Academy business. As a sampling this list includes 58 from their collection.

Principal Locations

The largest single collection of Garland's letters is at the Doheny Library. Some 8,500 letters deposited there consist of letters Garland received from almost 3,000 correspondents. An additional 1,587 are by Garland, most drafts or carbon copies, addressed to some 650 correspondents. Approximately 350 of this latter group are originals. Significant clusters of letters include those to members of the Vitagraph film company (James Blackton, Jasper Brady, William Wolbert); to his family—his parents, Richard and Isabelle, his wife, Zulime, his daughters, Mary Isabel and Constance, and his brother, Franklin; to his brother-in-law Lorado Taft; and to his friends Alexander G. Beaman, Henry B. Fuller, Hermann Hagedorn, Katherine Herne, Vachel Lindsay, and Augustus Thomas. Others are to various publishers (George Acklom, George Brett, Frederick Duneka, Henry Hoyns, Harold Latham, John Macrae, Edward Marsh). A finding aid to the entire Garland collection (which lists correspondence alphabetically) has been published as *Hamlin Garland: Centennial Tributes and a Checklist of the Hamlin Garland Papers in the University of Southern California Library*, compiled by Lloyd A. Arvidson, *USC Library Bulletin* No. 9 (Los Angeles: University of Southern California Press, 1962).

The Henry E. Huntington Library, San Marino, California, holds approximately 688 letters, most of which are undated and are directed to Garland's wife, Zulime, and to his daughters, Mary Isabel Johnson Lord and Constance Harper Doyle. These letters chiefly concern his lecture trips, his visits to England and Europe in 1924 and 1925, business matters, and a large number are devoted to his activities concerning *The Mystery of the Buried Crosses*.

Garland's correspondence with his *Century* publishers is located at the New York Public Library. About 300 letters are addressed to Richard Watson Gilder, Robert Underwood Johnson, Albert Shaw, Robert Sterling Yard, *New York Times* editor John H. Finley, and others. The Butler Library of Columbia University holds 238 letters addressed principally to Brander Matthews, Paul Revere Reynolds, Edmund Clarence Stedman and Arthur Stedman. Of the 511 letters housed in the archives of the National Institute and the American Academy of Art and Letters, the majority are about Academy business; a smaller portion concerns the composition of his literary logbooks.

Miami University, in Oxford, Ohio, holds some 365 letters, including 168 to Garland's first biographer, Eldon Hill, and clusters of others to the playwright Augustus Thomas, to Johnson Brigham, the editor of *Midland Monthly*, and to Albert Bigelow Paine, John Bradley, and Carl Van Doren. In addition, the library has a microfilm of about 100 letters to John H. Finley held at the New York Public Library. Alderman Library of the University of Virginia houses some 146 letters, 57 of which are addressed to William G. Chapman, the president of the International Press Bureau. The Library of Congress holds 138 letters to William Allen White, Theodore Roosevelt, Walt Whitman, Horace Traubel, and additional letters to others. Garland's correspondence with George Steele Seymour and Flora Warren Seymour, who formed the Bookfellows, amounts to 197 letters at the Seymour Library, Knox College, in Galesburg, Illinois.

Smaller collections include 77 letters at Harvard's Houghton Library, addressed to William Dean Howells, Mildred Howells, Amy Lowell, Walter Hines Page, and William R. Thayer, among others. Yale's Beinecke Library has 71 letters addressed to various correspondents, among them Wilbur Cross, Herbert Stone, Thomas Lounsberry, and William Lyon Phelps. The Van Pelt Library at the University of Pennsylvania holds 40 letters to Van Wyck Brooks, and 12 others to Theodore Dreiser and Arthur Hobson Quinn, among others. Indiana University's Lilly Library has 65 letters, 36 of them to James Whitcomb Riley and 4 to Upton Sinclair. The Newberry Library holds 56 letters to 16 correspondents, among them Henry B. Fuller, Alice French, and Herbert Stone. 30 letters to Stuart Pratt Sherman are at the University of Illinois Library; 28 to the poet Edwin Markham are held at the Horrmann Library of Wagner College, Staten Island; and 46 letters to Fred Lewis Pattee are at the Pattee Library, Pennsylvania State University. Finally, the following libraries have microfilmed their collections of Garland's letters: Doheny Library (University of Southern California), the New York Public Library, Butler Library (Columbia), Alderman Library (Virginia), and the Lilly Library (Indiana).

All bibliographers are greatly indebted to those who have scoured libraries and archives before them, and I am especially pleased to acknowledge the efforts of Donald Pizer, whose pioneering "Hamlin Garland: A Bibliography of Newspaper and Periodical Publications (1885-1895)" (*Bulletin of Bibliography* 22 [1957]: 41-44), provided the genesis for Garland's pre-1896 works and who kindly granted permission to incorporate his work into this bibliography. Garland's post-1895 works originally appeared, in somewhat different form, as "Hamlin Garland: A Bibliography (1896-1940)" (*Bulletin of Bibliography* 54 [1997]: 11-20), and I am grateful to the *Bulletin* for allowing me to include both bibliographies here. No work of bibliography is ever complete; scholars combing old newspapers continue to unearth Garland's syndicated work. I am particularly indebted to Gary Scharnhorst, who alerted me to several unknown newspaper items; to Charles Johanningsmeier, for his assistance in verifying Garland's syndicated publications; and to Joseph B. McCullough, for his aid in the original compilation of the checklist of letters. Finally, I would like to thank Madeleine Bombeld, Mary Corcoran, Louise Jackson, and Sophie Williams of Randall Library, University of North Carolina at Wilmington, for their cheerful help in discovering and acquiring copies of Garland's work. And to Robin, Michael, and Sarah Holowaty—Thanks, once more, for your patience and support.

Chronology

1860   Hannibal Hamlin Garland born, 14 September, near West Salem, Wisconsin.

1881   Graduates from Cedar Valley Seminary in Osage, Iowa.

1881-83   Travels and takes odd jobs; takes trip to the East with his brother, Franklin; returns to the West, where he takes up a claim in McPherson County, South Dakota.

1884   Goes to Boston in October; immerses himself in the study of literature, Charles Darwin, Herbert Spencer, and John Fiske; reads Henry George's *Progress and Poverty*.

1885   Begins teaching in Moses True Brown's Boston School of Oratory. "Ten Years Dead," his first published story, appears in *Every Other Saturday*.

1886-88   Writes to E. W. Howe, George Washington Cable, Walt Whitman, William Dean Howells, and James Whitcomb Riley and forms his understanding of "realism." Meets Howells in mid-1887, Riley in late 1887. Makes an extended visit West in 1887 and again in 1888 to gather material for fiction.

1889   Submits first stories to the *Century* in September; meets James A. Herne and begins campaign for realism in drama.

1891   *Main-Travelled Roads* published. Meets Stephen Crane; campaigns in Iowa for the Farmers' Alliance. With Herne, Garland forms the Boston Independent Theater Association.

1892   Publishes *Jason Edwards, A Member of the Third House, A Little Norsk*. Teaches at the Seaside Assembly, Avon by the Sea, New Jersey; campaigns in Iowa for the People's Party; visits Colorado and the West Coast.

1893   Delivers a paper at the World's Columbian Exposition on "Local Color in Fiction." Buys a home in West Salem, Wisconsin, variously referred to as the "Homestead" and "Mapleshade," and moves his parents to it. Moves to New York City in the fall to live with his brother. *Prairie Songs* (poetry) and *Prairie Folks* (fiction) are published.

1894   Settles in Chicago (474 Elm Street), making periodic lecture trips to the Eastern, Southern, and Western United States. *Crumbling Idols* published. Meets Henry B. Fuller, who becomes a close friend.

1895   *Rose of Dutcher's Coolly* published; travels to Colorado and New Mexico with Chicago artists Charles Francis Browne and Hermon Atkins MacNeil, gathering material on American Indians.

1897   Takes a trip through the West, living on several Indian reservations. Joins the Players Club (New York).

1898   Returns to Washington, D.C., to complete Ulysses S. Grant biography; leaves for a trip to the Alaskan gold fields. Becomes a charter member of the National Institute of Arts and Letters. Publishes *Ulysses S. Grant: His Life and Character*.

1899   Takes first trip to England. Marries Zulime Taft, 18 November.

1901   Becomes involved in agitation for Indian rights. *Her Mountain Lover* published.

1902   *The Captain of the Gray-Horse Troop* published.

1903   Mary Isabel Garland born, 15 July. *Hesper* published.

1906   Takes second trip to England.

1907   Constance Garland born, 18 June. Forms the Cliff-Dwellers, a Chicago literary club modeled after the Players Club and named for the novel by Fuller. Moves to 6427 Greenwood Avenue, Chicago.

1909   *Miller of Boscobel*, Garland's first performed play, is presented in Wisconsin and Chicago. 10-volume "Sunset Edition" issued by Harpers.

1910   *Cavanagh, Forest Ranger* published.

1911   Becomes Secretary of the Chicago Theater Society.

1912   The Garland Homestead, in West Salem, Wisconsin, burns.

1913   Organizes a Chicago meeting of the National Institute of Arts and Letters.

1914   Serializes "A Son of the Middle Border" in *Collier's*.
1916   Vitagraph Studios begins filming four of Garland's novels. Buys a summer cottage in Tannersville, New York, "Camp Neshonoc." Moves to 71 E. 92nd Street, New York City, to be closer to his publishers and literary life.
1917   Organizes a dinner to commemorate Howells's 80th birthday on 21 March. Goes to Battle Creek Sanitarium in April for treatment of sciatica. Attempts to get women elected into the National Institute. *A Son of the Middle Border* published.
1918   Elected to the American Academy of Arts and Letters. Becomes a member of the Century Club. Begins service on Pulitzer Prize juries.
1919   Theodore Roosevelt dies, 6 January. Begins work for the Roosevelt Memorial Association.
1920   William Dean Howells dies, 11 May.
1921   Chair of Pulitzer Prize juries for both the novel and the drama. *A Daughter of the Middle Border* published.
1922   12-volume "Border Edition" issued by Harpers. Receives Pulitzer Prize for *Daughter*. Takes family to England for six weeks.
1923   *The Book of the American Indian* published. Agitates for a more active role for the American Academy.
1924   Spends summer alone in England. Meets Edith Wharton.
1925   Begins correspondence with Van Wyck Brooks. Moves to 507 Cathedral Parkway, New York. Buys a summer house in the club community of Onteora, New York, "Grey Ledge."
1926   Mary Isabel Garland marries Hardesty Johnson, a singer. Presents the American Academy's Howells Medal for Fiction to Mary Wilkins Freeman. *Trail-Makers of the Middle Border* published.
1927   Constance Garland marries Joseph Harper, of the publishing firm.
1928   *Back-Trailers from the Middle Border* published.
1929   Begins an annual "Award for Good Diction on the Radio," sponsored by the American Academy. Moves to Hollywood, California, in August. Henry B. Fuller dies, 28 July.

1930   *Roadside Meetings* published. Begins to sell his collection of autographed books. Builds a house at 2045 DeMille Drive, Hollywood.

1931   *Companions on the Trail* published. Receives the Roosevelt Memorial Medal of Honor.

1932   *My Friendly Contemporaries* published.

1934   *Afternoon Neighbors* published.

1936   *Forty Years of Psychic Research* published. An exhibit of Garland's books, manuscripts, and memorabilia begins a four-year tour. Lorado Taft dies, 30 October. Zulime becomes seriously ill with Parkinson's disease.

1937   Guy D. Haselton makes a two-reel biographical film of Garland. Garland becomes obsessively involved in psychic investigation of buried objects.

1939   Garland's last book, *The Mystery of the Buried Crosses,* is published. Garland worries about the disposition of his papers after his death.

1940   Garland dies, on 4 March, of a cerebral hemorrhage.

Abbreviations

I. In bibliography

BAI	*Book of the American Indian*
BET	*Boston Evening Transcript*
MTR	*Main-Travelled Roads*
PF	*Prairie Folks*
PS	*Prairie Songs*
TGS	*Trail of the Gold-Seekers*
THT	*They of the High Trails*
W C	*Wayside Courtships*

II. In checklist of letters

Description of letters

AL	autograph letter
ALC	autograph letter, carbon (from Garland's Letterbook, 1901-1904, USC)
ALD	autograph letter, draft
ALS	autograph letter, signed
AnS	autograph note, signed
ApcS	autograph postcard, signed
Tpc	typed postcard
tel	telegram
TL	typed letter
TLC	typed letter, copy
TLS	typed letter, signed
trL	transcribed letter
*	included in *Selected Letters of Hamlin Garland*

Location of letters

Allegheny	Allegheny College, Meadville, Pennsylvania
Am Acad	American Academy of Arts and Letters, New York City
Amherst	Amherst College, Massachusetts
Bancroft	University of California, Berkeley
Boston PL	Boston Public Library
Bowdoin	Bowdoin College, Brunswick, Maine
Brigham Young	Brigham Young University, Provo, Utah
Bryn Mawr	Bryn Mawr College, Bryn Mawr, Pennsylvania
Brown	Brown University, Providence, Rhode Island
Cal St Lib	California State Library, Sacramento
Clark	Clark University, Worcester, Massachusetts
Colby	Colby College, Waterville, Maine
Colorado C	Colorado College, Colorado Springs
Columbia	Columbia University, New York City
Congress	Library of Congress, Washington, DC
Dartmouth	Dartmouth College, Hanover, New Hampshire
DePauw	DePauw University, Greencastle, Indiana
Dickinson	Dickinson College, Carlisle, Pennsylvania
Duke	Duke University, Durham, North Carolina
Emory	Emory University, Atlanta
Harvard	Harvard University, Cambridge, Massachussets
Homestead	Garland Homestead, West Salem Historical Society, Wisconsin
Hunt	Henry E. Huntington Library, San Marino, California
In HS	Indiana Historical Society, Indianapolis
In St Lib	Indiana State Library, Indianapolis
Indiana U	Lilly Library, Indiana University, Bloomington
Iowa HS	Iowa State Historical Society, Iowa City
Knox	Knox College Archives, Galesburg, Illinois
Louisiana St	Louisiana State University, Baton Rouge
Miami U	Miami University, Oxford, Ohio
Middlebury	Middlebury College, Middlebury, Vermont
Minn HS	Minnesota Historical Society, St. Paul
Morgan	Pierpont Morgan Library, New York City
Mt Holyoke	Mount Holyoke College, South Hadley, Massachusetts
Nat'l Arch	National Archives, Washington, DC
Newberry	Newberry Library, Chicago
Northwestern	Northwestern University, Evanston, Illinois

NY HS	New York Historical Society, New York City
NY State	New York State Library, Albany
NYPL	New York Public Library, New York City
NYU	New York University, New York City
Ohio St	Ohio State University, Columbus
Penn HS	Historical Society of Pennsylvania, Philadelphia
Penn State	Pennsylvania State University, University Park
Players	Hampden-Booth Theater Collection and Library, The Players Club, New York City
Princeton	Princeton University, Princeton, New Jersey
Pulitzer	Pulitzer Archives, Columbia University, New York City
Purdue	Purdue University, West Lafayette, Indiana
R. B. Hayes	Rutherford B. Hayes Library, Fremont, Ohio
Rochester	University of Rochester, Rochester, New York
Rosenberg	Rosenberg Library, Galveston, Texas
S Dak HS	South Dakota State Historical Society, Pierre
SE MO St	Southeast Missouri State University, Cape Girardeau
Smith	Smith College, Northampton, Massachusetts
Southwest	Southwest Museum Library, Los Angeles
St Mary	Saint Mary College, Leavenworth, Kansas
Stanford	Stanford University, Stanford, California
Swarthmore	Swarthmore College, Swarthmore, Pennsylvania
Syracuse	Syracuse University, Syracuse, New York
Temple	Temple University, Philadelphia
Tenn-Nash	Joint University Libraries, Nashville
Trinity	Trinity College, Hartford, Connecticut
Tulane	Tulane University, New Orleans
U Cal-Davis	University of California, Davis
U Chicago	University of Chicago
U of AZ	University of Arizona, Tucson
U of Del	University of Delaware, Newark
U of Ill	University of Illinois Library, Urbana
U of Iowa	University of Iowa, Iowa City
U of KY	University of Kentucky, Lexington
U of Mich	University of Michigan, Ann Arbor
U of OK	University of Oklahoma, Norman
U of Oregon	University of Oregon, Eugene
U Pacific	University of the Pacific, Stockton, California
U Penn	University of Pennsylvania, Philadelphia
U Texas	University of Texas, Austin

U Vermont	University of Vermont, Burlington
U Wis-LaCrosse	University of Wisconsin, LaCrosse
U Wis-Mil	University of Wisconsin, Milwaukee
UCLA	University of California, Los Angeles
UNC-CH	University of North Carolina, Chapel Hill
USC	University of Southern California, Los Angeles
USC LB	Garland's Letterbook (1901-04), University of Southern California, Los Angeles
Virginia	University of Virginia, Charlottesville
W Vir U	West Virginia University, Morgantown
Wagner	Wagner College, Staten Island, New York
Wis HS	State Historical Society of Wisconsin, Madison
Yale	Yale University, New Haven, Connecticut

Common abbreviations in annotations

Acad	American Academy of Arts and Letters. Elected in 1918, Garland became a member of the Board of Directors and served as its secretary, and was acting secretary of the Academy from 1920-1921.
Chicago Thea Soc	The Chicago Theatre Society. Garland was a founding member and its secretary, from 1911-1913.
Com Lit Art	Joint Committee of Literary Arts. Formed in 1916 (with Garland as chair) to promote the New York arts during World War I.
crosses	Letters which deal with Garland's obsessive quest to discover and authenticate buried objects, with the results published as *The Mystery of the Buried Crosses* (1939).
exhib	Travelling exhibits: one from 1936 to 1939, entitled "The Makers of American Literature," which showcased Garland and his literary friends and travelled to universities and libraries across the country. Another consisted of 5 touring exhibits of material promoting *The Mystery of the Buried Crosses*.
Indian	Contents about Garland's activities on behalf of Native American rights.

Institute   The National Institute of Arts and Letters.
                     Formed in 1898, Garland drafted its consti-
                     tution and became a vice-president in 1907.

porno rant   Letters (many repetitive) detailing Gar-
                     land's denouncements of current writing as
                     "pornographic" pandering.

renaming   Letters about Garland's involvement in a
                     government project to regularize the
                     names of Native Americans, from 1901 to
                     1905.

Trans-Miss   The Trans-Mississippi Exposition, June-
                     November 1898, in Omaha. Modeled after
                     Chicago's Columbian Exposition of 1893,
                     Garland was chairman of the Literary
                     Congress. Letters are circular letters gather-
                     ing participants.

Short titles

Afternoon	*Afternoon Neighbors*, 1934
Back-Trailers	*Back-Trailers from the Middle Border*, 1928
Captain	*The Captain of the Gray-Horse Troop*, 1902
Cavanagh	*Cavanagh, Forest Ranger*, 1910
Companions	*Companions on the Trail*, 1931
Contemporaries	*My Friendly Contemporaries*, 1932
Crosses	*The Mystery of the Buried Crosses*, 1939
Daughter	*A Daughter of the Middle Border*, 1921
Eagle's	*The Eagle's Heart*, 1900
Folks	*Prairie Folks*, 1893
Forester's	*The Forester's Daughter*, 1914
Forty	*Forty Years of Psychic Research*, 1936
Grant	*Ulysses S. Grant: His Life and Character*, 1898
Hesper	*Hesper*, 1903
High Trails	*They of the High Trails*, 1916
Joys	*Joys of the Trail*, 1935
Idols	*Crumbing Idols*, 1894
Moccasin	*The Moccasin Ranch*, 1909
Money Magic	*Money Magic*, 1907
Mountain	*Her Mountain Lover*, 1901
MTR	*Main-Travelled Roads*, 1891
Roadside	*Roadside Meetings*, 1930
Rose	*Rose of Dutcher's Coolly*, 1895

Shadow World	*The Shadow World*, 1908
Son	*A Son of the Middle Border*, 1917
Songs	*Prairie Songs*, 1893
Trail-Makers	*Trail-Makers of the Middle Border*, 1926
Tyranny	*The Tyranny of the Dark*, 1905
Wayside	*Wayside Courtships*, 1897

Bibliography

A. Books

A1   *Under the Wheel, A Modern Play in Six Scenes.* Boston: Barta Press, 1890. [51 pp.]

A2   *Main-Travelled Roads: Six Mississippi Valley Stories.* Boston: Arena, 1891. 260 pp. [**Contents**: "A Branch Road," "Up the Coulé," "Among the Corn Rows," "The Return of the Private," "Under the Lion's Paw," "Mrs. Ripley's Trip."]
- As *Main-Travelled Roads: Being Six Stories of the Mississippi Valley.* Introduction by W. D. Howells. Decorations by H. T. Carpenter. Chicago: Stone and Kimball, 1893. 251 pp.
- New York and London: Macmillan, 1899. 299 pp. [Adds "The Creamery Man," "A Day's Pleasure," "Uncle Ethan Ripley."]
- Sunset edition, 1909. [Rpt. of 1899 ed.]
- New York: Harper, 1912. 2 vols. [Rpt. of 1899 ed.]
- New York: Harper, 1920. 377 pp. [Rpt. of 1899 ed. Adds "God's Ravens," "A 'Good Fellow's' Wife."]
- Border edition, 1922. [Rpt. of 1920 ed.]
- Illus. Constance Garland. New York and London: Harper, 1930. 406 pp. [Rpt. of 1920 ed. Adds "The Fireplace."]

A3   *A New Declaration of Rights.* Boston: Arena, 1891. 64 pp. [Pamphlet publication of "A New Declaration of Rights" (1891).]

A4   *Jason Edwards: An Average Man.* Boston: Arena, 1892.
      213 pp.
      • New York: Appleton, 1897. 213 pp.
      • Sunset edition, 1909.

A5   *A Member of the Third House: A Dramatic Story.*
      Chicago: F. J. Schulte, 1892. 239 pp.
      • As *A Member of the Third House: A Story of Political
      Warfare.* Rev. ed. New York: Appleton, 1897.
      239 pp.
      • As *A la Troisième chambre.* Trans. Alice Foulon de
      Vaulx. Paris: Calman-Lévy, 1897.

A6   *A Little Norsk: or, Ol' Pap's Flaxen.* New York: D. Apple-
      ton, 1892. 157 pp.
      • Sunset edition, 1909.

A7   *A Spoil of Office: A Story of the Modern West.* Boston:
      Arena, 1892. 385 pp.
      • Rev. ed. New York: Appleton, 1897. 375 pp.
      • Sunset edition, 1909.

A8   *Prairie Folks.* Chicago: F. J. Schulte, 1893. 255 pp.
      [**Contents**: "Uncle Ethan's Speculation," "The Test
      of Elder Pill," "William Bacon's Hired Man," "Sim
      Burn's Wife," "Saturday Night on the Farm," "Vil-
      lage Cronies," "Drifting Crane," "Old Daddy Deer-
      ing," "The Sociable at Dudley's."]
      • Chicago: Stone and Kimball, 1895. 255 pp.
      • Rev. ed.   New York: Macmillan, 1899.   284 pp.
      [**Contents, stories**: "William Bacon's Man," "Elder
      Pill, Preacher," "A Day of Grace," "Lucretia Burns,"
      "Some Village Cronies," "Drifting Crane," "Daddy
      Deering," "Black Ephraim," "The Wapseypinnicon
      Tiger," "Aidgewise Feelin's," "The Sociable at Dud-
      ley's"; **poems**: "Then It's Spring," "April Days," "A
      Farmer's Wife," "Logan at Peach Tree Creek," "The
      War of Race," "Paid His Way," "Horses Chawin'
      Hay," "Across the Picket-Line," "Goin' Back t'mor-
      rer," "Growing Old," "An Afterword: Of Winds,
      Snows, and the Stars."]
      • Sunset edition, 1909.

A9   *Prairie Songs: Being Chants Rhymed and Unrhymed of the Level Lands of the Great West.* Illus. by H. T. Carpenter. Cambridge and Chicago: Stone and Kimball, 1893. 164 pp. [**Contents**: "Prairie Memories," "The West Wind," "Coming Rain on the Prairie," "Massasauga—The Meadow Rattlesnake," "Spring on the Prairie," "A Song of Winds," "Indian Summer," "Color in the Wheat," "The Meadow Lark," "The Rush of the Plains," "Pioneers," "Settlers," "Prairie Fires," "Drought," "At Dusk," "A Winter Brook," "The Voice of the Pines," "Corn Shadows," "The Herald Crane," "Sundown," "In the Autumn Grass," "Dreams of the Grass," "Meadow Memories," "The Whip-Poor-Will's Hour," "A Summer Mood," "Atavism," "In a Lull in the Splendors of Brahms," "The Passing of the Buffalo," "An Apology," "Home from the City," "April Days," "By the River," "A Mountain-Side," "In August," "The Blue Jay," "The Mountains," "My Cabin," "Beneath the Pines," "The Striped Gopher," "The Prairie to the City," "A Human Habitation," "A River Gorge," "Altruism," "Return of the Gulls," "Early May," "The Wind's Notice," "On the Mississippi," "A Brother's Death Search," "Spring Rains," "A Dakota Harvest Field," "The Noonday Plain," "Midnight Snows," "In Stacking Time," "Prairie Chickens," "A Town of the Plain," "In the Gold Country," "Home from the Wild Meadows," "Fighting Fire," "Boyish Sleep," "The Herdsman," "Rushing Eagle," "September," "The Stampede," "Sport," "The Cool Gray Jug," "The Gray Wolf," "Plowing," "A Tribute of Grasses," "Moods of the Plain," "Lost in a Norther," "Ladrone," "Across the Picket Line," "Then It's Spring," "Logan at Peach Tree Creek," "Paid His Way," "Horses Chawin' Hay," "Growing Old," "A Farmer's Wife," "Pom, Pom, Pull-Away," "Goin' Back t' Mother," "On Wing of Steam," "My Prairies," "Midway on the Trail."]

A10   *Crumbling Idols: Twelve Essays on Art Dealing Chiefly
      with Literature, Painting and the Drama.* Chicago
      and Cambridge: Stone and Kimball, 1894. 192 pp.
      [**Contents**: "A Personal Word," "Provincialism,"
      "New Fields," "The Question of Success," "Literary
      Prophecy," "Local Color in Art," "The Local
      Novel," "The Drift of the Drama," "The Influence
      of Ibsen," "Impressionism," "Literary Centres,"
      "Literary Masters," "A Recapitulatory Afterword."]

A11   *Impressions on Impressionism: Being a Discussion of the
      American Art Exhibition at the Art Institute,
      Chicago, by A Critical Triumvirate.* Chicago: Cen-
      tral Art Association, 1894. 24 pp. Pamphlet.

A12   *Five Hoosier Painters: Being a Discussion of the Holiday
      Exhibit of the Indianapolis Group, in Chicago, by
      The Critical Triumvirate.* Chicago: Central Art As-
      sociation, 1894. 16 pp. Pamphlet.

A13   *Rose of Dutcher's Coolly.* Chicago: Stone and Kimball,
      1895. 403 pp.
      • London: N. Beeman, 1896.
      • Rev. ed. New York and London: Macmillan, 1899.
      354 pp.

A14   *Wayside Courtships.* New York: Appleton, 1897. 281 pp.
      [**Contents**: "At the Beginning," "A Preacher's Love
      Story," "A Meeting in the Foothills," "A Stop-Over
      at Tyre," "An Alien in the Pines," "The Owner of
      the Mill Farm," "Of Those Who Seek," "The
      Prisoned Soul," "A Sheltered One," "A Fair Exile,"
      "The Passing Stranger," "Before the Low Green
      Door," "Upon Impulse," "The End of Love is Love
      of Love."]
      • London: N. Beeman, 1898. 320 pp.
      • Sunset edition, 1909.

A15   *The Spirit of Sweetwater.* Philadelphia: Curtis, 1898.
      100 pp.
      • New York: Doubleday and McClure, 1898. 100 pp.
      • London: Service and Paton, 1898. 100 pp.
      • Rev. and enlarged as *Witch's Gold* (1906).

A16 *Ulysses S. Grant: His Life and Character.* New York: Doubleday and McClure, 1898. 524 pp.
• New York: Macmillan, 1920. 524 pp.

A17 *Boy Life on the Prairie.* Illus. E. W. Deming. New York
and London: Macmillan, 1899. 423 pp.
• Every Boy's and Girl's Series. New York: Macmillan,
1907. 423 pp.
• Sunset edition, 1909.
• Border edition, 1922.
• Academy Classics for Junior High Schools. New York:
Allyn and Bacon, 1926. 354 pp. [With an introduc-
tion and author's notes.]

A18 *The Trail of the Gold Seekers: A Record of Travel in Prose
and Verse.* New York and London: Macmillan,
1899. 264 pp. [**poems:** "Anticipation," "Where the
Desert Flames with Furnace Heat," "The Cow-Boy,"
"From Plain to Peak," "Momentous Hour," "A
Wish," "The Gift of Water," "Mounting," "The Ea-
gle Trail," "Moon on the Plain," "The Whooping
Crane," "The Loon," "Yet Still We Rode," "The
Gaunt Gray Wolf," "Abandoned on the Trail," "Do
You Fear the Wind?" "Siwash Graves," "Line Up,
Brave Boys," "A Child of the Sun," "In the Grass,"
"The Faithful Broncos," "The Whistling Marmot,"
"The Clouds," "The Great Stikeen Divide," "The
Ute Lover," "Devil's Club," "In the Cold Green
Mountains," "The Long Trail," "The Greeting of
the Roses," "The Vulture," "Campfires," "The
Footstep in the Desert," "So This is the End of the
Trail to Him," "The Toil of the Trail," "The Gold-
seekers," "The Coast Range of Africa," "The Free-
man of the Hills," "The Voice of the Maple Tree,"
"A Girl on the Trail," "O the Fierce Delight," "The
Lure of the Desert," "This Out of All Will Remain,"
"Here the Trail Ends."]
• Sunset edition, 1909.

A19 *The Eagle's Heart.* New York: Appleton, 1900. 369 pp.
• London: Heineman, 1900. 369 pp.
• Sunset edition, 1909.
• Border edition, 1922.

A20 *Her Mountain Lover.* New York: Century, 1901. 396 pp.
     [From "Jim Matteson of Wagon Wheel Gap"
     (1900).]
     • New York: Grosset and Dunlap, 1901. 396 pp.
     • London: Heinemann, 1901. 396 pp.
     • Appleton Dollar Library. New York: Appleton, 1939.
       396 pp.

A21 *The Captain of the Gray-Horse Troop.* New York and
     London: Harper, 1902. 414 pp.
     • London: Grant Richards, 1902. 414 pp.
     • Special, Limited Edition. New York: Grosset and Dun-
       lap, 1920. 415 pp.
     • Border edition, 1922.

A22 *Hesper.* New York and London: Harper, 1903. 444 pp.
     • New York: Grosset and Dunlap, 1903. 444 pp.
     • Border edition, 1922.

A23 *The Light of the Star.* New York and London: Harper,
     1904. 277 pp.

A24 *The Tyranny of the Dark.* New York and London: Harper,
     1905. 438 pp.

A25 *Witch's Gold.* New York: Doubleday and Page, 1906. 231
     pp. [Expanded from *The Spirit of Sweetwater*
     (1898).]

A26 *The Long Trail: A Story of the Northwest Wilderness.*
     New York and London: Harper, 1907. 262 pp.
     • Border edition, 1922.
     • Ed. Barbara Grace Spayd. New York: Harper, 1935. 332
       pp. [Adds "Return of the Private."]

A27 *Money Magic.* Illus. J. N. Marchand. New York and Lon-
     don: Harper, 1907. 354 pp.
     • As *Mart Haney's Mate*, Border edition, 1922.

A28 *The Shadow World.* New York and London: Harper,
     1908. 294 pp.

A29   *The Moccasin Ranch: A Story of Dakota.* New York and
      London: Harper, 1909. 136 pp. [From "The Land of
      the Straddle-Bug" (1894).] Rpt. as "La Ferme du
      Moggason" (1917).

A30   Sunset Edition. New York and London: Harper, 1909. 10
      vols. *Boy Life on the Prairie, The Eagle's Heart, Ja-
      son Edwards, A Little Norsk, Main-Travelled
      Roads, Prairie Folks, Rose of Dutcher's Coolly, A
      Spoil of Office, Trail of the Gold-Seekers, Wayside
      Courtships.*

A31   *Cavanagh, Forest Ranger: A Romance of the Mountain
      West.* New York and London: Harper, 1910. 300 pp.
      • Border edition, 1922.

A32   *Other Main-Travelled Roads.* New York and London:
      Harper, 1910. 349 pp. [Compiled from *Prairie Folks*
      and *Wayside Courtships.* **Contents**: "William
      Bacon's Hired Man," "Elder Pill, Preacher," "A Day
      of Grace," "Lucretia Burns," "Daddy Deering," "A
      Stop-Over at Tyre," "A Division in the Coolly," "A
      Fair Exile," "An Alien in the Pines," "Before the
      Low Green Door," "A Preacher's Love Story."]
      • Border edition, 1922.

A33   *Victor Ollnee's Discipline.* New York and London:
      Harper, 1911. 307 pp.

A34   *The Forester's Daughter: A Romance of the Bear-Tooth
      Range.* New York and London: Harper, 1914. 286 pp.
      • Border edition, 1922.

A35   *They of the High Trails.* New York and London: Harper,
      1916. 381 pp. [**Contents**: "The Grub-Staker," "The
      Cow-Boss," "The Remittance Man," "The Lone-
      some Man," "The Trail Tramp," "The Prospector,"
      "The Outlaw," "The Leaser," "The Forest Ranger."]
      • New York: Harper, 1917. 453 pp. [With an Introduction
      by W. D. Howells, an Appreciation by Theodore
      Roosevelt, and "The Tourist."]
      • Border edition, 1922.

A36   *A Son of the Middle Border.* Illus. Alice Barber Stephens.
       New York: Macmillan, 1917. 467 pp.
       • London: John Lane, 1921.
       • Modern Reader's Series. Ed. for school use by E. H.
       Kemperer McComb. Illus. Alice Barber Stephens.
       New York: Macmillan, 1923. 478 pp.
       • New York: Grosset and Dunlap, 1928. 467 pp.

A37   *A Daughter of the Middle Border.* Illus. with pho-
       tographs. New York: Macmillan, 1921. 405 pp.
       • New York: Grosset and Dunlap, 1926. 405 pp.
       • Illus. Constance Garland. New York: Macmillan, 1929.
       399 pp.

A38   *Commemorative Tribute to James Whitcomb Riley.*
       Academy Notes and Monographs 24. New York:
       American Academy, 1922. 9 pp. Pamphlet.

A39   *A Pioneer Mother.* Chicago: The Bookfellows, 1922. 21 pp.
       [From "The Wife of a Pioneer" (1903).]

A40   Border Edition. New York and London: Harper, 1922. 12
       vols. *Main-Travelled Roads, Other Main-Travelled
       Roads, Boy Life on the Prairie, Rose of Dutcher's
       Coolly, The Eagle's Heart, The Captain of the Gray-
       Horse Troop, Hesper, Cavanagh, Forest Ranger, The
       Long Trail, Mart Haney's Mate [Money Magic], The
       Forester's Daughter, They of the High Trails.*

A41   *The Book of the American Indian.* Illus. Frederic Rem-
       ington. New York and London: Harper, 1923. 274
       pp. [**Contents**: "Wahiah—A Spartan Mother,"
       "Nistina," "The Iron Khiva," "The New Medicine
       House," "Rising Wolf—Ghost Dancer," "The
       River's Warning," "Lone Wolf's Old Guard," "Big
       Moggasen," "The Storm-Child," "The Blood Lust,"
       "The Remorse of Waumdisapa," "A Decree of
       Council," "Drifting Crane," "The Story of Howling
       Wolf," "The Silent Eaters."]

A42 *Trail-Makers of the Middle Border.* Illus. Constance Garland. New York: Macmillan; London: John Lane,
1926. 426 pp.
• Illus. Constance Garland. New York: Grosset and Dun-
lap, 1927. 426 pp.

A43 *The Westward March of American Settlement.* Reading
With a Purpose 29. Illus. Constance Garland.
Chicago: American Library Association, 1927. 35 pp.

A44 *Prairie Song and Western Story: Selections.* Comp. by
Stella S. Center. Illus. Constance Garland.
Academy Classics for Junior High Schools. Boston
and New York: Allyn and Bacon, 1928. 368 pp.
[Selections of poems and stories and "Hotan, the
Red Pioneer."]

A45 *Back-Trailers from the Middle Border.* Illus. Constance
Garland. New York: Macmillan, 1928. 379 pp.

A46 *Roadside Meetings.* Illus. Constance Garland. New York:
Macmillan, 1930. 474 pp.
• London: John Lane, 1931.

A47 *Companions on the Trail: A Literary Chronicle.* Illus.
Constance Garland. New York: Macmillan, 1931.
539 pp.

A48 *My Friendly Contemporaries: A Literary Log.* Illus. Constance Garland. New York: Macmillan, 1932. 544 pp.

A49 *Afternoon Neighbors: Further Excerpts from a Literary
Log.* New York: Macmillan, 1932. 589 pp.

A50 *Iowa, O Iowa.* Whirling Wind Series 4. Iowa City: Clio
Press, 1935. 58 pp. [Mostly rpt. from *Prairie Songs*
(1893). **Contents**: "Early May," "To a Winter Brook,
of June," "Color in the Wheat," "In August," "The
Cool Gray Jug," "In Stacking Time," "In the Au-
tumn Grass," "Home from the Wild Meadows,"
"Indian Summer," "Plowing," "My Cabin," "By the
River," "Fighting Fire," "Prairie Chickens," "The

Striped Gopher," "The Herald Crane," "Massas-
auga—The Meadow Rattlesnake," "The Passing of
the Buffalo," "At Dusk," "The Whip-poor-will's
Hour," "Corn Shadows," "A Farmer's Wife,"
"Pom-pom-pullaway," "Horses Chawin' Hay,"
"The Plowman of Today," "The Prisoned Fool,"
"The Sword Two-Edged," "Vanishing Trails."]

A51   *Joys of the Trail.* Chicago: Bookfellows, 1935. 46 pp.

A52   *Forty Years of Psychic Research: A Plain Narrative of Fact.*
      New York: Macmillan, 1936. 394 pp.

A53   *The Mystery of the Buried Crosses: A Narrative of Psychic
      Exploration.* New York: Dutton, 1939. 351 pp.

B. Contributions to periodicals and books

1885

B1   "Ten Years Dead." *Every Other Saturday* 2 (28 March
      1885): 97-99. Fiction.

B2   "Three Great Novels." *Portland Transcript* (Maine) 20
      May 1885: 60. Review of Victor Hugo's *Les Miser-
      ables*, Jean Paul Richter's *Titan*, and Walter Scott's
      Ivanhoe.

1886

B3   "Edwin Booth." *BET* 2 January 1886: 7. Poem.

B4   "The Moonlight Boy." *BET* 16 July 1886: 6. Review of the
      novel by E. W. Howe.

1887

B5   "Logan at Peach Tree Creek." *BET* 1 January 1887: 6. Rpt.
      PS (1893). Poem.

B6　"Lemuel Barker." *BET* 31 January 1887: 6. Review of W. D. Howells' *The Minister's Charge.*

B7　"Bret Harte's New Book." *BET* 3 February 1887: 6. Review of *A Millionaire of Rough-and-Ready.*

B8　"Confessions of Claude." *BET* 4 May 1887: 6. Review of the novel by Edgar Fawcett.

B9　"Zury, 'The Meanest Man in Spring County.'" *BET* 16 May 1887: 3. Review of the novel by Joseph Kirkland.

B10　"Wheat Harvesting in the West." Syndicated 31 July 1887, McClure Syndicate. Article.

B11　"Carlyle as a Poet." *BET* 2 August 1887: 5. Article.

B12　"Prairie Memories." *American* 6 (October 1887): 653. Rpt. *PS* (1893). Poem.

B13　"Seth's Brother's Wife." *BET* 11 November 1887: 6. Review of the novel by Harold Frederic.

B14　"Beneath the Pines." *American* 7 (November 1887): 87. Rpt. *PS* (1893). Poem.

B15　"Lost in the Norther." *Harper's Weekly* 31 (3 December 1887): 883. Rpt. *PS* (1893). Poem.

B16　"James Whitcomb Riley." *BET* 21 December 1887. Review of *Afterwhiles* and other works.

B17　"My Cabin." *American* 7 (December 1887): 232. Rpt. *PS* (1893). Poem.

1888

B18　"Boy Life on the Prairie." *American* 7-8. "The Huskin'" (January 1888): 299-303; "The Thrashin'" (March 1888): 570-577; "The Voice of Spring" (April 1888): 684-690; "Between Hay an' Grass" (June 1888): 148-

155; "Meadow Memories" (July 1888): 296-302;
(October 1888): 712-717. As *Boy Life on the Prairie*
(1899). Articles.

B19   "Land at Ten Cents an Acre." *BET* 12 January 1888: 6.
Letter.

B20   "Holding Down a Claim in a Blizzard." *Harper's Weekly*
32 (28 January 1888): 66-67. Fiction.

B21   "Hunger for Land." *BET* 30 January 1888: 6. Letter.

B22   "April Hopes." *BET* 1 March 1888: 6. Review of the novel
by W. D. Howells.

B23   "High Ground." *BET* 21 March 1888: 6. Review of the
book by Augustus Jacobson.

B24   "The Coming Storm." *BET* 28 March 1888: 6. Poem.

B25   "Paid His Way." *America* 1 (19 May 1888): 6. Rpt. *P S*
(1893). Poem.

B26   "Professor Garland's Western Trip." *Standard* 23 June
1888: 3. Article.

B27   "A Common Case." *Belford's* 1 (July 1888): 188-199. Rpt.
as "Before the Low Green Door," *WC* (1897).
Fiction.

B28   "In Minneapolis." *Standard* 28 July 1888: 2. Article.

B29   "American Novels." *Literary News* 9 (August 1888): 236-
237. Article.

B30   "Work in New Fields." *Standard* 25 August 1888: 8.
Article.

B31   "Major Kirkland's Second Novel." *BET* 20 October 1888: 6.
Review of *The McVeys*.

B32 "A Man Story." *BET* 7 November 1888: 6. Review of the novel by E. W. Howe.

B33 "Whitman's 'November Boughs.'" *BET* 15 November 1888: 6. Review.

B34 "Cheering Words from Professor Garland." *Standard* 17 November 1888: 3. Article.

B35 "Mrs. Ripley's Trip." *Harper's Weekly* 32 (24 November 1888): 894-895. Rpt. *MTR* (1891). Rpt. 1931. Fiction.

B36 "Annie Kilburn." *BET* 27 December 1888: 6. Review of the novel by W. D. Howells.

1889

B37 "Another American Play." *BET* 12 January 1889: 10. Letter.

B38 "For Club Houses at Small Expense." *Standard* 12 January 1889: 2. Article.

B39 "A Wind from the East Sea." *Standard* 9 March 1889: 11. Poem.

B40 "The Tragedy of a Town." *BET* 6 April 1889: 10. Article.

B41 "Hints for a Spring and Summer Campaign in Massachusetts." *Standard* 13 April 1889: 13. Article.

B42 "The Greek Play." *BET* 1 May 1889: 2. Article.

B43 "Apology." *Literary World* 20 (8 June 1889): 92. Rpt. *PS* (1893). Poem.

B44 "The Cause of Poverty." *Dawn* 1 (15 June 1889): 1-2. Article.

B45 "Points of View." *Standard* 22 June 1889: 15. Poem.

B46 "Whitman at Seventy. How the Good Gray Poet Looks and Talks." *New York Herald* 30 June 1889: 7. Article.

B47 "A Dakota Wheat-Field." *Youth's Companion* 62 (18 July 1889): 366. Rpt. as "A Dakota Harvest Field," *P S* (1893). Poem.

B48 "The Average Man." *America* 2 (25 July 1889): 526. Poem.

B49 "I Am Very Sorry I Cannot Be with You." *Standard* 3 August 1889: 4. Letter.

B50 "By the River." *Youth's Companion* 62 (15 August 1889): 410. Rpt. *PS* (1893). Poem.

B51 "Scepterless Kings." *Standard* 17 August 1889: 9. Poem.

B52 "In New Hampshire." *Standard* 24 August 1889: 5. Article.

B53 "Single Tax Cat." *Standard* 7 September 1889: 14. Poem.

B54 "Under the Lion's Paw." *Harper's Weekly* 33 (7 September 1889): 726-727. Rpt. *MTR* (1891). Fiction.

B55 "Truth in the Drama." *Literary World* 20 (14 September 1889): 307-308. Letter.

B56 "The 'Single-Tax' Theory." *BET* 16 September 1889: 6. Letter.

B57 "An Interesting Announcement." *Standard* 28 September 1889: 3. Article.

B58 "Words! Words! Words!" *BET* 9 October 9 1889: 6. Letter.

B59 "Herbert Spencer on Property." *Standard* 12 October 1889: 6. Article.

B60 "An Ibsen Club." *BET* 9 November 1889: 5. Letter.

B61   "'Single-Tax' and Woman Suffrage." *Woman's Journal* (Boston) 19 October 1889: 330. Letter.

B62   "Mr. Howells's Latest Novel." *BET* 14 December 1889: 10. Review of *A Hazard of New Fortunes.*

B63   "Old Sid's Christmas." *Harper's Weekly* 33 (28 December 1889): 1038-1040. Fiction.

B64   "The Teacher." *Camden's Compliments to Walt Whitman.* Ed. Horace L. Traubel. Philadelphia: D. McKay, 1889. 40-42. Article.

1890

B65   "Mark Twain's Latest." *BET* 10 January 1890: 6. Review of *A Connecticut Yankee in King Arthur's Court.*

B66   "A Great Book." *Standard* 5 February 1890: 5-6. Review of W. D. Howells' *A Hazard of New Fortunes.*

B67   "Mr. Howells's Latest Novels." *New England Magazine,* n.s. 2 (May 1890): 243-250. Digested in *Review of Reviews* 1 (June 1890): 497. Article.

B68   "The Massachusetts Plan." *Standard* 7 May 1890: 12. Article.

B69   "Miss Shaw's Production." *BET* 17 May 1890: 8. Letter.

B70   "Drifting Crane." *Harper's Weekly* 34 (31 May 1890): 421-422. Rpt. *PF* (1893). Fiction.

B71   "Ibsen as a Dramatist." *Arena* 2 (June 1890): 72-82. Rpt. *Crumbling Idols* (1894). Article.

B72   "She Passed Me on the Street." *Arena* 2 (July 1890): 187. Rpt. *Jason Edwards* (1892). Poem.

B73   "Among the Corn-Rows." *Harper's Weekly* 34 (28 June 1890): 506-508. Rpt. *MTR* (1891). Rpt. 1924. Fiction.

B74   "Under the Wheel: A Modern Play in Six Scenes." *Arena*
       2 (July 1890): 182-228. As *Under the Wheel* (1890).
       Play.

B75   "Mr. Herne's New Play." *BET* 8 July 1890: 6. Review of
       Margaret Fleming.

B76   "Women and Their Organization." *Standard* 8 October
       1890: 5-6. Article.

B77   "The Return of A Private." *Arena* 3 (December 1890): 97-
       113. Rpt. *MTR* (1891). Fiction.

B78   "The Verestchagin Collection." *BET* 3 December 1890: 3.
       Letter.

                                    1891

B79   "Music Land: At a Symphony." *New England Magazine*
       n.s. 3 (January 1891): 628-630. Poem.

B80   "A New Declaration of Rights." *Arena* 3 (January 1891):
       157-184. Rpt. in pamphlet form [A3]. Article.

B81   "Rhymes of Childhood." *BET* 12 February 1891. Unsigned
       review of the book by James Whitcomb Riley.

B82   "The Test of Elder Pill." *Arena* 3 (March 1891): 480-501.
       Rpt. *PF* (1893). Fiction.

B83   "Going for the Doctor." *Youth's Companion* 64 (12 March
       1891): 151. Fiction.

B84   "The Question of an Independent Theatre." *BET* 29 April
       1891: 6. Letter.

B85   "The Morality of Margaret Fleming." *BET* 7 May 1891: 6.
       Letter.

B86   "The New Drama." *BET* 9 May 1891: 12. Letter.

B87 "A Spring Romance." *Century* 42 (June 1891): 296-302.
Rpt. as "William Bacon's Hired Man," *PF* (1893).
Rpt. as "William Bacon's Man" (1929). Fiction.

B88 "A Prairie Heroine." *Arena* 4 (July 1891): 223-246. Rpt. as
"Sim Burns's Wife," *PF* (1893). Fiction.

B89 "Canada and the Canadian Question." *Arena* 4 (August
1891): xxiv. Review of the book by Goldwin Smith.

B90 "The Silver Question." *Arena* 4 (August 1891): xxv. Review of *Silver in Europe* by S. Dana Horton.

B91 "I Saw with Consternation." *Standard* 19 August 1891: 6.
Letter.

B92 "The Future of 'The Standard.'" *Standard* 26 August 1891:
9. Article.

B93 "An Evening at the Corner Grocery: A Western Character
Sketch." *Arena* 4 (September 1891): 504-512. Rpt. as
"Village Cronies," *PF* (1893). Fiction.

B94 "A Plea for Liberty." *Arena* 4 (September 1891): xvii-xxiv.
Review of the collection of essays.

B95 "Mr. and Mrs. Herne." *Arena* 4 (October 1891): 543-560.
Digested in *Review of Reviews* 4 (November 1891):
455-456. Article.

B96 "Wallace's 'Natural Selection.'" *Arena* 4 (October 1891):
xxv-xxviii. Review of the book by Alfred R. Wallace.

B97 "Mr. George's Work on Free Trade." *Arena* 4 (November
1891): xlii-xliii. Review of Henry George's *Protec-
tion and Free Trade*.

B98 "Two New Novels." *Arena* 5 (December 1891): xxxvi-
xxxviii. Review of Ignatius Donnelly's *Dr. Huguet*
and Joseph Kirkland's *The Captain of Company K*.

B99   "Uncle Ripley's Speculation." *Arena* 5 (December 1891):
      125-135. Rpt. as "Uncle Ethan's Speculation," *PF*
      (1893). Fiction.

1892

B100 "'A Spoil of Office: A Story of the Modern West." *Arena* 5-
      6 (January 1892): 253-268; (February 1892): 376-400;
      (March 1892): 495-522; (April 1892): 619-644; (May
      1892): 749-744; (June 1892): 104-132. As *A Spoil of
      Office* (1892). Fiction.

B101 "Mr. Howells's Plans." *BET* 1 January 1892: 6. Article.

B102 "The Alliance Wedge in Congress." *Arena* 5 (March 1892):
      447-457. Digested in *Review of Reviews* 5 (April
      1892): 359. Article.

B103 "Ol' Pap's Flaxen." *Century* 43 (March 1892): 743-751;
      (April 1892): 912-923; 44 (May 1892): 39-47. As *A Lit-
      tle Norsk* (1892). Fiction.

B104 "A Queer Case." *Youth's Companion* 65 (3 March 1892):
      105-106; (10 March 1892): 121-122; (17 March 1892):
      133-134. Fiction.

B105 "Daddy Deering." *Belford's* 8 (April 1892): 152-161. Rpt. as
      "Old Daddy Deering," *PF* (1893). Fiction.

B106 "At the Brewery." *Cosmopolitan* 13 (May 1892): 34-42.
      Rpt. as "Saturday Night on the Farm," *PF* (1893).
      Fiction.

B107 "Sprigs of Lilac for Walt Whitman." *Conservator* 3 (June
      1892): 26. Rpt. in *At the Graveside of Walt Whit-
      man*. Ed. Horace L. Traubel. Philadelphia: D.
      McKay, 1892. 32. Article.

B108 "Psychography. Mr. Garland's Report." *Psychical Review*
      1 (August 1892): 43-44. Article.

B109 "Salt Water Day." *Cosmopolitan* 13 (August 1892): 387-394. Article.

B110 "Under the Dome of the Capitol: A Prose Etching." *Arena* 6 (September 1892): 468-470. Rpt. as "The Prisoned Soul," *WC* (1897). Fiction.

B111 "Matter, Ether and Motion." *Arena* 6 (October 1892): 1. Review of the book by Amos E. Dolbear.

B112 "Onoqua." *Arena* 6 (October 1892): l-li. Review of the novel by Frances C. Sparhawk.

B113 "Opie Read's Novels." *Arena* 6 (October 1892): xlix. Review of Read's *Emmett Benlore.*

B114 "The Sociable at Dudley's." *Los Angeles Times* 27 November 1892: 10; *Chicago Inter-Ocean* 27 November 1892. Syndicated, McClure Syndicate. Rpt. *PF* (1893). Fiction.

B115 "An Experiment in Psychography." *Psychical Review* 1 (November 1892): 136-137. Article.

B116 "Who Pays Your Taxes?" *Arena* 6 (November 1892): lxxi-lxxii. Review of the collection of essays.

B117 "The West in Literature." *Arena* 6 (November 1892): 669-676. Rpt. *Crumbling Idols* (1894). Article.

B118 "In Winter Night." *Literary Northwest* 2 (December 1892): 96. Rpt. as "An Afterword," *PF* (1893). Poem.

B119 "Forgetting." *Ladies' Home Journal* 10 (December 1892): 17. Rpt. as "The End of Love is Love," *WC* (1897). Fiction.

B120 "On the Oregon Trail." *Bookbuyer* 9 (December 1892): 500-503. Review of a new edition of the book by Francis Parkman.

1893

B121 "Sounds, Voices, and Physical Disturbances in the Pres-
ence of a Psychic." *Psychical Review* 1 (February
1893): 226-229. Article.

B122 "The Future of Fiction." *Arena* 7 (April 1893): 513-524.
Digested in *Review of Reviews* 7 (May 1893): 475-
476. Rpt. *Crumbling Idols* (1894). Article.

B123 "Before the Overture." *Ladies' Home Journal* 10 (May
1893): 13. Rpt. as "At the Beginning," *WC* (1897).
Fiction.

B124 "An Ambitious French Novel and A Modest American
Story." *Arena* 8 (June 1893): xi-xii. Review of Paul
Bourget's *Cosmopolis* and Stephen Crane's *Maggie*.

B125 "A Short-Term Exile." *Literary Northwest* 3 (July 1893):
308-315. Rpt. as "A Fair Exile," *WC* (1897). Fiction.

B126 "I Had My Share in the General Hearty Laugh." *Chicago
Record* 28 July 1893: 4. [In Eugene Field's "Sharps
and Flats" column.] Letter.

B127 "Real Conversations.—II. A Dialogue Between Eugene
Field and Hamlin Garland. Recorded by Hamlin
Garland." *McClure's* 1 (August 1893): 195-204. Digested in *Review of Reviews* 8 (September 1893):
334. Article.

B128 "There Is Very Little To Add." *Chicago Record* 1 August
1893: 4. [In Eugene Field's "Sharps and Flats" column.] Letter.

B129 "A Ridge of Corn." *Harper's Weekly* 37 (12 August 1893):
763. Rpt. *PS* (1893). Poem.

B130 "O Cool Gray Jug!" *Harper's Weekly* 37 (19 August 1893):
786. Rpt. *PS* (1893). Poem.

B131 "A Summer Mood." *New England Magazine* n.s. 9
(September 1893): 64. Rpt. *PS* (1893). Poem.

B132 "Washington Brown, Farmer." *Arena* 8 (September 1893): xxiii. Review of the novel by Leroy Armstrong.

B133 "Prairie Fires." *Youth's Companion* 64 (14 September 1893): 444. Rpt. *PS* (1893). Poem.

B134 "Literary Emancipation of the West." *Forum* 16 (October 1893): 156-166. Rpt. *Crumbling Idols* (1894). Article.

B135 "Sport." *New England Magazine* n.s. 9 (October 1893): 240. Rpt. *PS* (1893). Poem.

B136 "Prairie Chickens." *Independent* 16 (5 October 1893): 1329. Rpt. *PS* (1893). Poem.

B137 "Co-Operative Banking." *Arena* 8 (November 1893): xv. Review of the book by W. H. Van Ornum.

B138 "Money Found." *Arena* 8 (November 1893): xv-xvi. Review of the book by Thomas E. Hill.

B139 "Report of Dark Séances, With a Non-Professional Psychic, For Voices and the Movement of Objects Without Contact." *Psychical Review* 2 (November 1893-February 1894): 152-177. [Written in collaboration with T. E. Allen and B. O. Flower. Garland's contributions are on pages 155-158, 163-165, 167-170, 174-176.] Article.

B140 "A Human Habitation." *Arena* 4 (December 1893): 130. Rpt. *PS* (1893). Poem.

B141 "A Graceless Husband." *Northwestern Miller*, Extra Christmas Number (December 1893): 57-62. Rpt. as "The Owner of the Mill Farm," *WC* (1897). Fiction.

B142 "A Pioneer Christmas." *Ladies' Home Journal* 11 (December 1893): 11. Article.

B143 "Western Landscapes." *Atlantic Monthly* 72 (December 1893): 805-809. Article.

B144 "Walt Whitman." *In Re Walt Whitman.* Ed. Horace L.
      Traubel. Philadelphia: D. McKay, 1893. 328. Poem.

1894

B145 "'Prairie Songs.' Selections from the Advance Sheets of a
      Book of Poems by Hamlin Garland." *Midland
      Monthly* 1 (January 1894): 22-27. [**Contents**: "Mas-
      sasauga" (in ms. facsimile), "Horses Chawin' Hay,"
      "A Winter Brook," "April Days," "The Wind's
      Voice," "A Summer Mood," "In the Autumn
      Grass," "Dreams of the Grass," "The Herald Crane,"
      and "Boyish Sleep."] A number of other magazines
      and newspapers also printed poems from *Prairie
      Songs* in December 1893 and January 1894.

B146 "In Re Walt Whitman." *Arena* 9 (January 1894): i-ii. Re-
      view of the book edited by Horace L. Traubel.

B147 "The Land Question, and Its Relation to Art and Litera-
      ture." *Arena* 9 (January 1894): 165-175. Digested in
      Review of Reviews 9 (February 1894): 214. Article.

B148 "Boy Life in the West—Winter." *Midland Monthly* 1
      (February 1894): 113-122. Article.

B149 "Real Conversations.—IV. A Dialogue Between James
      Whitcomb Riley and Hamlin Garland. Recorded by
      Mr. Garland." *McClure's* 2 (February 1894): 219-234.
      Digested in *Review of Reviews* 9 (March 1894): 356.
      Article.

B150 "Realism and Romanticism in Literature." *Conservator* 5
      (April 1894): 30. Article.

B150a "A Realist at Homestead." *Syracuse Evening Herald* 13
      May 1894: 12. Syndicated, McClure Syndicate.
      Article.

B151 "God's Ravens." *Harper's Monthly* 89 (June 1894): 142-
      148. Rpt. *MTR* (1920). Fiction.

B152 "Homestead and Its Perilous Trades. Impressions of a Visit." *McClure's* 3 (June 1894): 3-20. Article.

B153 "The Single Tax in Actual Application." *Arena* 10 (June 1894): 52-58. Article.

B154 "An American Tolstoi. Hamlin Garland Describes a Visit to Joaquin Miller's Farm." *Philadelphia Press* 17 June 1894: 26. Syndicated, Bacheller Syndicate. Article.

B155 "Productive Conditions of American Literature." *Forum* 17 (August 1894): 690-698. Article.

B155a "Our Pioneer Sculptor. A Visit and Talk With Edward Kemeys—His Surroundings and Appearance." *Syracuse Evening Herald* 9 September 1894: 11. Syndicated, McClure Syndicate. Article.

B156 "Old Mosinee Tom." *Syracuse Daily Journal* 1 November 1894: 3; *Utica Daily Observer* 1 November 1894: 3; and *New York Press* 4 November 1894, Part 4: 4. Syndicated, Bacheller Syndicate. Fiction.

B157 "A Lynching in Mosinee." *Syracuse Daily Journal* 2 November 1894: 3; *New York Press* 11 November 1894, Part 5: 4. Rpt. *Pocket Magazine* 2 (July 1896): 5-6. Syndicated, Bacheller Syndicate. Fiction.

B158 "The Land of the Straddle-Bug." *Chap-Book* 2 (15 November 1894): 5-11; (1 December 1894): 73-76; (15 December 1894): 134-142; (1 January 1895): 182-189; (15 January 1895): 223-29; (1 February 1895): 261-271; (15 February 1895): 304-319. As *The Moccasin Ranch* (1909).

B159 "Personal Tribute to Dr. Holmes." *Writer* 7 (November 1894): 167. Letter.

B160 "Mount Shasta." *Midland Monthly* 2 (December 1894): 481-483. Article.

B161 "A Woman in the Camp: A Christmas Sketch." *Arena* 11
      (December 1894): 90-97. Fiction.

B162 "Only a Lumber Jack." *Harper's Weekly* 38 (8 December
      1894): 1158-1159. Rpt. as "An Alien in the Pines,"
      WC (1897). Fiction.

                              1895

B163 "Art Conditions in Chicago." *Catalogue, United Annual
      Exhibition of the Palette Club and the Cosmopoli-
      tan Art Club.* Chicago: The Art Institute, 24 January
      1895. Introduction, dated 12 January 1895. 5-8.

B164 "A Night Landing on the Mississippi River." *Midland
      Monthly* 3 (February 1895): 142-143. Article.

B165 "The Wapseypinnicon Tiger.   A Pioneer Sketch."
      Philadelphia Press 28 February 1895: 11, and 1
      March 1895: 11; *Utica Daily Observer* 1 March 1895:
      7, and 2 March 1895: 7. Syndicated, Bacheller Syndi-
      cate. Rpt. *PF* (1899). Fiction.

B166 "My Grandmother of Pioneer Days." *Ladies' Home Jour-
      nal* 12 (April 1895): 10. Article.

B167 "Whitman and Chicago University." *Conservator* 6 (June
      1895): 60-61. Article.

B168 "Edward Kemeys. A Sculptor of Frontier Life and Wild
      Animals." *McClure's* 5 (July 1895): 120-131. Digested
      in *Review of Reviews* 12 (July 1895): 103. Article.

B169 "Work of an Art Association in Western Towns." *Forum*
      19 (July 1895): 606-609. [Part of a symposium enti-
      tled "Successful Efforts to Teach Art to the Masses."]
      Article.

B170 "Round Up on the Grange." *New York Herald* 18 August
      1895, sec. 4: 7. Syndicated, Bacheller Syndicate.
      Article.

B171 "Hamlin Garland's Rambles." *Chicago Times-Herald* 23 August 1895: 6. Syndicated, Bacheller Syndicate. Article.

B172 "A Grim Experience." *Utica Daily Observer* 23 August 1895: 7; *Philadelphia Press* 24 August 1895: 9. Syndicated, Bacheller Syndicate. Fiction.

B173 "An Evangel in Cyene." *Harper's Monthly* 91 (August 1895): 375-390. Rpt. as "A Preacher's Love Story," *WC* (1897). Fiction.

B174 "Wagner." *Chap-Book* 3 (1 October 1895): 379-380. Poem.

B175 "Torture of Branding." *Chicago Daily News* 2 October 1895: 9. Syndicated, Bacheller Syndicate. Article.

B176 "Grace . . . A Reminiscence." *Utica Daily Observer* 16 October 1895: 7; *Philadelphia Press* 17 October 1895: 11. Syndicated, Bacheller Syndicate. Rpt. as "A Day of Grace," *PF* (1899). Fiction.

B177 "Opposites." *Bookman* 2 (November 1895): 196-197. Rpt. as "A Sheltered One," *WC* (1897). Fiction.

B178 "The Cry of the Artist." *Chap-Book* 4 (15 November 1895): 7-8. Poem.

1896

B179 "A Girl from Washington." *Syracuse Daily Journal* 15 January 1896: 3; 16 January 1896: 3; 17 January 1896: 3; 18 January 1896: 3; *Philadelphia Press* 16 January 1896: 11; 17 January 1896: 10; 18 January 1896: 12; *Chicago Tribune* 19 January 1896: 37, 39. Syndicated, Bacheller Syndicate. Rpt. as "A Meeting in the Foothills," *WC* (1897). Fiction.

B180 "Into the Happy Hunting-Grounds of the Utes." *Harper's Weekly* 40 (11 April 1896): 350-351. Syndicated as "Among the Utes," Albert Bigelow Paine Syndicate. Article.

B181 "Ouray in the Heart of the Rockies." *The Letter* 4 (1 May 1896): 129-130. Article.

B182 "In the Klondike; The Grim Realities of the Overland Trail." *Cleveland Leader* 31 July 1896. Article.

B183 "Among the Moki Indians." *Harper's Weekly* 40 (15 August 1896): 801-807. Syndicated, Albert Bigelow Paine Syndicate. Article.

B184 "With the Placer Miners; A Glimpse of Cripple Creek in 1896." Syndicated 6 September 1896, McClure Syndicate. Article.

B185 "The Most Mysterious People in the America: The Cliff Dwellers and Pueblo People of Arizona." *Ladies' Home Journal* 8 (October 1896): 5-6. Syndicated, Albert Bigelow Paine Syndicate. Article.

B186 "Captain Hance." *Los Angeles Times* 1 November 1896: 13, 14. Syndicated, Bacheller Syndicate. Fiction.

B187 "A Division in the Coulé." *New York Press* 1 November 1896: 3; *Chicago Sunday Tribune* 15 November 1896, sec. 6: 42, 43 [with altered text at beginning]. Syndicated, Bacheller Syndicate. Rpt. as "Aidgewise Feelin's," *PF* (1899). Fiction.

B188 "The Whole Troop Was Water Drunk." Syndicated 7 November 1896, Bacheller Syndicate. Article.

B189 "A Stern Fight With Cold and Hunger." Syndicated 16 November 1896, Bacheller Syndicate. Article.

B190 "Home from the City." 1893. *McClure's* 8 (November 1896): 96. Poem.

B191 "The Early Life of Ulysses S. Grant." *McClure's* 8 (December 1896): 125. Syndicated, McClure Syndicate. Article.

B192 "The Dance at Acoma." Syndicated, Albert Bigelow Paine Syndicate, 1896. Article.

B193 "With the Silver Miner; Hard Luck Story of the Small Prospector." Syndicated 1896, McClure Syndicate. Article.

B194 "A Hard Citizen and His Side of It." Syndicated 1896, McClure Syndicate. Article.

1897

B195 "Grant's First Command." Syndicated 24 January 1897, McClure Syndicate. Article.

B196 "Grant at West Point." *McClure's* 8 (January 1897): 195-210. Digested as "Grant as a Cadet," *Living Age* 9 January 1897: 143-144. Syndicated, McClure Syndicate. Article.

B197 "Upon Impulse." *Bookman* 4 (January 1897): 428-432. Rpt. *WC* (1897). Fiction.

B198 "Grant in the Mexican War." *McClure's* 8 (February 1897): 366-380. Article.

B199 "Grant's Quiet Years at Northern Posts." *McClure's* 8 (March 1897): 402-412. Article.

B200 "Grant's Life in Missouri." *McClure's* 8 (April 1897): 514-520. Article.

B201 "Grant at the Outbreak of War." *McClure's* 8 (May 1897): 601-610. Article.

B202 "An Anglo-American Club." *Critic* n.s. 27 (12 June 1897): 402. Letter.

B203 "Grant's First Great Work in the War." *McClure's* 9 (June 1897): 721-726. Article.

B204 "A Girl of Modern Tyre." *Century* 53 (July 1897): 401-423. Rpt. as "A Stop-Over at Tyre," *WC*. Fiction.

B205 "Grant in a Great Campaign." *McClure's* 9 (July 1897): 805-811. Article.

B206 "Plot to Kidnap Grant." Syndicated 15 August 1897, Mc-Clure Syndicate. Article.

B207 "Grant, His First Meeting With Lincoln." *McClure's* 9 (August 1897): 892.

B208 "*The Descendent* and its Author." *Bookbuyer* n.s. 15 (August 1897): 45-46. Review of the novel by Ellen Glasgow.

B209 "The Spirit of Sweetwater." *Ladies' Home Journal* 14 (August 1897): 5-6; (September 1897): 9-10; (October 1897): 11-12. As *The Spirit of Sweetwater* (1898). Fiction.

B210 "Joe, the Navajo Teamster." *Youth's Companion* 71 (18 November 1897): 579-580. Fiction.

B211 "The Story of Buff." *Youth's Companion* 71 (2 December 1897): 606-607. Fiction.

B212 "The Creamery Man of Molasses Gap: A Character Sketch." *Outlook* 57 (4 December 1897): 838-845. Rpt. as "The Creamery Man," *MTR* (1899). Fiction.

B213 "The Stony Knoll." *Youth's Companion* 71 (18 December 1897): 635. Fiction.

B214 "The Doctor." *Ladies' Home Journal* 15 (December 1897): 7-8; (January 1908): 7-8; (February 1908): 9-10; (March 1898): 9-10. Fiction.

1898

B215 "Outlines in Local Color." *Bookbuyer* 4 (January 1898): 690-692. Review of the novel by J. B. Matthews.

B216 "Henry George's Last Book." *McClure's* 10 (February 1898): 386. Review of *A Perplexed Philosopher.*

B217 "Ho, for the Klondike." *McClure's* 10 (March 1898): 443-454. Digested as "Overland Routes to the Klondike," *National Geographic* 9 (April 1898): 113-116; and as "Nine Routes to the Klondike," *Review of Reviews* 17 (March 1898): 331-332. Article.

B218 "The Grant and Ward Failures." *McClure's* 10 (April 1898): 498-505.

B219 "A 'Good Fellow's' Wife." *Century* 55 (April 1898): 936-952. Rpt. *MTR* (1920). Fiction.

B220 "Ulysses S. Grant, His Last Year." *McClure's* 11 (May 1898): 86-96. Article.

B221 "Sam Markham's Wife." *Ladies' Home Journal* 15 (July 1898): 8. Rpt. as "A Day's Pleasure," *Main-Travelled Roads* (1899). Fiction.

B222 "General Custer's Last Fight as Seen by Two Moon." *McClure's* 11 (September 1898): 443-448. Article.

B223 "Ulysses S. Grant (1822-1885)." *A Library of the World's Best Literature, Ancient and Modern.* Vol. 16. Ed. Charles D. Warner. New York: International Society, 1898. 6593-6600. Article.

1899

B224 "The Prairie Route to the Golden River." *Independent* 51 (20 January 1899): 245-251. Article.

B225 "Rising Wolf, Ghost Dancer." *McClure's* 12 (January 1899): 241-248. Rpt. 1902; *BAI* (1923). Fiction.

B226 "Hitting the Trail." *McClure's* 12 (January 1899): 298-304. Rev. as "Vanishing Trails" (1905). Article.

B227 "Trampers on the Trail." *Cosmopolitan* 26 (March 1899): 515-522. Article.

B228 "The Golden Seekers." *McClure's* 12 (April 1899): 505. Rpt. as "The Gold Seekers," *TGS* (1899). Poem.

B229 "The Long Trail." *McClure's* 12 (April 1899): 505. Rpt. *TGS* (1899). Poem.

B230 "The Freeman of the Hills." *McClure's* 12 (April 1899): 506. Rpt. *TGS* (1899). Poem.

B231 "Do You Fear the Wind?" *McClure's* 12 (April 1899): 507. Rpt. *TGS* (1899). Poem.

B232 "Cry of the Age." *Outlook* 62 (6 May 1899): 37. Rpt. 1902, 1933. Poem.

B233 "The Loon." *McClure's* 13 (May 1899): 65. Rpt. *TGS* (1899). Poem.

B234 "Camp Fires." *McClure's* 13 (May 1899): 65. Rpt. *TGS* (1899). Poem.

B235 "O, The Fierce Delight." *McClure's* 13 (May 1899): 66. Rpt. *TGS* (1899). Poem.

B236 "Relentless Nature." *McClure's* 13 (May 1899): 67. Rpt. *TGS* (1899). Poem.

B237 "A Mountain Pass." *McClure's* 13 (May 1899): 67. Rpt. *TGS* (1899). Poem.

B238 "The End of the Trail." *McClure's* 13 (May 1899): 67. Rpt. *TGS* (1899). Poem.

B239 "The Ute Lover." *Century* 58 (June 1899): 218-220. Rpt. *TGS* (1899). Poem.

B240 "Beacons Through the Gloom." *Outlook* 62 (1 July 1899): 527. Poem.

B241 "The Man at the Gate of the Mountains." *Ladies' Home Journal* 16 (August 1899): 9-10. Rpt. as "The Lonesome Man," *THT* (1916). Fiction.

B242 "The Average Man." 1889 [B48]. *Outlook* 63 (2 September 1899): 75. Poem.

B243 "Theodore Robinson." *Brush and Pencil* [Chicago Art Institute] 4 (September 1899): 285-286. Article.

B244 "Dakota." *Independent* 51 (19 October 1899): 2808-2809. Poem.

B245 "I. Zangwill." *Conservative Review* 2 (November 1899): 402-412. Article.

B246 "Impressions of Paris in Times of Turmoil." *Outlook* 63 (16 December 1899): 968-973. Article.

1900

B247 "The Electric Lady." *Cosmopolitan* 29 (May 1900): 73-83. Fiction.

B248 "The Eagle's Heart." *Saturday Evening Post* 172-173 (16 June 1900): 1170-1172; (23 June 1900): 1203-1205; (30 June 1900): 1227-1229; (7 July 1900): 14-16; (14 July 1900): 9-11; (21 July 1900): 14-16; (28 July 1900): 11-13; (4 August 1900): 14-16; (11 August 1900): 14-16; (18 August 1900): 10-11; (25 August 1900): 12-13, 19; (1 September 1900): 14-15; (8 September 1900): 14-17; (15 September 1900): 14-16; (22 September 1900): 16-18; (29 September 1900): 16-19. As *The Eagle's Heart* (1900). Fiction.

B249 "Stephen Crane: A Soldier of Fortune." *Saturday Evening Post* 183 (28 July 1900): 16-17. Rpt. as "Stephen Crane." *Book-Lover* 1 (September-November 1900): 6-9. Article.

B250 "Big Moggasen." *Independent* 52 (1 November 1900): 2622-2624. Rpt. *BAI* (1923). Fiction.

B251 "Jim Matteson of Wagon Wheel Gap." *Century* 61 (November 1900): 136-149; (December 1900): 287-302; (January 1901): 438-453; (February 1901): 612-622; (March 1901): 736-740; (April 1901): 869-891. As *Her Mountain Lover* (1901). Fiction.

B252 "Bad Medicine Man." *Independent* 52 (6 December 1900): 2899-2904. Fiction.

B253 "People of the Buffalo." *McClure's* 16 (December 1900): 153-159. Rev. as "The Storm Child," *BAI* (1923). Fiction.

1901

B254 "Yellow Horse." *Collier's* 26 (16 February 1901): 19. Fiction.

B255 "The Drummer Boy's Alarum." *Saturday Evening Post* 173 (9 March 1901): 7. Fiction.

B256 "Whiteman's Court." *Collier's* 27 (1 June 1901): 11. Fiction.

B257 "Homeward Bound." *Living Age* 1 June 1901: 594-596. [From *Her Mountain Lover* (1901).] Fiction.

B258 "Death in the Desert." *Munsey's* 25 (June 1901): 395. Poem.

B259 "A Tale of a Tenderfoot." *Saturday Evening Post* 174 (24 August 1901): 8-9. Fiction.

B260 "Herne's Sincerity as a Playwright." *Arena* 26 (September 1901): 282-284. [Part of "James A. Herne: Actor, Dramatist, and Man." By Garland, J. J. Enneking, and B. O. Flower, 282-291.] Article.

B261 "The Captain of the Gray-Horse Troop." *Saturday Evening Post* 174 (14 December 1901): 3-5, 19; (28 December 1901): 6-8, 18; (4 January 1902): 12-13, 18; (11 January 1902): 6-8; (18 January 1902): 10-11, 18; (25 January 1902): 13-16; (1 February 1902): 8-9, 18; (8

February 1902): 8-9; (15 February 1902): 10-11, 14; (22 February 1902): 8-10, 20; (1 March 1902): 8-9; (8 March 1902): 10-11; (15 March 1902): 10-11, 15; (22 March 1902): 10-11; (29 March 1902): 10-11. As *The Captain of the Gray-Horse Troop* (1902). Fiction.

B262 "Realism vs. Romanticism, Speech of Hamlin Garland at the Eighty-Second Dinner of the Sunset Club (January 31, 1895)." *Modern Eloquence.* Ed. Thomas B. Reed. Vol. 2. Philadelphia: Morris, 1901. 518-521. Article.

B263 "Out-of-Door Men and Books: A Talk." *Out-of-Door Americans, Talks and Lectures.* By David Starr Jordan, Ernest Ingersoll, and Hamlin Garland; editorial notes by Fred Lewis Pattee. Philadelphia: Booklover's Library, 1901. 57-62. Article.

1902

B264 "The River's Warning." *Frank Leslie's* 53 (January 1902): 297-304. Rpt. *BAI* (1923). Fiction.

B265 "Delmar of Pima." *McClure's* 17 (February 1902): 340-348. Fiction.

B266 "The Red Man's Present Needs." *North American Review* 174 (April 1902): 476-488. Article.

B267 "The Steadfast Widow Delaney." *Saturday Evening Post* 174 (14, 28 June 1902). Rpt. as "The Grub-Staker," *THT* (1916). Fiction.

B268 "Hamlin Garland Misquoted." *New York Times Saturday Review of Books* 12 July 1902: 473. Letter.

B269 "Automobiling in the West." *Harper's Weekly* 46 (6 September 1902): 1254. Article.

B270 "Hippy, the Dare-Devil." *McClure's* 19 (September 1902): 474-480. Fiction.

B271 "Will the Novel Disappear?" *North American Review* 175 (September 1902): 289-196. [A symposium; Garland contributed 295-196.] Article.

B272 "Cry of the Age." 1899 [B232]. *Outlook* 72 (29 November 1902): 740. Poem.

B273 "Sitting Bull's Defiance." *McClure's* 20 (November 1902): 35-40. Fiction.

B274 "Culture or Creative Genius?" *Outlook* 72 (6 December 1902): 780-781. Article.

B275 "New Medicine House." *Harper's Weekly* 46 (6 December 1902): 36-37. Rpt. *BAI* (1923). Fiction.

B276 "Rising Wolf—Ghost Dancer." 1899 [B225]. *Idler* 20 (1902): 471-80. Rpt. *BAI* (1923). Fiction.

B277 "The Grand Canyon at Night" and "John Hance, A Study." *The Grand Canyon of Arizona.* Chicago: Passenger Dept. of the Santa Fe, 1902. 61-62, 106-109. Articles.

1903

B278 "The Din of Inkpots." *Booklover's Magazine* 1 (February 1903): 117-118. Article.

B279 "Sanity in Fiction." *North American Review* 176 (March 1903): 336-348. Article.

B280 "The Work of Frank Norris." *Critic* 42 (March 1903): 216-218. Article.

B281 "Nistina." *Harper's Weekly* 46 (4 April 1903): 544-545. Rpt. *BAI* (1923). Fiction.

B282 "Lone Wolf's Old Guard." *Harper's Weekly* 47 (2 May 1903): 716-718. Rpt. *BAI* (1923). Fiction.

B283 "The Faith of His Fathers." *Harper's Weekly* 47 (30 May 1903): 892-893. Fiction.

B284 "The Outlaw." *Harper's Weekly* 47 (13 June 1903): 972-973; (20 June 1903): 1036-38. Rev. as "The Story of Howling Wolf," *BAI* (1923). Rpt. as "Histoire de l'Indian Loup Houlant" (1933). Fiction.

B285 "The Iron Khiva." *Harper's Weekly* 47 (29 August 1903): 1416-1419. Rpt. *BAI* (1923). Rpt. as "La Maison d'Ecole des Hommes Blancs" (1939). Fiction.

B286 "The Red Man as Material." *Booklover's Magazine* 2 (August 1903): 196-198. Article.

B287 "The Wife of a Pioneer." *Ladies' Home Journal* 20 (September 1903): 8, 42. As *A Pioneer Mother* (1922). Fiction.

B288 "New York: A City of Power." *Metropolitan Magazine* 19 (December 1903): 376-380. Article.

1904

B289 "The Light of the Star." *Ladies' Home Journal* 21 (January 1904): 13-14; (February 1904): 7-8; (March 1904): 11-12; (April 1904): 14; (May 1904): 11-12. As *The Light of the Star* (1904). Fiction.

B290 "Little Squatters." *Youth's Companion* 78 (9 June 1904): 280-281; (16 June 1904): 292; (23 June 1904): 302-303. Fiction.

B291 "Two Stories of Oklahoma. I: Nuko's Revenge. II: A Red Man's View of Evolution." *Century* 68 (June 1904): 328-329. Fiction.

B292 "The City's Allurement." *Collier's* 33 (23 July 1904): 19. Article.

B293 "The Marshall's Capture." *Harper's Weekly* 48 (10 December 1904): 1894-1900. Fiction.

1905

B294 "The Tyranny of the Dark." *Harper's Weekly* 49 (28 January 1905): 124-126; (4 February 1905): 165-167; (11
February 1905): 208-211; (18 February 1905): 244-247,
255, 257; (25 February 1905): 280-283; (4 March 1905):
326-329; (11 March 1905): 360-363, 368-369; (18 March
1905): 396-399; (25 March 1905): 432-435; (1 April
1905): 469-471; (8 April 1905): 504-506, 511; (15 April
1905): 541-543, 547; (22 April 1905): 580, 584-586; (29
April 1905): 615, 620-622; (6 May 1905): 653-655, 664-
665; (13 May 1905): 691, 696-698. As *The Tyranny of
the Dark* (1905). Fiction.

B295 "The Spartan Mother." *Ladies' Home Journal* 22
(February 1905): 10, 50. Rpt. as "Wahiah—A Spartan Mother," *BAI* (1923). Fiction.

B296 "The Doctor's Visit." *Pall Mall Magazine* 35 (May 1905):
558-590. Fiction.

B297 "Building a Fireplace in Time for Christmas." *Country
Life in America* 8 (October 1905): 645-647. Article.

B298 "Mart Haney's Mate" [Ch. 1-6]. *Saturday Evening Post* 178
(18 November 1905): 1-3, 27-32. Rev. as *Money
Magic* (1907). Fiction.

B299 "The Fireplace." *Delineator* 66 (December 1905): 1051-1056,
1140-1142. Rpt. *MTR* (1930). Fiction.

B300 "Vanishing Trails." *University Record* [University of
Chicago] 10 (1905): 53-61. Article.

B301 "Oh, The Good Days on the Trail." *University Record*
[University of Chicago] 10 (1905): 61. Poem.

B302 "A Wish." *University Record* [University of Chicago] 10
(1905): 61. Poem.

1906

B303 "The Noose: A Story of Love and the Alien." *Saturday Evening Post* 178 (6 June 1906): 3-5, 18. Fiction.

B304 "Manhattan." *Century* 72 (June 1906): 301. Poem.

B305 "The Long Trail: A Story of the Klondike." *Youth's Companion* 80-81 (6 December 1906): 621-622; (13 December 1906): 636-637; (20 December 1906): 648-649; (27 December 1906): 664-665; (3 January 1907): 1-2; (10 January 1907): 13-14; (17 January 1907): 28-29; (24 January 1907): 40-41; (31 January 1907): 52-53; (7 February 1907): 64-65. As *The Long Trail* (1907). Fiction.

1907

B306 "Money Magic." *Harper's Weekly* 51 (17 August 1907): 1198-1201; (24 August 1907): 1240-1203; (31 August 1907): 1276-1209; (7 September 1907): 1312-1305; (14 September 1907): 1350-1353; (21 September 1907): 1386-1389; (28 September 1907): 1422-1425; (5 October 1907): 1456-1459; (12 October 1907): 1492-1495. As *Money Magic* (1907). Fiction.

B307 "A Splendid Land of Giants: Our Wind River Mountains Compare Favorably with the Alps." *Pinedale Roundup* [Pinedale, Wyoming] 4.4 (September 1907): 1. Article.

B308 "The Stricken Mountaineer." *Century* 74 (October 1907): 928-930. Poem.

B309 "In That Far Land." *Circle* 2 (October 1907): 204-205; (November 1907): 298-300. Fiction.

B310 "Red Plowman." *Craftsman* 13 (November 1907): 180-182. Fiction.

B311 "In the Autumn Grass." 1893 [A9]. *Craftsman* 13 (November 1907): 182. Rpt. *Iowa, O Iowa* (1935). Poem.

1908

B312 "The Healer of Mogalyon." *Circle* 3 (March 1908): 140-145. Fiction.

B313 "The Shadow World." *Everybody's Magazine* 18-19 (April 1908): 485-493; (May 1908): 670-680; (June 1908): 797-807; (July 1908): 77-87; (August 1908): 199-211; (September 1908): 388-399. As *The Shadow World* (1908). Article.

B314 "The Outlaw and the Girl." *Ladies' Home Journal* 25 (May 1908): 7-8; (June 1908): 17-18; (July 1908): 8. Rpt. as "The Outlaw," *THT* (1916). Fiction.

B315 "A Night Raid at Eagle River." *Century* 76 (September 1908): 725-734. Rpt. as "The Cow-Boss," *THT* (1916). Fiction.

B316 "Shadow World Prize Winners." *Everybody's Magazine* 19 (November 1908): 665-679. Article.

B317 "Prairie Chickens." 1893 [A9]. *Independent* 65 (10 December 1908): 1410. Rpt. *Iowa, O Iowa* (1935). Poem.

1909

B318 "Ernest Howard Crosby and His Message." *Twentieth Century Magazine* 1 (October 1909): 27-28. Article.

1910

B319 "My Aim in 'Cavanagh.'" *World's Work* 20 (October 1910): 13569. Article.

B320	"Local Color as the Vital Element of American Fiction."
	*Proceedings of the American Academy of Arts and
	Letters and the National Institute of Arts and Let-
	ters* 1 (December 1910): 41-45. Article.

1911

B321	"'Starring' the Play." *Nation* 93 (20 July 1911): 54. Letter.

B322	"To the Editor." *Chicago Record Herald* 23 July 1911.
	[Same as "'Starring' the Play."] Letter.

B323	"My First Christmas Tree." *Ladies' Home Journal* 28
	(December 1911): 13. Article.

B324	"The Trail Makers." *Twentieth Century Magazine* 5
	(December 1911): 156-158. Poem.

B325	"The Magic Spring: Lines Read in Acceptance of the
	Punch Bowl." *Cliff-Dwellers' Yearbook*. Chicago:
	Cliff-Dwellers, 1911. 37. Poem.

1912

B326	"Middle West—Heart of the Country." *Country Life in
	America* 22 (15 September 1912): 19-24, 44. Article.

B327	"Roosevelt Praised as Man and Leader by Hamlin Gar-
	land." *Chicago Evening Post* 21 October 1912.
	Article.

1913

B328	"Nugget." *Sunset* 30 (April 1913): 335-342. Fiction.

B329	"Legitimize Every Child." *Chicago Tribune* 23 April 1913:
	8. Letter.

B330 "Sin No More Against 'Nature Children,' Says Novelist: Let Us Make Them Legitimate." *Cleveland Press* 2 June 1913: 5. Syndicated, Newspaper Enterprise Association. Article.

B331 "It's Full Time to End Our Pitiless Injustice Toward Unwed Mothers, Says Author." *Cleveland Press* 3 June 1913: 6. Syndicated, Newspaper Enterprise Association. Article.

B332 "Must Men Always Be Beasts, Trampling Women in the Mire?" *Cleveland Press* 4 June 1913: 6. Syndicated, Newspaper Enterprise Association. Article.

B333 "The Wisconsin Dramatic Society in Chicago." *Play-Book* 1 (June 1913): 20-23. Article.

B334 "The Poet of the Sierras." *Sunset* 30 (June 1913): 765-770. Article.

B335 "The New Chicago." *Craftsman* 24 (September 1913): 555-565. Article.

B336 "Kelly Afoot." *Sunset* 31 (November 1913): 919-926. Rev. as "The Trail Tramp," *THT* (1916). Fiction.

B337 "Magic." *Poetry* 3 (November 1913): 37. Poem.

B338 "A Gray Sunset." *Poetry* 3 (November 1913): 38. Poem.

B339 "To a Captive Crane." *Poetry* 3 (November 1913): 39. Poem.

B340 "The Mountains are a Lonely Folk." *Poetry* 3 (November 1913): 39. Poem.

1914

B341 "Partners for a Day." *Collier's* 52 (14 March 1914): 5-6. Rev. as "The Trail Tramp," *THT* (1916). Fiction.

B342 "A Son of the Middle Border: A Personal History" *Collier's* 53. "I, Half-Lights" (28 March 1914): 5-7, 22-23; "II, Following the Sunset" (18 April 1914): 11-12, 21-22, 24-25; "III, Woods and Prairie Lands" (9 May 1914): 15-16, 26, 28-30; "IV, The Passing of the Prairie" (27 June 1914): 13-14, 31-32; "V, Lincoln Enters Hostile Territory" (8 September 1914): 20-21, 31-32. Autobiography.

B343 "Stephen Crane as I Knew Him." *Yale Review* 3 (1 April 1914): 494-506. Article.

B344 "Shakespeare. Distinguished Men and Women Quote Favorite Lines." *New York Times* 23 April 1914: 12. Letter.

B345 "On the Road With James A. Herne." *Century* 88 (August 1914): 574-581. Article.

1915

B346 "Kelley of Brimstone Basin." *National Sunday Magazine* 28 March 1915: 387-388, 392-394. Rev. as "The Trail Tramp," *THT* (1916). Fiction.

B347 "The Ranger and the Woman." *Collier's* 55. "The Murder" (24 July 1915): 5-7; "A Meeting in the Garden" (31 July 1915): 20-22; "The Flight" (7 August 1915): 20-24; "The Jail and the Jailer" (14 August 1915): 21-23; "The Inquest" (21 August 1915): 12-13; "Helen Helps Out" (18 August 1915): 20-21. Fiction.

1916

B348 "Emily's Horse Wrangler." *Collier's* 57. "Infatuation" (5 August 1916): 5-7; "Defiance" (12 August 1916): 18-19; "Flight" (14 August 1916): 17-18. Rpt. as "The Tourist," *THT* (1917). Fiction.

B349 "The Lure of the Bugle." *Current Opinion* 61 (September 1916): 199-200. Poem.

1917

B350 "A Son of the Middle Border." *Collier's* 59. "Golden Days at Cedar Valley Seminary" (31 March 1917): 9-10, 25-26; (21 April 1917): 8-9, 27-30; "A Prairie Outpost" (26 May 1917): 13-14, 49. Autobiography.

B351 "Meetings With Howells." *Bookman* 45 (March 1917): 1-7. Article.

B352 "William Dean Howells: Master Craftsman." *Art World* 1 (March 1917): 411-412. Article.

B353 "The Graven Image." *Art World* 2 (May 1917): 127-230. Rpt. in *Prairie Gold, by Iowa Authors and Artists.* Chicago: Reilly-Britton, 1917. 21-37. Fiction.

B354 "A Place for Roosevelt." *New York Times* 7 July 1917: 8. Letter.

B355 "La Ferme du Moggason." *Revue Politique et Littéraire* 55 (28 July-27 October 1917). [*The Moccasin Ranch* (1909).] Fiction.

B356 "Hillquit Not the Man." *New York Times* 19 October 1917: 12. [Opposes socialist mayoral candidate.] Letter.

B357 "Going to School in Iowa in 1871." *Educational Review* 54 (December 1917): 495-499. [Excerpt from *A Son of the Middle Border.*] Article.

1918

B358 "A Word About Bacheller." *American* 85 (April 1918): 19. Article.

B359 "Our Alien Press." Syndicated 16 May 1918, Wheeler Syndicate. Article.

B360 "Universal Military Training." Syndicated 31 May 1918, Wheeler Syndicate. Article.

B361 "The Crime of Profiteering." *Colorado Springs Gazette* 24
      September 1918: 4. Syndicated, Wheeler Syndicate.
      Article.

B362 "No Negotiated Peace." Syndicated 2 November 1918,
      Wheeler Syndicate. Article.

                              1919

B363 "Reading Aloud to the Child." *Kindergarten Primary
      Magazine* 31 (January 1919): 134. Article.

B364 "Wants Roosevelt Stories." *New York Times* 6 February
      1919: 10. Letter.

B365 "Intellectuals' Appeal." *New York Times* 28 June 1919: 8.
      Letter.

B366 "The Passing of the Frontier." *Dial* 67 (4 October 1919):
      285-286. Review of Emerson Hough's *Passing of
      the Frontier* and Stewart Edward White's *The Forty
      Niners*.

B367 "My Neighbor, Theodore Roosevelt." *Everybody's Maga-
      zine* 41 (October 1919): 9-16, 94. Article.

                              1920

B368 "The English in Jerusalem." *New York Times* 4 January
      1920, sec. 3: 20. Letter.

B369 "The Coming of Sir Oliver Lodge." *Touchstone* 6 (January
      1920): 217. Article.

B370 "Theodore Roosevelt." *Mentor* 7 (2 February 1920): 1-12.
      Article.

B371 "The Spirit World on Trial." *McClure's* 52 (March 1920):
      33-34. Article.

B372 "Irving Bacheller, Interpreter of the Old America to the
      New." *Red Cross Magazine* March 1920: 11-12.
      Article.

B373 "William Dean Howells' Boston: A Posthumous Pilgrim-
      age." *Boston Transcript* 22 May 1919. Article.

B374 "Ulysses S. Grant." *Mentor* 8 (1 July 1920): 1-11. Article.

1921

B375 "A Great American." *New York Evening Post,* Literary
      Review, 5 March 1921: 1-2. [About Howells.] Article.

B376 "Westward Migrations.   Westward Ho!—Fourth and
      Final Stage." *New York Times* 14 August 1921, sec.
      3: 8. Article.

B377 "My Friend, John Burroughs." *Century* 102 (September
      1921): 731-742. Article.

1922

B378 "Popular Misconceptions of Grant." *New York Times* 30
      April 1922, sec. 8: 4. Article.

B379 "In the Days of My Youth." *New York Herald* 4 June 1922:
      3. Article.

B380 "John Burroughs, Poet-Naturalist." *Landmark* 4 (October
      1922): 725-728. Article.

B381 "An Appreciation." Foreword to *Roughing It.* By Mark
      Twain. New York: Gabriel Wells, 1922. xi-xiii.

B382 "Burroughs the Man." *Public Meeting of the American
      Academy and the National Institute of Arts in Let-
      ters in Honor of John Burroughs.* Academy Notes
      and Monographs 35.   New York: American
      Academy, 1922. 43-55. Article.

1923

B383 "The American Academy: Its History and Purpose." *Landmark* 5 (January 1923): 47-50. Article.

B384 "'The Fifty Immortals' Open Their New Home." *New York Times* 18 February 1923, sec. 8: 2, 7. Article.

B385 "A Midwestern Sculptor: The Art of Lorado Taft." *Mentor* 11 (October 1923): 19-34. Article.

B386 "The American Academy of Arts and Letters." *Bookman* [London] 65 (November 1923): 89-92. Article.

B387 "Current Fiction Heroes." *New York Times Book Review* 23 December 1923: 2, 23. Article.

B388 "Pioneers and City Dwellers." *Bookman* 58 (December 1923): 369-372. Article.

B389 Introduction. *The Autobiography of Davy Crockett.* Modern Students' Library. New York: Scribner's, 1923.

B390 "Joys of the Trail" and "In Praise of Booth Tarkington." *Modern Eloquence.* Vol. 2: After-Dinner Speeches. Ed. Ashley H. Thorndike. New York: Modern Eloquence Corp., 1923. 67-76.

B391 Foreword. *The Pioneer West: Narratives of the Westward March of Empire.* Selected and ed. Joseph Lewis French. Illus. Remington Schuyler. Boston: Little, Brown, 1923.

1924

B392 "Limitations of Authorship in America." *Bookman* 59 (May 1924): 257-262. Article.

B393 "A Citizen of Chicago." *New York Times* 19 October 1924, sec. 8: 14. [About Charles L. Hutchinson.] Letter.

1925

B394 "An Un-American Art." *New York Times* 3 March 1925:
      22. [About O'Neill's *Desire Under the Elms*.] Letter.

B395 "Roosevelt House." *Landmark* 7 (May 1925): 273-277.
      Article.

B396 "Memories of Henry George." *Libertarian* 5 (November
      1925): 280. Article.

B397 "Among the Corn Rows." 1890 [B73]. *Golden Book* 2 (July
      1925): 88-98. Fiction.

1926

B398 "Hope for a Clean City." *New York Times* 25 May 1926: 26.
      Letter.

B399 "The White Weasel: A True Indian Story." *Dearborn In-
      dependent* 27 (18 December 1926): 4, 5, 27. Article.

B400 "Roosevelt as Historian." Preface to *The Winning of the
      West, I.* Vol. 8 of *The Works of Theodore Roo-
      sevelt.* National Edition. New York: Scribner's,
      1926. xxvii-xxxiv.

B401 "Biographic Note" [of Fenton B. Turck]. *Bulletin of the
      Turck Foundation for Biological Research* 1 (1926):
      18. Article.

1927

B402 "Mexico." *Dearborn Independent* 8 January 1927. Poem.

B403 "John Burroughs." *World Review* 4 (6 June 1927): 265.
      Article.

B404 "Doris Ullman's Photographs." *Mentor* 15 (July 1927): 41-
      47. Article.

B405   "The Dark Side of the Moon." *Dearborn Independent* 2
        July 1927: 3, 18, 19. Rpt. 1932. Article.

B406   "The Westward March of American Settlement." *Dear-*
        born Independent 9 July 1927: 1-2, 25-26.
        [Republication, with revisions, of A43.] Article.

B407   "The Human Side of the Redman." *Current Literature* 3
        (28 November 1927): 25-26; (2 December 1927): 41-42.
        Article.

B408   "Recollections of Roosevelt." *Roosevelt As We Knew*
        Him. Ed. Frederick S. Wood. Philadelphia: John C.
        Winston, 1927. Article.

B409   "Stuart Pratt Sherman." *Commemorative Tributes of the*
        American Academy. Academy Notes and Mono-
        graphs 60. New York: American Academy, 1927.
        Article.

                                1928

B410   "I Don't Know What Happened at Those Séances."
        American 105 (March 1928): 42-43, 142-148. Article.

B411   "First and Last—The Artist." *Percy MacKaye, A Sympo-*
        sium on His Fiftieth Birthday, 1925. Hanover, New
        Hampshire: Dartmouth Press, 1928. 22. Article.

B412   Foreword. *Warpath and Cattle Trail.* By Hubert E.
        Collins. New York: Morrow, 1928. ix-xi.

                                1929

B413   "Songs and Shrines of Old New England." *Current Litera-*
        ture 6 (25-29 March 1929): 38-40. Article.

B414   "William Bacon's Man." 1891 [B87]. *Golden Book* 9
        (April 1929): 72-78. Fiction.

B415 "The Late Henry Fuller." *New York Times* 1 August 1929:
26. Letter.

B416 "Roadside Meetings of a Literary Nomad." *Bookman* 70-
71 (October 1929) 138-152; (November 1929): 246-257;
(December 1929): 392-406; (January 1930): 514-528;
(February 1930): 625-638; (March 1930): 44-57; (April
1903): 196-208; (May 1930): 302-313; (June 1930): 423-
434. Autobiography.

B417 "The Value of Melodious Speech." *Emerson Quarterly* 9
(November 1929): 5-6, 22, 24. Article.

B418 "Color in the Wheat." 1893 [A9]. *Bookman* 70 (December
1929): 394. Rpt. *Iowa, O Iowa* (1935). Poem.

B419 "From Hamlin Garland." *Tributes to Henry Blake Fuller.*
Comp. and ed. by Anna Morgan. Chicago: Ralph
Bletcher Seymour, 1929. 91-93. Article.

1930

B420 "Fortunate Coast." *Saturday Evening Post* 5 April 1930: 31.
Article.

B421 "Books of My Childhood." *Saturday Review of Literature*
7 (15 November 1930): 347. Article.

B422 Introduction. *The Oregon Trail.* By Francis Parkman.
New York: Macmillan, 1930. vii-xv.

B423 "Mark Twain's Freshness of Diction." Foreword to *A Vo-
cabulary Study of the Gilded Age.* By Alma Borth
Martin. Webster Groves, Missouri: Mark Twain
Society, 1930. 3.

B424 "Announcement of Award of the Medal of the Academy
for Good Diction on the Radio to Mr. Milton Cross
by Mr. Hamlin Garland." *Proceedings in Com-
memoration of the 25th Anniversary of the Found-
ing of the American Academy of Arts and Letters.*
Academy Notes and Monographs 72. New York:
American Academy, 1930. 41-52. Speech.

1931

B425 "Mrs. Ripley's Trip." 1888 [B35]. *Golden Book* 13 (April 1931): 45-49. Fiction.

B426 "Some of My Youthful Enthusiasms." *English Journal* 20 (May 1931): 355-362. Article.

B427 "How I Got My Literary Start." *Scholastic Magazine* June 1931: 355. Article.

B428 "Irving Bacheller, My Friend and Yours." *American Legion Monthly* September 1931: 6, 36. Article.

B429 "The American Academy of Arts and Letters and Its Campaign for Better Speech." *Education on the Air, Second Yearbook of the Institute for Education by Radio.* Ed. Josephine H. MacLatchy. Columbus: Ohio State Univ. Press, 1931. 233-236. Article.

B430 "Mr. Hamlin Garland, Member of the American Academy of Arts and Letters, Presents the Medal for Good Diction on the Radio to Mr. Alwin Bach." *Proceedings of Ceremonies to Mark the Formal Opening of the New Building of the American Academy of Arts and Letters.* Academy Notes and Monographs 75. New York: American Academy, 1931. 357-362. Speech.

B431 "Howells." *American Writers on American Literature: By Thirty-Seven Contemporary Writers.* Ed. John Macy. New York: Liveright, 1931. 285-297. Article.

1932

B432 "The Dark Side of the Moon." 1927 [B405]. *Forum of Psychic and Scientific Research* July 1932: 5-6, 23. Article.

B433 "For A Practical Man." *New York Times* 1 November 1932: 20. [Urges re-election of Hoover.] Letter.

B444 "A Camping Trip." *America in Story: A Collection of Short Stories for the Junior High School Years.* Ed. Mary C. Foley and Ruth G. Gentles. New York and London: Harper, 1932. Fiction.

1933

B445 "Histoire de l'Indien Loup Hurlant." Trans. Mme. P. Chène. *Revue Politique et Littéraire* 71 (18 February 1933): 103-107; (4 March 1933): 138-143. ["The Story of Howling Wolf" (B284)] Fiction.

B446 "Cry of the Age." 1899 [B232]. *Saturday Review of Literature* 10 (29 July 1933): 12. Poem.

1935

B447 "Le Vengeur." Trans. Mme. P. Chène. *Revue Politique et Littéraire* 73 (4 May 1935): 312-316. ["The Lonesome Man" (*THT*, 1916).] Fiction.

B448 "The Westward March of Settlement." *Frontier Times* 12 (August 1935): 499-505. Article.

B449 "Adventurous Boyhood." *Frontier Times* 12 (August 1935): 503. Poem.

B450 "Osceola's Defiance." *The American Historical Scene.* As Depicted by Stanley Arthurs and Interpreted by Fifty Authors. Philadelphia: University of Pennsylvania Press, 1935. 118-20. Fiction.

1936

B451 "John Charles Van Dyke" and "Augustus Thomas." *Commemorative Tributes.* Academy Notes and Monographs 88. New York: American Academy, 1936. 71-75, 149-153. Articles.

1937

B452 "The Late Sir James Barrie." *New York Times* 22 June 1937: 22. Letter.

B453 "A Man Most Favored." *Mark Twain Quarterly* 1 (Summer 1937): 3. Article.

B454 Rev. of *Why Was Lincoln Murdered*, by Otto Eisenschiml. *Stepladder* 23 (July 1937): 132-133.

B455 "Homage to the Pioneers." *Stepladder* 23 (September 1937): 162-163. Article.

B456 "Houtan, le Courrier Rouge." Trans. Mme. P. Chène. *Revue Politique et Littéraire* 75 (18 December 1937): 777-778. ["Hotan, the Red Pioneer."] Fiction.

B457 "We Go Up the Hill." *Stepladder* 23 (December 1937): 218-219. Article.

B458 "The Reformer Tolstoy." Preface to *Recollections & Essays*. By Leo Tolstoy. Trans. Aylmer Maude. Centenary Edition. London: Oxford University Press, 1937. vii-x.

1938

B459 "Two Excellent Bookmen." *Stepladder* 24 (January 1938): 3. Article.

B460 "A Word About Bacheller from His Friend Hamlin Garland." Introduction to *From Stores of Memory*. By Irving Bacheller. New York: Farrar and Rinehart, 1938. vii-viii.

1939

B461 "La Maison d'Ecole des Hommes Blancs." Trans. Mme. P. Chène. *Revue Politique et Littéraire* 77 (February 1939): 56-60. ["The Iron Khiva" (1903).] Fiction.

B462 "Literary Fashions Old and New." *Think* 4 (March 1939): 14, 24-27. Article.

B463 "Frontiersman of the Spirit." *News of Books and Authors* [E. P. Dutton] 1 (May-June 1939): 7. Article.

B464 "Le Vagabond." Trans. Ferron-Chene. Illus. Paul Coze. *La Petite Illustration*, no. 3 (3 June 1939): 32. ["The Trail Tramp," *THT* (1916).] Fiction.

B465 "Mystery of the Buried Crosses." *Saturday Review of Literature* 29 July 1939: 9. Letter.

B466 "Plowman Today." *Rotarian* 55 (September 1939): 6. Poem.

B467 "Let the Sunshine In." *Rotarian* 55 (October 1939): 8-11. Article.

B468 "Walt Whitman." 1893 [B144]. *Rotarian* 55 (October 1939): 9. Poem.

B469 Foreword. *Badger Saints and Sinners.* By Fred L. Holmes. Milwaukee: E. M. Hale, 1939. 13-14.

B470 Foreword. *Hamlin Garland Memorial.* American Guide Series. Mitchell, S. D.: Federal Writers Project, 1939. 7.

1940

B471 "Quiet Acceptance." *Mark Twain Quarterly* 3 (Spring 1940): 11. Article.

B472 "Dan Beard and the Scouts." *Mark Twain Quarterly* 4 (Summer 1940): 12. Article.

B473 "Twain's Social Conscience." *Mark Twain Quarterly* 4 (Summer 1940): 13. Article.

B474 Foreword. *A Chat with Robert Frost.* By Cyril Clemens. Biographical series no. 9. Webster Groves, Missouri: International Mark Twain Society, 1940. 5.

B475 "Sponsor's Message." *Gondolier* (Venice, California, High School Yearbook) 1940. Letter.

C. Articles which quote Garland extensively and verbatim

C1 "An Anti-Poverty Lecture in Boston." *Standard* 10 December 1887: 5. Lecture.

C2 "Anti-Poverty in Boston." *Standard* 3 March 1888: 8. Lecture.

C3 "The Conference . . . Full Report of the Proceedings." *Standard* 10 September 1890: 13, 25, 27-28. Speeches at the First National Single Tax Conference.

C4 "Howells Discussed at Avon-By-The-Sea." *New York Tribune* 18 August 1891: 5. Lecture.

C5 "For a 'Theatre Libre.' Prof. Hamlin Garland's Plans." *Chicago Daily News* 30 January 1892 [morning issue]: 1. Interview.

C6 "Single Tax News . . . Illinois." *Standard* 3 February 1892: 7-8. Address.

C7 "He Criticizes His Own Books. Hamlin Garland Talks about His Literary Work." *Los Angeles Herald* 27 November 1892: 3. Interview.

C8 "New York Notes." *Literary World* 24 (8 April 1893): 112. Interview.

C9 "All Men Are Equal. Hamlin Garland of 'The Arena' Speaks at the First Congregational Church." *Denver Daily News* 1 May 1893. Lecture.

C10   "Hamlin Garland. A Virile New Force in Our Literature."
      Chicago Inter-Ocean 18 February 1894: 31. Inter-
      view.

C11   "Realism and Romanticism." *New York Times* 14 March
      1894: 4. Debate.

C12   Bentzon, Th. [Pseud. of Marie Thérèse Blanc.] "Un Radi-
      cal de la Prairie" *Revue Des Deux Mondes* 157
      (1900): 139-80. Essay and interview.

C13   "Hamlin Garland Suggests for Colorado New National
      Playground," *Rocky Mountain News* 6 August 1905,
      sec. 1. Interview.

C14   "Good Evening: Hamlin Garland." *Wisconsin State Jour-
      nal* 30 January 1909: 3. [About the production of
      Garland's play, *Miller of Boscobel.*] Interview.

C15   "Why Hamlin Garland Find Wider Fields in the Drama
      Than in the Writing of Novels." *New York Times*
      11 April 1909, sec. 5: 4. Interview.

C16   "Music and Drama: Chicago Theater Society's Repertory
      Announced." *Chicago Daily Tribune* 18 August
      1911: 8, 9. Article and interview.

C17   Hackett, Carleton. "Have We Progressed? Hear Hamlin
      Garland." *Chicago Evening Post* 29 December 1911:
      5. [About the Chicago Theater Society.] Interview.

C18   Woods, Mary Katherine. "Hamlin Garland Attacks 'The
      American Drama'; Thinks Dramatic Quality Sacri-
      ficed to Greed." *New York Morning Telegraph* 7
      January 1912, sec. 2: 2. Interview.

C19   Kilmer, Joyce. "Says New York Makes Writers Trades-
      men." *New York Times Magazine* 28 May 1916: 13-
      14. Interview.

C20   "One Side of Roosevelt." *New York Times* 18 April 1920,
      sec. 6: 5. Interview.

C21   "In Honor of Howells." *New York Times* 27 February
       1921, sec. 4: 6. Interview.

C23   Faris, John T. "Life on the Middle Border." *Forward, A
       Paper for Young People* 57 (22 January 1938): 12-13.
       Essay and interview.

C24   "Academy Elects Benet and Cather." *New York Times* 11
       November 1938: 26. [About Garland's last address
       to the American Academy of Arts and Letters.]
       Article.

C25   "Gregory Parent's Diary." *Journal of the American Society
       for Psychical Research* 33 (1939): 257-269. Article.

A Checklist of Hamlin Garland's Letters

To unknown or incomplete recipients

ALS	? [first 2 pgs. missing]	n.d.	USC	
TC	"Please speak your mind..."	n.d.	USC	
TC	"To American Authors"	[1917-18]	USC	re: American Authors Fund
ALS	to [Maurique, Mrs.?]	June 15	Virginia	
ALS	to [obliterated]	April 26 [1917]	Morgan	Crane material turned over to Des Moines Lib.
ALS	to [Plauplon], George A.	Nov. 24	Virginia	
AnS	[incomplete note or letter]	June 6, 1896	Newberry	
ALS	to ?	Aug. 15, 1894	U of Iowa	[incomplete]
TLC	to "Harper's Young People"	Feb. 14, 1912	USC	re: Authors League
ALS	to Dear Friends	Aug. 3, 1894	Yale	at work on homestead
ALS	to Dear Friends	May 3	Homestead	bon voyage
ALS	to Dear Friends	June 24 [1894]	Yale	at work fixing up homestead
ALC	to Dear Madam	Aug. 11 [1902]	USC LB 79	wants to buy pottery collection
TLC	to Dear Maidie	Oct. 28	USC	
TLC	to Dear Maidie	n.d.	USC	re: benefits of Turck's treatment
ALS	to Dear Sir	March 31 [1910]	Homestead	no degrees; books only claim to respect
ALC	to Dear Sir	Oct. 11 [1902]	USC LB 102	re: lectures
ALS	to Dear Sir	May 20	Duke	is not responsible for grammar of characters
ALC	to Dear Sir	Oct. 14 [1902]	USC LB 103	re: lectures
ALC	to Dear Sir	June 18 [1903]	USC LB 164	bill for photos
ALC	to Dear Sir	[Nov. 18, 1901]	USC LB 11	re: lectures
ALS	to Dear Sir	Feb. 9	Brigham Young	sending lithographs
ALS	to Dear Sir	May 2, 1894	Colorado C	re: wants to appear last on a program
ALS	to Dear Sir	Dec. 24, 1894	Yale	difficulty writing short humorous stories

ALS	to Dear Sir	March 8, 1899	Virginia	at work on *Trail of the Goldseekers*
ALC	to Dear Sir	[Sept. 22, 1902]	USC LB 84	re: lectures
ALC	to Dear Sir	Oct. 27 [1902]	USC LB 108	re: hearing device for father
ALC	to Dear Sir	Feb. 9 [1903]	USC LB 126	is "tempted" to do story of Klondike/ Black Hawk
ALC	to Dear Sir	June 4, 1902	USC LB 69	prints are satis- factory
ALC	to Dear Sir	Oct. 8 [1902]	USC LB 97	
ALS	to Dear Sir	Sept. 23, 1900	Virginia	sends 2 Indian stories
ALC	to Dear Sir	[June 1903]	USC LB 165	re: bill for photos
ALC	to Dear Sir	Nov. 25 [1903]	USC LB 176	re: "The Squatters"
TLC	to Dear Sir	n.d.	USC	sympathizes with what Pattee & Brownell say
ALC	to Dear Sir	[Jan. 1901]	USC LB 35	establ. PO on Kansas land
ALC	to Dear Sir	June 26 [1902]	USC LB 76	settles bill
ALC	to Dear Sir	June 24 [1902]	USC LB 74	re: lectures
ALC	to Dear Sir	May 12 [1904]	USC LB 198-9	re: newspaper serial of *Captain*
ALC	to Dear Sir	July 20, 1903	USC LB 174	re: donating Zulime's land for school
ALC	to Dear Sir	[Feb. 14-June 1903]	USC LB 128	
ALS	to Dear Sir	n.d.	Harvard	
ALS	to Dear Sir	Sept. 12, 1896	Yale	re: *Grant*, future forthcoming works
TLS	to Dear Sir	July 22 [1920]	Boston PL	wishes to publicize Turck's treatment
ALS	to Dear Sir	Jan. 10, 1895	U of Iowa	stories, poems that are "successful readings"
ALC	to Dear Sir	May 12 [1902]	USC LB 53	re: excessive bills
ALC	to Dear Sir	Sept. 3 [1902]	USC LB 81	re: lectures
ALC	to Dear Sir	Sept. 22 [1904]	USC LB 210	
ALC	to Dear Sir	Aug. 15 [1902]	USC LB 80	when will "Corn Dance at Acoma" be publ?
TLS	to Taft Committee	n.d.	Hunt	re: Academy testimonial
TLC	to Whom It May Concern	n.d.	USC	
TLC	to Whom It May Concern	July 13	USC	
ALS	to Whom It May Concern	Dec. 22, 1938	Miami U	letter of introd. for Eldon Hill

Alphabetical by correspondent

TLS	to Aawn, D. H.	May 19 [1923]	USC	residences of the McClintocks
ALS	to Abbott, Edgar	Feb. 27, 1896	Bowdoin	thanks for rev. of *Rose*; begins *Grant*
TLC	to Abbott, Miss	Nov. 23, 1911	USC	thanks for interest in unspec. article
TLC	to Abel, Max	March 3, 1913	USC	re: slides
TLC	to Acklom, George Moreby	Nov. 30 [1938]	USC	crosses
TLC	to Acklom, George Moreby	n.d.	USC	crosses
TLD	to Acklom, George Moreby	Jan. 27, 1939	USC	crosses
TLC	to Acklom, George Moreby	n.d.	USC	crosses; design of book
TLD	to Acklom, George Moreby	n.d.	USC	crosses
TLC	to Acklom, George Moreby	n.d.	USC	crosses
TLD	to Acklom, George Moreby	Feb. 4 [1939]	USC	crosses
TLD	to Acklom, George Moreby	June 21, 1939	USC	crosses
TLC	to Acklom, George Moreby	n.d.	USC	crosses; Parent ms
TLC	to Acklom, George Moreby	Aug. 1, 1939	USC	crosses
TLC	to Acklom, George Moreby	June 20, 1938	USC	crosses; design of book
ALS	to Acklom, George Moreby	n.d.	USC	crosses; royalties
TLC	to Acklom, George Moreby	Nov. 17, 1938	USC	crosses
TLC	to Adams, Charles S.	n.d.	Hunt	crosses; aid to deposit his papers
ALS	to Adams, Dr.	Jan. 31 [1931]	U of Iowa	visit to Mt. Wilson
TLCS	to Adams, J. Donald	[Sept. 12, 1939]	Hunt	crosses; arguments for thanks for review
TLS	to Adams, J. T.	Oct. 23, 1939	Columbia	Acad; re: Taylor as candidate
ALS	to Adcock, St. John	July 21	U Wis-Mil	introd. of Richard Jones
TLS	to Adcock, St. John	Dec. 5 [1925]	U Wis-Mil	*Trail-Makers*
ALS	to Adcock, St. John	March 28	U Wis-Mil	re: comment on "Silent Eaters"
TLC	to Adcock, St. John	Sept. 21	USC	suggests article for *Bookman* on English visit
ALS	to Ade, George	Dec. 3, 1896	Purdue	
ALS	to Ade, George	Jan. 12 [1902]	Purdue	
ALS	to Ade, George	Oct. 12, 1995	Purdue	
TLS	to Ade, George	March 1917	Purdue	Com Lit Art circular
TLS	to Ade, George	Sept. 25, 1916	Purdue	re: endorsement of Hughes
ALS	to Ade, George	Oct. 19	Purdue	
ALS	to Ade, George	n.d.	Purdue	invites to join Little Room
ALS	to Ade, George	Feb. 28	Purdue	
TLS	to Ade, George	Sept. 14, 1916	Purdue	re: endorsement of Hughes

TLS	to Ade, George	Dec. 11	Purdue tribute	Acad; Howells
ALS	to Ade, George	Dec. 21	Purdue	Midland Authors Soc.
ALS	to Ade, George	Feb. 19	Purdue	
ALS	to Ade, George	Dec. 28	Purdue	
TLC	to Agar, John G.	April 17	USC	accepts life membership in National Arts Club
TLC	to Agar, John G.	May 31	USC	re: formation of Com Lit Art
ALS	to Ainsworth, Ed.	July 28, 1939	USC	crosses
TLD	to Ainsworth, Ed.	June 9, 1939	USC	crosses
TLC	to Akely, Carl	July 7 [1919]	USC	
TLC	to Akely, Carl Ethan	April 3 [1919]	USC	Roosevelt Memorial
ALS	to Alberti, William	Jan. 30, 1891	NY State	re: payment for potential work
ALS	to Alberti, William	[April 14-16, 1891]	NY State	single-tax address
ALS	to Alberti, William	n.d.	NY State	re: photo of HG for advertising
ALS	to Alberti, William	Jan. 26, 1891	NY State	re: payment for potential work
*ALS	to Aldrich, Lillian Woodman	[May 1891]	Harvard	*Margaret Fleming* promo
TLC	to Alexander, John W.	Feb. 10, 1913	USC	re: dinner meeting
TLC	to Alexander, John W.	March 31, 1913	USC	re: 1913 Chicago Institute meeting
TLC	to Alexander, John W.	Feb. 11, 1913	USC	Cliff Dwellers dinner
TLC	to Alexander, John W.	Feb. 17, 1913	USC	re: dinner meeting
TLS	to Alexander, William Albert	Feb. 19 [1937]	Indiana U	exhib; IU
TLD	to Aley, Maxwell	April 6	USC	re: P.E.N. election
TLC	to Allen, Edmund N.	Aug. 5. 1914	USC	re: prisons
TLC	to Allison, Mattie M.	Feb. 14, 1940	USC	re: anthologizing stories from *High Trails*
TLC	to Allison, W. S.	Nov. 28. 1911	USC	re: lectures
TLC	to Amderson, John D.	Dec. 8	USC	re: anthology
ALS	to America's Pioneers	Aug. 11, 1936	Hunt	
TLS	to American Academy	March 23 [1923]	U of Ill	
TLS	to American Academy	Oct. 15, 1931	U of Iowa	Acad; good diction
TLD	to Amsdem, Charles	May 12, 1937	USC	crosses; req. SW Museum authority
TLC	to Amsden, Charles	Oct. 16, 1939	Hunt	crosses; exhib
TLS	to Andrews	Feb. 23 [1917]	Princeton	"prize"; refuses vote for "creeds"
TLC	to Andrews, Albert	March 18, 1913	USC	
ALS	to Anthony, Alfred W.	Jan. 20 [1932]	NYPL	re: honorary degree
ALS	to Appleton Co.	Aug. 3	Indiana U	

ALS	to Appleton Co.	May 4, 1910	Indiana U	re: expiration of contract for *Eagle's*
ALS	to Appleton Co.	n.d.	Indiana U	re: new ed. of *Mountain*
ALS	to Appleton Co.	Jan. 6, 1939	Indiana U	accepts contract for *Mountain* Dollar Lib. ed.
ALS	to Appleton, William	Dec. 3, 1920 [1900?]	Columbia	
TLS	to Art Dept, *Review of Reviews*	March 8 [1922]	NYPL	re: photo of Zulime
TLS	to Art Dept, *Review of Reviews*	Feb. 24 [1922]	NYPL	
TLC	to Arthur, Helen	March 13, 1914	USC	re: favor for "Miss Lee"
TLC	to Atkinson, J. Brooks	Sept. 21	USC	re: writing for NYT
TLC	to Atkinson, J. Brooks	Jan. 10	USC	re: rate of pay for NYT
TLC	to Atkinson, J. Brooks	June 25	USC	opening of *Rip Van Winkle*
TLC	to Atkinson, Will	Oct. 18, 1912	USC	thanks for concern for Homestead fire
ALS	to Austin, Mary	March 13 [1928]	Hunt	arranging work for Mary Isabel and Hardesty
TLS	to Austin, Mary	May 3 [1925]	Hunt	re: protest of play rev. in *Step Ladder*
TLC	to Ayer, Edward E.	Dec. 5, 1911	USC	receives painting for Cliff Dwellers
ALS	to Babbitt, Irving	Oct. 29	USC	re: good diction medal; goals
ALD	to Babbitt, Irving	Sept. 24	USC	re: good diction medal
AL	to Babcock, Burton	Feb. 27, 1888	USC	re: status of HG's work
TLC	to Bacheller, Irving	June 5, 1912	USC	travel plans
ALS	to Bacheller, Irving	[1923?]	USC	re: English visits, lecture dates
TLC	to Bacheller, Irving	May 31, 1913	USC	travel plans
*TLC	to Bacheller, Irving	[after Jan. 16, 1940]	USC	contemplates approaching death
TLC	to Bacheller, Irving	May 7, 1914	USC	arranging meeting
TLC	to Bailey	Jan. 21 [1919]	USC	thanks for praise of *Son*; health status
ALS	to Bailey, L. M.	May 12	USC	
ALS	to Baker, George P.	June 16	USC	good diction medal
TLC	to Baker, Harry T.	May 29, 1912	USC	good diction medal
TLC	to Baker, Harry T.	May 20, 1912	USC	offers article to *Country Gentleman*

TLC	to Baldwin, Charles C.	Feb. 2 [1919]	Miami U	about B's use of HG's work on Howells
TLC	to Baldwin, Charles C.	Jan. 16 [1919]	USC	encl. clippings re: HG's work
TLC	to Baldwin, Charles C.	Dec. 27	USC	encl. clippings re: HG's work
*TLC	to Baldwin, Charles C.	Jan. 25 [1919]	USC	HG evals. his own work
TLC	to Ballou, Walter	April 20, 1912	USC	
TLC	to Balmer, Edwin L.	Dec. 13, 1913	USC	
ALS	to Bancroft, Frederic	Feb. 10, 1898	Columbia	thanks for use of "club"
ALS	to Bangs, John Kendrick	Jan. 3 [1903]	Swarthmore	re: article for *New Metropolitan*
TLC	to Banning, Kendall	March 27 [1916]	USC	
TLS	to Barbe, Waitman	Dec. 17 [1920]	W Vir U	
TLS	to Barbe, Waitman	May 5 [1920]	W Vir U	dislikes work of English teachers
TLC	to Barclay, Dr.	April 2	USC	re: HG's arthritis
TLC	to Barmby	Feb. 28	Miami U	arranging lecture management
TLC	to Barney, Danford	March 25 [1924]	USC	
ALS	to Barney, Danford	April 30 [1924]	Yale	
TLS	to Barney, Danford	April 16 [1924]	Yale	eval. Barney's verse
TLS	to Barney, Danford	March 25 [1924]	Yale	re: photos
ALS	to Barney, Danford	May 30 [1924]	Yale	re: Barney's verse & photos
TLS	to Barney, Danford	April 27 [1924]	Yale	
TLS	to Barney, Danford	May 2 [1924]	Yale	
ALS	to Barney, Danford	April 6 [1924]	Yale	
TLS	to Barney, Danford	April 22 [1924]	Yale	re: Barney's photos of HG
ALS	to Barney, Danford	April 12 [1924]	Yale	eval. Barney's verse
TLC	to Barnhart, Mrs. A. M.	Jan. 8, 1914	USC	
*ALD	to Barrie, Sir James M.	[Jan. 8, 1921]	USC	resp. to *Mary Rose*
TLC	to Barry, John	Feb. 11, 1940	USC	crosses; exhib.
TLC	to Bartlett, Frederick C.	June 15, 1914	USC	invite Joseph Husband to Cliff Dwellers
ALC	to Bashford, Dr.	Oct. 31 [1901]	USC LB 3	re: lectures
ALC	to Bate, Miss	Aug. 13 [1904]	USC LB 209	has no duplicate of "Spartan Mother"
ALS	to Baumgardt, Prof.	March 27 [1930?]	USC	arranging work for Mary Isabel and Hardesty
TLS	to Baxter	n.d.	U of Iowa	re: lectures
TLC	to Bay, J. Christian	Feb. 7, 1913	USC	autographs books for Bay

TLC	to Beach, Rex	Sept. 18 [1916]	USC	Com Lit Art dinner for South Amer. writers
TLC	to Beach, Rex	Jan. 9 [1919]	USC	re: lecture on death of T. Roosevelt
Tpc	to Beaman, Alexander G.	June 18, 1938	USC	
TLS	to Beaman, Alexander G.	[Feb. 21, 1936]	USC	
ALS	to Beaman, Alexander G.	May 4 [1934]	USC	
ALS	to Beaman, Alexander G.	Dec. 30 [1934]	USC	
ALS	to Beaman, Alexander G.	July 16 [1934]	USC	
TL	to Beaman, Alexander G.	Feb. 22 [1939]	USC	
Tpc	to Beaman, Alexander G.	June 18, 1938	USC	
TL	to Beaman, Alexander G.	Tue. [1937]	USC	
TLS	to Beaman, Alexander G.	Aug. 18 [1929]	USC	
ALS	to Beaman, Alexander G.	[1938]	USC	
Tpc	to Beaman, Alexander G.	July 31, 1935	USC	
TLS	to Beaman, Alexander G.	March 15	USC	
ALS	to Beaman, Alexander G.	Jan. 31	USC	
TLS	to Beaman, Alexander G.	[Sept. 9, 1934]	USC	
ALS	to Beaman, Alexander G.	April 8 [1932]	USC	
TL	to Beaman, Alexander G.	Jan. 2, 1935	USC	
ALS	to Beaman, Alexander G.	Sun. 17	USC	
ApcS	to Beaman, Alexander G.	[Aug. 10, 1929]	USC	
ALS	to Beaman, Alexander G.	Jan. 23	USC	
ApcS	to Beaman, Alexander G.	Oct. 6, 1934	USC	
ALS	to Beaman, Alexander G.	Mon.	USC	
TLS	to Beaman, Alexander G.	[1938]	USC	crosses; s/dup of n.d. ltr
TL	to Beaman, Alexander G.	[1938]	USC	
ALS	to Beaman, Alexander G.	Jan. 30, 1939	USC	
ALS	to Beaman, Alexander G.	April 12 [1934]	USC	
ALS	to Beaman, Alexander G.	Sept. 17	USC	
TLS	to Beaman, Alexander G.	May 16	USC	
ALS	to Beaman, Alexander G.	June 13 [1934]	USC	
ALS	to Beaman, Alexander G.	July 8 [7] [1930]	USC	
ALS	to Beaman, Alexander G.	April 3 [1935]	USC	
ALS	to Beaman, Alexander G.	[1938?]	USC	
ALS	to Beaman, Alexander G.	Aug. 14 [1929]	USC	
ALS	to Beaman, Alexander G.	May 4 [1934]	USC	
TLS	to Beaman, Alexander G.	April 12, 1936	USC	
ALS	to Beaman, Alexander G.	[Aug. 17, 1937]	USC	crosses
ALS	to Beaman, Alexander G.	Feb. 6. [1929]	USC	
ALS	to Beaman, Alexander G.	Dec. 24. [1930]	USC	
TL	to Beaman, Alexander G.	[Sept. 22, 1936]	USC	
TLS	to Beaman, Alexander G.	Feb. 9 [1934]	USC	
ALS	to Beaman, Alexander G.	Nov. 29	USC	
TL	to Beaman, Alexander G.	Mon.	USC	
ALS	to Beaman, Alexander G.	[Dec. 19, 1937]	USC	
ALS	to Beaman, Alexander G.	[Oct. 27, 1936]	USC	in Mexico

TL	to Beaman, Alexander G.	Sun. 4 [1937]	USC	
ALS	to Beaman, Alexander G.	July 27 [1929]	USC	
ALS	to Beaman, Alexander G.	Tue [Dec. 1934]	USC	
ALS	to Beaman, Alexander G.	[June 28, 1936]	USC	
ALS	to Beaman, Alexander G.	Jan. 25. [1929]	USC	
ALS	to Beaman, Alexander G.	Dec. 11, 1939	USC	
TLS	to Beaman, Alexander G.	March 25 [1929]	USC	
TLS	to Beaman, Alexander G.	Sept. 2 [1929]	USC	
TL	to Beaman, Alexander G.	[1938]	USC	crosses; exhib.
ALS	to Beaman, Alexander G.	Nov. 28 [27], 1934	USC	
ALS	to Beaman, Alexander G.	Dec. 10 [1931]	USC	
ALS	to Beaman, Alexander G.	Aug. 16	USC	
ALS	to Beaman, Alexander G.	Thurs.	USC	
ALS	to Beaman, Alexander G.	Jan. 5 [1931]	USC	
ALS	to Beaman, Alexander G.	[1938]	USC	
TLS	to Beaman, Alexander G.	Sept. 12	USC	
ALS	to Beaman, Alexander G.	March 18 [1929]	USC	
TL	to Beaman, Alexander G.	[March-April 1937]	USC	crosses
ALS	to Beaman, Alexander G.	Feb. 16, 1939	USC	
ALS	to Beaman, Alexander G.	Nov. 26 [1931?]	USC	
AnS	to Beaman, Alexander G.	[1937]	USC	
ALS	to Beaman, Alexander G.	May 21 [1934]	USC	
ALS	to Beaman, Alexander G.	Feb. 16, 1939	USC	
ALS	to Beaman, Alexander G.	Dec. 17 [1935]	USC	
ALS	to Beaman, Alexander G.	July 14	USC	
TL	to Beaman, Alexander G.	[1938]	USC	crosses; exhib.
ALS	to Beaman, Alexander G.	Aug. 8 [1932]	USC	
TLS	to Beaman, Alexander G.	Aug. 11 [1931]	USC	
TL	to Beaman, Alexander G.	Sun. [1938]	USC	
ApcS	to Beaman, Alexander G.	n.d.	USC	
*TLS	to Beaman, Alexander G.	April 17, 1939	USC	solicits aid in disposing of mss
ALS	to Beaman, Alexander G.	March 29 [1939]	USC	declines membership/Calif. College in China
ALS	to Beaman, Alexander G.	Jan. 15 [1928-9?]	USC	
TL	to Beaman, Alexander G.	n.d.	USC	crosses
*TL	to Beaman, Alexander G.	Sept. 18, 1936	USC	crosses; 1st idea of story
TLC	to Becker, Walda	Nov. 10, 1911	USC	re: lectures
TL	to Beer, Thomas	Dec. 19 [1923]	Miami U	offers Crane materials
ALS	to Behymer, Lynden	Dec. 4, 1939	Hunt	
TLC	to Bell, Valerie	April 17, 1913	USC	Chicago Thea Soc
*TLC	to Benton, Prof. Elbert Jay	Feb. 3 [1920?]	USC	lecture: tends to "break out in song"
ALS	to Bessey, Mabel A.	Sun. [Mar-Apr 1929]	USC	re: publ. of "Songs & Shrines of New Eng"

ALD	to Bianchi, Martha Dickinson	July 24 [1932]	Miami U	apologies for ID error in *Companions*
ALC	to Biddle, A. J. Drexel	April 30 [1902]	USC LB 43	not ready to sign contract
TLC	to Biddle, Mrs.	Aug. 15	Miami U	now chair of Research Com, Soc. Psych. Res.
ALS	to Bigelow, Poultney	June 11 [1917]	Miami U	arranging meeting
ALS	to Bigelow, Poultney	Sept. 6 [1927]	NYPL	invites to Constance's wedding reception
ALS	to Bigelow, Poultney	Aug. 22	NYPL	Acad; candidates
ALS	to Bigelow, Poultney	Sept. 28 [1930?]	NYPL	
ALS	to Bigelow, Poultney	July 27, 1930	NYPL	re: Bigelow's appearance on bio. film
ALS	to Bigelow, Poultney	Aug. 7	NYPL	
TLS	to Bigelow, Poultney	Sept. 24	NYPL	re: pollution of rivers
ALC	to Bigelow, Rev. H. S.	Nov. 18 [1901]	USC LB 10	re: lectures
ALC	to Bigelow, Rev. H. S.	Nov. 18 [1901]	USC LB 12	re: lectures
TLD	to Birkenhead, Frederick, Lord	July 8 [1924]	USC	re: Prohibition's effect
TLC	to Bishop, Joseph B.	Feb. 2	USC	re: bio. of Roosevelt
ALC	to Bissell, Arthur	Oct. 3 [1911?]	USC LB 221	[incomplete]
TLC	to Bjorkman, Edwin	May 10	UNC-CH	arranges meeting
TLS	to Bjorkman, Edwin	May 10	Miami U	arranges meeting
TLS	to Bjorkman, Edwin	April 24 [1921]	UNC-CH	arranges meeting
TLS	to Bjorkman, Edwin	April 8, [1921]	UNC-CH	club meetings—no place for writers
TLS	to Bjorkman, Edwin	Nov. 22 [1920]	UNC-CH	HG resigns from Author's Club
TLC	to Black, Fred L.	May 29	USC	re: Ford; sends draft
*ALS	to Black, Fred L.	Dec. 20 [1926]	USC	re: meeting w/ Ford
TLC	to Black, Fred L.	June 27, 1939	Hunt	distrib. of his papers
TLC	to Black, Fred L.	April 2	USC	re: article on Henry Ford
TLC	to Black, Fred L.	Dec. 3 [1931]	USC	re: Ford
TLC	to Black, Fred L.	Jan. 2, 1927	USC	re: Ford
TLC	to Black, Regina M.	April 13	USC	re: Black's interest in HG's poetry
TLC	to Blackton, James Stuart	July 8 [1916]	USC	*Money Magic* adaptation
TLC	to Blackton, James Stuart	July 7 [1916]	USC	*Money Magic* adaptation
TLC	to Blackton, James Stuart	April 19 [1916]	USC	
TLC	to Blackton, James Stuart	May 30 [1916]	USC	
TLC	to Blackton, James Stuart	Feb. 27 [1917]	USC	re: Brady's resignation from Vitagraph
TLC	to Blackton, James Stuart	Jan. 13 [1917]	USC	concern re: *Captain*
TLC	to Blackton, James Stuart	May 10 [1916]	USC	

TLC	to Blackton, James Stuart	Jan. 7 [1917]	USC	resp. to film of *Cavanagh*
ALS	to Blackton, James Stuart	[April 1916]	USC	film; *Hesper* character sketch
TLC	to Blackton, James Stuart	March 26 [1916]	USC	re: film adaptation
TLC	to Blackton, James Stuart	March 29 [1916]	USC	re: film adaptation
TLC	to Blackton, James Stuart	July 23 [1916]	USC	re: location shots
ALS	to Blackton, James Stuart	Jan. 13 [1917]	USC	concern re: *Captain*
TLC	to Blackton, James Stuart	April 10 [1916]	USC	
TLC	to Blackton, James Stuart	May 1 [1916]	USC	
TLC	to Blackton, James Stuart	March 24 [1917]	USC	
TLC	to Blackton, James Stuart	Dec. 10 [1916]	USC	
TLC	to Blackton, James Stuart	March 21 [1916]	USC	re: film adaptation
TLC	to Blackton, James Stuart	July 14 [1917]	USC	revising *Cavanagh*
TLS	to Blackton, James Stuart	March 10 [1917]	USC	want to revise *Cavanagh*
TLC	to Blackton, James Stuart	[1917]	USC	positive reviews of *Captain*
TLC	to Blackton, James Stuart	Oct. 18 [1916]	USC	re: Eastman as actor in *Captain*
*TLC	to Blackton, James Stuart	June 29 [1916]	USC	dislikes *Hesper* film
*TLC	to Blackton, James Stuart	Jan. 10 [1917]	USC	upset re: name change for *Captain*
*TLC	to Blackton, James Stuart	April 4 [1916]	USC	dissatisfied w/ *Hesper* script
TLC	to Blackton, James Stuart	Nov. 10 [1916]	USC	
TLC	to Blackton, James Stuart	Jan. 31 [1917]	USC	
TLC	to Blackton, James Stuart	Feb. 2 [1917]	USC	
TLC	to Blackton, James Stuart	Oct. 6 [1916]	USC	
ALS	to Blashfield, Edwin H.	Mon.	NY HS	Acad; solicits drawings
TLC	to Blashfield, Edwin H.	March 28	USC	film: promote Institute connection
ALS	to Blashfield, Edwin H.	Nov. 25	NY HS	Institute
ALS	to Blashfield, Edwin H.	April 14	NY HS	Acad; solicits drawings
ALS	to Blashfield, Edwin H.	Nov. 10	NY HS	Institute; HG's portrait
ALS	to Blodgett	May 15	U of Iowa	has signed unspec. letter
TLC	to Boardman, Dixon	July 5	USC	re: investments
TLC	to Bok, Edward	Nov. 10, 1911	USC	lunch—Little Room; supper—Cliff Dwellers
TLC	to Bok, Edward	Jan. 22, 1913	USC	did you receive unspec. novelette?
ALS	to Bok, Edward	Aug. 8, 1899	Princeton	has been too busy to revise *Eagle's*
*ALS	to Booth, Edwin	Feb. 21, 1889	USC	re: perf. of *MacBeth*

*ALS	to Booth, Edwin	Jan. 22, 1886	USC	re: Booth's influence
TLC	to Borglum, Gutzon	May 28, 1914	USC	arranging meeting
ALS	to Bourne, Randolph	Oct. 27, [1917]	Columbia	re: effect of irrigation
TLC	to Bowers, Florence W.	April 20, 1939	USC	crosses; review copies
TLC	to Bowman, James C.	July 23, 1915	USC	re: contribution to anthology
TLC	to Bowman, Stanley	March 13 [1917]	USC	re: revision of *The Public*
TLC	to Boyer, Will R.	Feb. 3, 1913	USC	read *Shadow World*
ALS	to Braddock	Sat.	NYU	arranges meeting at Univ. Club of LA
ALS	to Bradford	Dec. 13	Harvard	thanks for encouragement
TLD	to Bradley	Aug. 28	USC	modif. of Cathedral Pkwy house
TpcS	to Bradley, John	[Sept. 2, 1937]	Miami U	
TLS	to Bradley, John	Sun. 17	Miami U	reading ms of book
ALS	to Bradley, John	Sat. 20, 1937	Miami U	crosses
ALS	to Bradley, John	Oct. 21, 1937	Miami U	
TpcS	to Bradley, John	[Sept. 21, 1936]	Miami U	reading Peattie's book
TpcS	to Bradley, John	[Sept. 9, 1936]	Miami U	to Tahoe
ALS	to Bradley, John	Oct. 1, 1938	Miami U	congrats. on book
ALS	to Bradley, John	Jan. 9, 1939	Miami U	
TLS	to Bradley, John	April 22, 1939	Miami U	
ALS	to Bradley, John	April 12, 1939	Miami U	
ALS	to Bradley, John	May 6, 1939	Miami U	
TLS	to Bradley, John	Feb. 19, 1939	Miami U	declining health
ALS	to Bradley, John	Thurs.	Miami U	likes latest chapter
ALS	to Bradley, John	Sept. 21	Miami U	
ALS	to Bradley, John	June 10, 1937	Miami U	progress on *Crosses*
TLS	to Bradley, John	Wed. 39.	Miami U	revising *Crosses*
ALS	to Bradley, John	Oct. 10 [1938]	Miami U	travel plans; Zulime's health
ALS	to Bradley, John	Sat. 14	Miami U	reads final chapter
TLS	to Bradley, John	Sat. 25	Miami U	re: Doheny exhib.
ALS	to Bradley, John	April 8, 1937	Miami U	crosses
ALS	to Bradley, John	April 20	Miami U	finishes *Parade of the Living*
ALS	to Bradley, John	July 18, 1938	Miami U	
ALS	to Bradley, John	Sept. 4	Miami U	eager to read *Parade of the Living*; first letter
ALS	to Bradley, John	March 19, 1939	Miami U	
ALS	to Bradley, John	Oct. 20, 1936	Miami U	reads chapt.; to Mexico
TLS	to Bradley, John	June 28, 1937	Miami U	crosses
TLS	to Bradley, John	Sept. 13, 1937	Miami U	crosses
ApcS	to Bradley, John	[Oct. 16, 1936]	Miami U	going to Mexico

TLS	to Bradley, John	Wed. [Sept. 1936]	Miami U	
ALS	to Bradley, John	Tue. [Nov. 24, 1936]	Miami U	effect of death of Taft
TLS	to Bradley, John	Oct. 6, 1939	Miami U	feels loss of his teeth
ALS	to Bradley, John	July 21, 1939	Miami U	
ALS	to Bradley, John	Feb. 9, 1937	Miami U	advice re: textbook
ALS	to Bradley, John	March 7, 1938	Miami U	re: flood
ALS	to Bradley, John	Sat. 19	Miami U	re: health, *Crosses*
TLS	to Bradley, John	March 29 [1939]	Miami U	rejoices B's book is done: addressed to "slave"
ALS	to Bradley, John	Feb. 6, 1937	Miami U	re: Constance's divorce
ALS	to Bradley, John	Jan. 1, 1937	Miami U	Zulime's health
ALS	to Bradley, John	April 8 [1938]	Miami U	reads *Is Man an Absurdity?*
ALS	to Bradley, John	May 3 [1937]	Miami U	progress on *Crosses*
ALS	to Bradley, John	April 25, 1938	Miami U	detailed critique of book
TLS	to Bradley, John	Dec. 30, 1938	Miami U	HG will review B's book
ALS	to Bradley, John	Nov. 11, 1936	Miami U	HG is sick; Taft has died: "my darkest week"
ALS	to Bradley, John	Dec. 16, 1938	Miami U	working on "Fortunate Exiles"; eval. B's book
ALS	to Bradley, John	Nov. 2 [1938]	Miami U	arranging meeting
ALS	to Bradley, John	Thurs 14, 1936	Miami U	
ApcS	to Bradley, John	Oct. 28 [1938]	Miami U	
ALS	to Bradley, John	[Nov.] Tues. 17	Miami U	
ALS	to Bradley, John	May 30, 1939	Miami U	feeling his age; crosses offer hope
AnS	to Bradley, John	Sun.	Miami U	don't discuss crosses
ALS	to Bradley, John	April 19 [1938]	USC	eval. ms. *Parade of the Living*
ALS	to Bradley, John	April 17 [1938]	USC	eval. ms. *Parade of the Living*
TLS	to Bradshaw, John H.	May 21 [1939]	Miami U	about growing old
TLC	to Brady	n.d.	USC	[incomplete]
ALS	to Brady	Feb. 2, 1897	Virginia	machine to "talk letters" to mother
TLC	to Brady, Jasper E.	March 10, 1915	USC	re: contract for film of *Hesper*
TLC	to Brady, Jasper E.	April 29 [1916]	USC	
TLC	to Brady, Jasper E.	n.d. [1915?]	USC	
TLC	to Brady, Jasper E.	April 24 [1916]	USC	
TLC	to Brady, Jasper E.	Oct. 26 [1916]	USC	re: Eastman as potential actor

TLC	to Brady, Jasper E.	April 4 [1916]	USC	disappointed w/ *Hesper* script
TLC	to Brady, Jasper E.	March 21 [1915]	USC	
TLC	to Brady, Jasper E.	June 8, 1916	USC	
TLC	to Brady, Jasper E.	[1916]	USC	no desire to see *Captain* film
TLC	to Brady, Jasper E.	Oct. 27 [1916]	USC	
TLC	to Brady, Jasper E.	April 11 [1916]	USC	
TLC	to Brady, Jasper E.	March 26 [1916]	USC	
TLC	to Brady, Jasper E.	n.d. [1916]	USC	
TLC	to Brady, Jasper E.	March 29 [1916]	USC	
TLC	to Brady, Jasper E.	Feb. 27 [1917]	USC	disappointed w/ Vitagraph
TLC	to Brady, Jasper E.	June 22 [1915]	USC	
TLC	to Brady, Jasper E.	May 7 [1916]	USC	
TLC	to Brady, Jasper E.	April 25 [1916]	USC	
TLC	to Brady, Jasper E.	May 3 [1916]	USC	
TLC	to Brady, Jasper E.	July 8 [1916]	USC	
TLC	to Brady, Jasper E.	March 21 [1916]	USC	
TLC	to Brady, Jasper E.	April 5 [1916]	USC	
TLC	to Brady, Jasper E.	Jan. 10 [1917]	USC	re: *Captain* name change
TLC	to Brady, Jasper E.	[June] 18 [1916]	USC	
TLC	to Brady, Jasper E.	June 29 [1916]	USC	resp. to *Hesper* film
*TLC	to Brady, Jasper E.	March 31 [1920?]	USC	sums up Vitagraph films
TLC	to Brady, Jasper E.	April 21 [1916]	USC	
TLC	to Brady, Jasper E.	May 9 [1916]	USC	
TLC	to Brady, Jasper E.	Aug. 3 [1916]	USC	
TLC	to Brady, Jasper E.	April 6 [1916]	USC	
ALS	to Branch, Anna Hempstead	Sept. 11, 1925	Smith	Town Hall Club; admissions
TLC	to Braun, Prof.	May 2 [1919]	USC	re: address on T. Roosevelt
TLC	to Bray	Dec. 23, 1912	USC	
ALS	to Brett, George	June 12, 1900	Columbia	rpt. poems for Stedman's anthology
TLC	to Brett, George	March 9	USC	re: serial of *Companions*
TLC	to Brett, George	July 8	USC	re: uniform edition
TLC	to Brett, George	Dec. 28	USC	interest in *Son*, other books?
ALD	to Brett, George	n.d.	USC	[incomplete]
ALC	to Brett, George	Nov. 13 [1901]	USC LB 9	re: lectures-Klondike photos
TLC	to Brett, George	Dec. 26	USC	re: contracts
ALD	to Brett, George	March 30	USC	Brett's influence on autobios

TLC	to Brett, George	Dec. 23	USC	reviews status of contracts
*ALC	to Brett, George	Dec. 30 [1901]	USC LB 28	*Captain*-negotiation
TLC	to Brett, George	Oct. 8, 1921	USC	re: English ed. of *Daughter, Son*
TLC	to Brett, George	n.d.	USC	
TLC	to Brett, George, Jr.	July 14, 1936	USC	re: marketing and foregoing royalties
ALS	to Bridges, Robert	May 22	Princeton	proposes collected ed. for Scribners
ALS	to Bridges, Robert	April 2 [1923]	Princeton	recommends Robert Halliburton
ALS	to Briggs, William H.	April 23	USC	re: keeping books in print
TLC	to Briggs, William H.	n.d.	USC	
TLC	to Briggs, William H.	[1916]	USC	re: methods of work
TLC	to Brigham, Alice	June 1, 1914	USC	
ALS	to Brigham, Johnson	[1894]	Miami U	enquires re: plate, *Midland Monthly* copy
ALS	to Brigham, Johnson	[Nov. 25, 1893?]	Miami U	offers several pieces of fiction
ALS	to Brigham, Johnson	Oct. 15, 1894	Miami U	haggling over prices
ALS	to Brigham, Johnson	Nov. 10, 1893	Miami U	encl. poem, sketch, plan for two volumes
ALS	to Brigham, Johnson	Dec. 15, 1893	Miami U	re: illustration
TLS	to Brigham, Johnson	May 24, 1926	Miami U	resp. to repub. req
ALS	to Brigham, Johnson	Sept. 7 [1926]	Miami U	returns draft of B's "Sketch" of HG
ALS	to Brigham, Johnson	May 29 [1931]	Miami U	thanks for sketch of HG, *Book of Iowa Authors*
ALS	to Brigham, Johnson	Oct. 14, 1894	Miami U	prices for story
ApcS	to Brigham, Johnson	[Jan. 21, 1896]	Miami U	asks for address of Leigh Leslie
AnS	to Brigham, Johnson	[after July 15, 1930]	Miami U	resp. to repub. req
ALS	to Brigham, Johnson	Jan. 5, 1894	Miami U	returns proof
*ALS	to Brigham, Johnson	Nov. 19, 1893	Miami U	selling Boy Life sketches
trL	to Brigham, Johnson	Sept. 16, 1894	Miami U	asks if interested in novelette
TLS	to Brigham, Johnson	April 12, 1898	Miami U	Trans-Miss circular
ALS	to Brigham, Johnson	[1894]	Miami U	selling "Division in the Coolly" for $175
*ALS	to Brigham, Johnson	Jan. 26, 1894	Miami U	re: "war" his verse has sparked
ALS	to Brigham, Johnson	Oct. 10, 1894	Miami U	selling stories: "Woman in Camp," "Metallus"

ALS	to Brigham, Johnson	n.d.	Miami U	re: selling "Shasta" for $30
ALS	to Brigham, Johnson	Nov. 5, 1893	Miami U	interested in new magazine-*Midland Monthly*
*ALS	to Brooks, Van Wyck	Dec. 27, 1938	U Penn	describes influence of Wilkins
*ALS	to Brooks, Van Wyck	May 24 [1925]	U Penn	commends *James*; influence of James
ALD	to Brooks, Van Wyck	Aug. 31, 1939	USC	draft of U Penn copy
*ALS	to Brooks, Van Wyck	Jan. 20, 1939	U Penn	crosses; gives B. Howells material
*ALS	to Brooks, Van Wyck	Nov. 8, 1936	U Penn	commends *Flowering*; HG's unmet aspirations
*ALS	to Brooks, Van Wyck	Dec. 5, 1937	U Penn	detailed sketch of Elinor Howells
ALS	to Brooks, Van Wyck	Dec. 17, 1939	U Penn	
TLS	to Brooks, Van Wyck	Dec. 7, 1938	U Penn	crosses; ms finished; offers Howells material
ALS	to Brooks, Van Wyck	July 14	U Penn	
ALS	to Brooks, Van Wyck	Oct. 23	U Penn	
ALS	to Brooks, Van Wyck	Aug. 14	U Penn	
ALS	to Brooks, Van Wyck	Dec. 2, 1938	U Penn	
*ALS	to Brooks, Van Wyck	Dec. 21 [1936]	U Penn	crosses; commends Hawthorne chapter
*ALS	to Brooks, Van Wyck	May 28 [1925]	U Penn	Twain; view of America
*TLS	to Brooks, Van Wyck	Aug. 31, 1939	U Penn	considers destroying mss
*ALS	to Brooks, Van Wyck	Jan. 31, 1939	U Penn	Howells; sketch of Wilkins, Jewett
ALS	to Brooks, Van Wyck	Jan. 12, 1939	U Penn	Howells material ready; Congress wants mss
*ALS	to Brooks, Van Wyck	June 16, 1939	U Penn	crosses; now interested only in 4th Dimension
ALS	to Brooks, Van Wyck	Nov. 2	U Penn	
ALS	to Brooks, Van Wyck	March 18, 1939	U Penn	
*ALS	to Brooks, Van Wyck	Nov. 5, 1934	U Penn	commends *Emerson*
ALS	to Brooks, Van Wyck	Jan. 23	U Penn	offers Howells letter
ALS	to Brooks, Van Wyck	June 4	U Penn	Town Hall Club; invites membership
ALS	to Brooks, Van Wyck	April 21	U Penn	
ALS	to Brooks, Van Wyck	Nov. 8 [1937]	U Penn	crosses; Dutton receptive
ALS	to Brooks, Van Wyck	Sept. 6	U Penn	interest in Emerson m

ALS	to Brooks, Van Wyck	April 10, 1939	U Penn	re: Howells' *Boys Town*
ALS	to Brooks, Van Wyck	May 16, 1939	U Penn	
ALS	to Brooks, Van Wyck	Jan. 4, 1940	U Penn	
ALS	to Brooks, Van Wyck	Sept. 30, 1936	U Penn	commends *Flowering of New England*
ALS	to Brooks, Van Wyck	April 10 [1932]	U Penn	rereads *Emerson*
ALS	to Brooks, Van Wyck	May 27, 1939	U Penn	Howells exhib. at Doheny; disposition of papers
ALS	to Brooks, Van Wyck	Dec. 13 [1931]	U Penn	
ALS	to Brooks, Van Wyck	April 17, 1937	U Penn	
ALS	to Brooks, Van Wyck	March 27	U Penn	
ALS	to Brooks, Van Wyck	Sept. 19 [1933]	U Penn	resp. to b-day greeting
ALS	to Brooks, Van Wyck	July 5, 1938	U Penn	
ApcS	to Brooks, Van Wyck	Oct. 29, 1938	U Penn	
ALS	to Brooks, Van Wyck	July 21	U Penn	
ALS	to Brooks, Van Wyck	Nov. 4 [1938]	U Penn	sends Howells material
ALS	to Brooks, Van Wyck	Oct. 20, 1936	U Penn	offers use of letters; exhib.
TLS	to Brooks, [William E.?]	Dec. 12 [1918]	USC	re: potential AEF service in France
TLC	to Brown	March 9	USC	re: lectures
*ALS	to Brown, Clarence	May 27, 1938	USC	praises *Conquest*, Garbo, Boyer
TLS	to Brown, Miss	Jan. 31	Virginia	sketch of MacDowell
TLC	to Brown, [Horace B.?]	Jan. 13, 1940	USC	crosses; refuses to sign article by W. Wellman
TLC	to Brown, [Howard Clark?]	Oct. 5 [1923]	USC	re: publ. of Academy article in NYT
ALS	to Browne, Charles Francis	April 26	USC	thanks for praise
ALS	to Browne, Charles Francis [?]	Mon. [1923?]	USC	
TLC	to Browne, Charles Francis	Feb. 18	USC	
TLC	to Browne, Charles Francis	Nov. 9, 1914	USC	
*ALS	to Browne, Francis F.	Oct. 21, 1893	Middlebury	*Dial* quarrel
*ALS	to Browne, Francis F.	Oct. 12, 1893	Middlebury	*Dial* quarrel
ALS	to Bryant, Mrs.	Aug. 8, 1939	USC	
TLC	to Buchanan, [Thompson?]	June 28	USC	refuses to sign "report"
*TLS	to Bull, Charles	March 21, 1939	USC	declines to be subject of thesis
ALS	to Burdette, Clara	Jan. 3 [1936]	Hunt	
TLC	to Burroughs, John	March 21 [1917]	USC	re: health; treatment at Battle Creek
ALC	to Burrows Bros, Cleveland	Dec. 7 [1903]	USC LB 179	declines unspec. work

ALC	to Burton, Richard	May 23 [1902]	USC LB 61	arranges meeting
TLS	to Bush	Sept. 1, 1939	Miami U	about ratio of men/ women on prairie
TLS	to Bush	Aug. 18, 1939	Virginia	agrees to aid w/ diss
TLC	to Butler, Ellis P.	May 22, 1913	USC	
TLS	to Butler, Ellis P.	June 4	NYPL	query re: potential anthology of HG
ApcS	to Butler, Ellis P.	Jan. 17, 1915	NYPL	
TLC	to Butler, Ellis P.	March 28, 1913	USC	
TLS	to Butler, Ellis P.	March 17, 1925	NYPL	Town Hall Club; meetings
TLS	to Butler, Ellis P.	Nov. 27, 1916	U of Iowa	Author's League; Com Lit Art
TLS	to Butler, Ellis P.	Dec. 1, 1916	U of Iowa	Author's League
TLS	to Butler, Ellis P.	March 4, 1913	NYPL	Author's League; formed
TLC	to Butler, Ellis P.	Feb. 26, 1913	USC	
ALS	to Butler, Ellis P.	Feb. 6	U of Iowa	Author's League; dissatis. w/ candidate
TLS	to Butler, Ellis P.	March 1917	NYPL	Com Lit Art circular
TLS	to Butler, Ellis P.	June 29	U of Iowa	
ALS	to Butler, Ellis P.	May 7	NYPL	
TLS	to Butler, Ellis P.	Dec. 14 [1916]	NYPL	Com Lit Art; dinner for South Amer. writers
ALS	to Butler, Nicholas M.	July 20, [1919]	Columbia	Acad
TLC	to Butler, Nicholas M.	Oct. 15, 1937	Am Acad	on death of R.U. Johnson
TLC	to Butler, Nicholas M.	Oct. 7 [1923]	USC	Acad; HG's service
ALS	to Butler, Nicholas M.	Oct. 1 [1932]	Am Acad	resigns from committee
TLC	to Butler, Nicholas M.	Jan. 22	USC	
TLS	to Butler, Nicholas M.	Jan. 10, 1919	Columbia	Com Lit Art; req fund for Carnegie Endow/ Peace
TLC	to Butler, Nicholas M.	May 2	USC	re: Roosevelt address
TLS	to Butler, Nicholas M.	Jan. 31 [1924]	Am Acad	re: exhib. of 1824 writers
TLC	to Butler, Nicholas M.	Dec. 16	USC	
*TLS	to Butler, Nicholas M.	May 11 [1920]	Pulitzer	Pulitzer; reluctantly votes for *Beyond the Horizon*
TLS	to Butler, Nicholas M.	Sept. 8 [1926]	Am Acad	nomination procedures
ALS	to Butler, Nicholas M.	Sept. 9 [1926]	Am Acad	nomination procedures
TLC	to Cable, George W.	June 20, 1921	Tulane	Acad; req. nominations

TLS	to Cable, George W.	Oct. 9, 1916	Tulane	invitation to National Arts Club exhib.
TLS	to Cable, George W.	April 12, 1898	Tulane	Trans-Miss circular
ALS	to Cable, George W.	May 29, 1896	Tulane	receives check for "Ouray"
ALS	to Cable, George W.	Jan. 26	Tulane	Institute; meeting
TLS	to Cable, George W.	March 1917	Tulane	Com Lit Art circular
TLS	to Cable, George W.	Oct. 26, 1916	Tulane	is pleased Cable will come to National Arts Club
ALS	to Cable, George W.	June 7 [1921]	Tulane	Acad; solicits books
ALS	to Cable, George W.	Feb. 21, 1896	Tulane	has no articles to submit to *The Letter*
ApcS	to Cable, George W.	[April 4, 1896]	Tulane	sells "Ouray" to *The Letter*
ALS	to Cable, George W.	Sept. 13 [1921]	Tulane	Acad; solicits books
ALS	to Cable, George W.	Oct. 4	Tulane	[incomplete]
TLS	to Cable, George W.	Nov. 9, 1916	Tulane	further invitation to National Arts Club
TLS	to Cable, George W.	April 21, 1921	Tulane	Acad; solicits books for new building
ALS	to Cable, George W.	Sept. 21 [1921]	Tulane	Acad; solicits books
*ALS	to Cable, George W.	July 29, 1886	Tulane	req. re: negroes
ALS	to Cable, George W.	Nov. 27	Tulane	rejoices over success of Cable's new book
*ALS	to Cable, George W.	Aug. 7, 1886	Tulane	req. info re: congo dance
ALS	to Caldwell	March 18, 1893	Morgan	arranging lecture, meeting
ALS	to Calver	May 18	U Wis-Mil	
TLC	to Campbell photographer	March 5	Miami U	destroy plates of photos
ALD	to Canby, Henry Seidel	n.d.	USC	porno rant; resp. to *Sat Rev Lit*
ALS	to Canfield, Dorothy	July 6, 1929	U Vermont	commends *Hillsboro People*
TLC	to Cannon, William M.	May 28, 1927	USC	arranges meeting
TLS	to Caplan, Albert	March 19 [1929]	Temple	declines to offer book to Scriptorum Press
TLS	to Caplan, Albert	Feb. 24, 1929	Temple	will consider offering book to Scriptorum Press
TLC	to Carlton	March 17, 1914	USC	re: resignation from unspec. group
TLC	to Carlton	Nov. 9, 1914	USC	thanks for list of unspec. mss
ALS	to Carlton, W. N. C.	Aug. 2	Newberry	
ALS	to Carlton, W. N. C.	Jan. 24	Newberry	

ALS	to Carlton, W. N. C.	June 14	Newberry	re: board meetings of Cliff Dwellers
ALS	to Carman, Bliss	Feb. 9	NYU	wishes success for unnamed periodical
*TLD	to Carr, Harry	Dec. 30, 1934	USC	Calif. lit as product of environment
TLS	to Carrel, Alexis	Jan. 29, 1936	USC	psychic; *Forty*
ALS	to Case, Leland	Nov. 3 [1938]	Miami U	re: pub. of last Academy address
ALS	to Cawein, Madison	Nov. 18, 1891	Penn HS	commends "Farmstead" & "Yule"; Riley
ALS	to Cawein, Madison	Jan. 30, 1912	Virginia	Institute; meeting
TLC	to Chamberlin, Joseph E.	Dec. 9 [1925]	USC	plans for logbooks
TLC	to Chamberlin, Joseph E.	May 20 [1920]	USC	re: dates of Howells poems
ALS	to Chambers, Julius	Jan. 4, 1893	NYU	suggests drama article
*ALS	to Chambers, Julius	Feb. 2, 1894	Virginia	introd. Crane
ALS	to Chambers, Julius	Nov. 14	Virginia	sends advance sheets of "new book"
ALS	to Chambers, Julius	Dec. 21, 1895	NYU	agrees to read unspec. mss
ALS	to Chambers, Julius	n.d.	Virginia	has too many commitments to promise article
TLC	to Chandler, Harry	Feb. 4, 1934	USC	S Calif Mus Hist Sculpture
TLC	to Chandler, Harry	Oct. 30, 1939	Hunt	crosses; depo artifacts
TLD	to Chandler, Harry	Dec. 10 [1933]	USC	S Calif Mus Hist Sculpture
ALS	to Chandler, Harry	[1934]	USC	S Calif Mus Hist Sculpture
ALS	to Chandler, Harry	Jan. 8 [1934]	USC	S Calif Mus Hist Sculpture
ALS	to Chapman, John Jay	May 6	Harvard	thanks for appreciation of unspec. book
*ALS	to Chapman, John Jay	Mon. [ca. April 1925]	Harvard	approves KKK
ALS	to Chapman, John Jay	Jan. 30	Harvard	thanks for dinner
ALS	to Chapman, John Jay	Nov. 6	Harvard	agrees w/ Chapman re: "our universities"
ALS	to Chapman, William G.	May 6 [1910]	Virginia	
ALS	to Chapman, William G.	May 8 [1910]	Virginia	
TLS	to Chapman, William G.	Nov. 28, 1911	Virginia	
ALS	to Chapman, William G.	May 17 [1910]	Virginia	
TLS	to Chapman, William G.	Nov. 6 [1916]	Virginia	
ALS	to Chapman, William G.	Nov. 11 [1915]	Virginia	

ALS	to Chapman, William G.	n.d.	Virginia	
ALS	to Chapman, William G.	Nov. 16	Virginia	
ALS	to Chapman, William G.	Nov. 17 [1910]	Virginia	
ALS	to Chapman, William G.	Jan. 2	Virginia	
ALS	to Chapman, William G.	April 29 [1910?]	Virginia	
ALS	to Chapman, William G.	April 22 [1910?]	Virginia	
ALS	to Chapman, William G.	June 4 [1914]	Virginia	
ALS	to Chapman, William G.	[Sept.] 22 [1914]	Virginia	
ALS	to Chapman, William G.	Aug. 22 [1910]	Virginia	
ALS	to Chapman, William G.	Aug. 18 [1914]	Virginia	proposes serial of *Son*
ALS	to Chapman, William G.	Feb. 17	Virginia	
ALS	to Chapman, William G.	July 17 [1910]	Virginia	sends 3 sketches for serialization
ALS	to Chapman, William G.	April 12 [1910?]	Virginia	
ALS	to Chapman, William G.	April 19 [1910?]	Virginia	
ALS	to Chapman, William G.	March 1 [1915]	Virginia	
TLS	to Chapman, William G.	March 11 [1915]	Virginia	
TLS	to Chapman, William G.	June 15, 1914	Virginia	
ALS	to Chapman, William G.	June 18 [1910]	Virginia	
ALS	to Chapman, William G.	March 24 [1914]	Virginia	offers *Forester's* for serialization
ALS	to Chapman, William G.	May 12 [1910]	Virginia	contract for serial of *Cavanagh*
TLS	to Chapman, William G.	June 11 [1919]	Virginia	
ALS	to Chapman, William G.	June 27 [1910]	Virginia	
ALS	to Chapman, William G.	July 21 [1910]	Virginia	sends "Black Eyed Norsk" for serialization
ALS	to Chapman, William G.	June 24, 1914	Virginia	
ALS	to Chapman, William G.	June 20, 1911	Virginia	
ALS	to Chapman, William G.	June 1 [1910]	Virginia	asks if C. could serialize *Hesper*
TLS	to Chapman, William G.	Jan. [1932]	Virginia	
TLC	to Chapman, William G.	April 28 [1910]	USC	re: serial rights to *Cavanagh*
TLS	to Chapman, William G.	Sept. 16, 1914	Virginia	
ALS	to Chapman, William G.	Sept. 12 [1914]	Virginia	
ApcS	to Chapman, William G.	Sept. 25, 1910	Virginia	
ApcS	to Chapman, William G.	Dec. 9, 1914	Virginia	
ApcS	to Chapman, William G.	Sept. 26, 1910	Virginia	
ALS	to Chapman, William G.	March 3 [1915]	Virginia	
ALS	to Chapman, William G.	Sept. 15 [1911]	Virginia	
ALS	to Chapman, William G.	Nov. 3 [1915]	Virginia	
ALS	to Chapman, William G.	May 12 [1910]	Virginia	
ALS	to Chapman, William G.	May 14 [1914]	Virginia	
ALS	to Chapman, William G.	May 13, 1915	Virginia	
ALS	to Chapman, William G.	Oct. 9 [1915]	Virginia	desire to film *Captain*
ALS	to Chapman, William G.	[May 1910]	Virginia	

ALS	to Chapman, William G.	March 1910	Virginia	
ALS	to Chapman, William G.	Aug. 8 [1910]	Virginia	"Black Eyed Norsk" is rejected
ALS	to Chapman, William G.	July 13 [1910]	Virginia	
ALS	to Chapman, William G.	Oct. 5 [1910]	Virginia	
ALS	to Chapman, William G.	March 8 [1915]	Virginia	
ALS	to Chapman, William G.	Aug. 8 [1910]	Virginia	
ALS	to Chapman, William G.	Oct. 3 [1906]	Virginia	
ALS	to Chapman, William G.	Oct. 1 [1911]	Virginia	
TLS	to Chapman, William G.	Oct. 13, 1916	Virginia	
ALS	to Chapman, William G.	Oct. 27 [1915]	Virginia	
ALS	to Chapman, William G.	Oct. 2 [1910]	Virginia	
ALS	to Chapple, Joe Mitchell	July 21 [1932]	USC	
TLC	to Charlton, George J.	June 4, 1912	USC	re: decorating Cliff Dwellers
TLC	to Charlton, George J.	June 6, 1912	USC	re: decorating Cliff Dwellers
TLC	to Chatfield-Taylor, Hobart	May 20, 1913	USC	Cliff Dwelers: banquet committee
TLC	to Chatfield-Taylor, Hobart	May 27, 1913	USC	re: Cliff Dwellers
ALS	to Cheney, John Vance	May 22, 1893	Hunt	
ALS	to Cherry, Thomas Crittendon	Feb. 19 [1927]	USC	likes C's history of Kentucky
ALD	to Cherry-Garrard, Apsley George	Oct. 16	USC	re: bio of Shaw
TLD	to Cherry-Garrard, Apsley George	Oct. 17	USC	[incomplete]
TLC	to Cherry-Garrard, Apsley George	[Oct. 17]	USC	re: bio of Shaw
ALS	to Chichester, Charles F.	Dec. 11	Indiana U	re: book edition of *Mountain*
TLC	to Chollett, Mrs. Calvin [by sec'y]	May 16, 1913	USC	
TLC	to Chollett, Mrs. Calvin	April 29, 1912	USC	
TLC	to Chollett, Mrs. Calvin	May 8, 1913	USC	
TLC	to Chollett, Mrs. Calvin	May 8, 1913	USC	re: Booth lectures
ALS	to Christensen, Frances	[July 24, 1939]	USC	re: exhib. at Doheny
ALS	to Christensen, Frances	July 26 [1939]	USC	re: exhib. at Doheny
TLS	to Christensen, Frances	[July 28, 1939]	USC	crosses; re: exhib. at Doheny
ALS	to Christensen, Frances	Aug. 20, 1939	USC	re: exhib. at Doheny
TLS	to Christensen, Frances	March 22 [1936]	USC	re: exhib. at Doheny
TLC	to Christie, Gerald	n.d.	USC	solicits English lectures
ALS	to Chubb, Thomas C.	Dec. 17 [1920]	Miami U	praises poems
TLC	to Churchill, Winston	June 30, 1916	USC	opposed to affiliating w/ "labor"

TLC	to Churchill, Winston	May 3 [1912]	USC	arranging "Roosevelt" meeting
TLS	to Clampitt	Friday 27 [1922]	USC	re: dislike for farm work
ALS	to Clark	Jan. 27 [1930]	Yale	
ALS	to Clark	Feb. 29	NYU	will attend performance of C's plays
TLS	to Clark	May 17	Yale	
ALS	to Clark	July 9 [1911-13]	NYU	Chicago Thea Soc: will read C's play
*ALS	to Clark, Barrett H.	Feb. 22 [1930]	USC	porno rant: O'Neill
*TLC	to Clark, Barrett H.	March 7, 1934	USC	history of *Under the Wheel*
ALS	to Clarke, Donald	Jan. 21, 1937	USC	crosses; no $ interest
ALC	to Clarke, H.	[Dec. 1903]	USC LB 187	*Hesper*-newspaper serial
ALC	to Clarke, H.	[Dec. 1903]	USC LB 187	*Hesper*-newspaper serial
ALC	to Clarke, H.	Dec. 30 [1903]	USC LB 190	potential serial of *Hesper*
ALS	to Clemens, Cyril	April 18	U of Iowa	re: missed meeting
TL	to Clemens, Cyril	Jan. 18 [1929]	U of Iowa	re: *Life and Letters of Howells*
TLS	to Clemens, Cyril	Jan. 13, 1940	U of Iowa	re: Opie Read, Zane Grey
ALS	to Clemens, Cyril	March 27	U of Iowa	thanks for election of Knight of MT
ALS	to Clemens, Cyril	Oct. 31	U of Iowa	
ALS	to Clemens, Cyril	Oct. 28	U of Iowa	re: meeting
TLS	to Clemens, Cyril	Oct. 27, 1939	U of Iowa	crosses; controv; *Son* history
TLS	to Clemens, Cyril	July 19, 1937	U of Iowa	re: Gilbert Chesterton
ALS	to Clemens, Cyril	March 23 [1930]	Dickinson	re: J. Hawthorne's address
TLS	to Clemens, Cyril	[Nov. 16, 1936]	U of Iowa	when is "introduction" due?
ALS	to Clemens, Cyril	Nov. 27	U of Iowa	
TLS	to Clemens, Cyril	[Oct. 26, 1938]	U of Iowa	has read C's *Nasby*
TLS	to Clemens, Cyril	March 15, 1936	U of Iowa	re: Dan Beard
TL	to Clemens, Cyril	April 2, 1937	Dickinson	re: Drinkwater & *Lincoln*
TLS	to Clemens, Cyril	Feb. 19, 1939	U of Iowa	crosses; lectures
ALS	to Clemens, Cyril	Aug. 13 [1927]	U of Iowa	accepts honorary VP
*ALS	to Clemens, Samuel	July 7 [1905]	Bancroft	re: praise for *Tyranny*
ALS	to Clemens, Samuel	Feb. 26 [1903]	Bancroft	thanks for visit
*ALS	to Clemens, Samuel	March 21, 1889	Bancroft	ltr of introd; solicits rev. of lectures
ALS	to Clement, Edward H.	July 3	Duke	req. clipping re: false report of lecture

ALS	to Clement, Edward H.	n.d.	Duke	re: proof of Indian article
ALS	to Cliff Dwellers	Jan. 10, 1935	Miami U	letter of intro—Eldon Hill
TLC	to Clyde, Judge	March 4, 1912	USC	can't be at Seminary celebration
TLC	to Coburn	March 9 [1920s]	Miami U	wants Coburn to be tenant
TLC	to Cochems, Henry S.	Oct. 10, 1912	USC	arranging meeting
*TLC	to Collins, Hubert E.	July 2 [1924]	USC	re: Seger and Seger ms theft
ALS	to Collins, James	Aug. 18, 1939	Miami U	re: Crosses, testing
TLS	to Collins, James	Aug. 10 [1939]	Miami U	re: Crosses, testing
ALS	to Collins, Seward	Dec. 22, 1937	Virginia	commends American Review
TLC	to Collins, Seward	May 24 [1936]	USC	re: psychic sittings
ALS	to Connelly, John R.	April 14	U of Iowa	re: WWI: should ally w/ England, France
ALS	to Connolly, James B.	April 8 [1919]	Colby	req. stories for Roosevelt Mem. vol.
ALS	to Cooke, John D.	Wed. 14	Hunt	
ALS	to Cooke, John D.	March 25, 1939	Hunt	
TLS	to Cooke, John D.	May 5, 1939	Hunt	
ALS	to Cooke, John D.	March 16, 1939	Hunt	
TLS	to Cooke, John D.	May 15	Hunt	
ALS	to Cooke, John D.	May 24, 1936	Hunt	
ALS	to Cooke, John D.	[June 25, 1939]	Hunt	
ALS	to Cooke, John D.	Nov. 23 [1939]	Hunt	
ALS	to Cooke, John D.	March 22, 1937	Hunt	
TLS	to Cooke, John D.	Sun. 18	Hunt	
ALS	to Cooke, John D.	July 25 [1939]	Hunt	
TLS	to Cooke, John D.	April 8, 1938	Hunt	
ALS	to Cooke, John D.	Nov. 9, 1939	Hunt	
ALS	to Cooke, John D.	June 7	Hunt	
TLS	to Cooke, John D.	July 3 [1939]	Hunt	
ALS	to Cooke, John D.	Dec. 18 [1939]	Hunt	
ALS	to Coolbrith, Ina D.	Oct. 29	Bancroft	
TLC	to Cooper, Clayton S.	July 3 [1916]	USC	High Trails is doing well
TLS	to Cooper, Miss	Oct. 23 [1924]	UCLA	re: rpt. of HG's prose
TLS	to Cooper, Miss	March 2 [1925]	UCLA	
TLS	to Cooper, Miss	Oct. 6 [1924]	UCLA	re: rpt. of HG's poems
ALD	to Corbaley, Kate	Aug. 16, 1934	USC	thanks for interest in Captain film; [incomplete]
ALS	to Cortissoz, Royal	May 30 [1921]	Yale	Acad; re: Rouland portrait of Burroughs
TLD	to Cosgrave, Jessica G.	July 16	USC	

ALS	to Costain, Thomas B.	Feb. 12 [1929]	USC	suggests serial *Roadside*
ALS	to Cottman, George S.	[April 14, 1898]	Ind St Lib	is leaving for Yukon
TLC	to Cotton, Fassett A.	April 19, 1913	USC	re: lectures
TLC	to Coursey, Oscar William	April 8 [1916]	USC	re: contribution to anthology
TLC	to Courtney	June 29 [1916]	USC	
TLC	to Couse, Eanger Irving	May 3 [1916]	USC	
TLC	to Cowan,	n.d.	USC	
TLC	to Craft, Claude	Sunday 12 [1939]	USC	crosses; lecture; dep. in museum
TLC	to Craft, Claude	Nov. 27, 1939	USC	crosses
ALS	to Craig, Miss	March 18	Stanford	
ALS	to Cram, Ralph	Jan. 16 [1930]	Newberry	thanks for praise of *Back-Trailers*
ALS	to Cram, Ralph	July 18 [1922]	Newberry	thanks for priase of *Son, Daughter*
TLC	to Crane, Charles R.	Feb. 20, 1913	USC	invites lunch at Cliff Dwellers
TLC	to Crane, Charles R.	March 9, 1912	USC	invites lunch at Cliff Dwellers
ALS	to Crane, Stephen	May 8, 1894	Columbia	asks whether McClure accepted *Red Badge*
ApcS	to Crane, Stephen	April 17, 1894	Columbia	is at home; how are things?
*ALS	to Crane, Stephen	Nov. 29, 1897	Columbia	re: Conrad
*ALS	to Crane, Stephen	April 22, 1894	Columbia	lends money
TLC	to Cross, Ethan Allen	March 11, 1914	USC	
TLC	to Cross, Ethan Allen	Dec. 26, 1912	USC	Chicago Thea Soc
TLC	to Cross, Ethan Allen	Feb. 20, 1914	USC	
ALS	to Cross, Harold H. U.	Sept. 10, 1938	USC	
ALS	to Cross, Wilbur	Aug. 17 [1914]	Yale	can you pay more?
ALS	to Cross, Wilbur	Sept. 27 [1914]	Yale	encloses 2 chapters from *Son*
TpcS	to Cross, Wilbur	May 18, 1918	Yale	
ALS	to Cross, Wilbur	July 24 [1913]	Yale	re: Crane article
ALS	to Cross, Wilbur	Aug. 12 [1913]	Yale	thanks for interest in *Son*
ALS	to Cross, Wilbur	Feb. 19 [1913]	Yale	
ALS	to Cross, Wilbur	June 23 [1913]	Yale	sends revision of Crane article
TLS	to Cross, Wilbur	June 15 [1919]	Yale	encloses James article
TLS	to Cross, Wilbur	Jan. 25 [1922]	Yale	
ALS	to Cross, Wilbur	Feb. 12 [1922]	Yale	arranging meeting
*ALS	to Cross, Wilbur	Aug. 8 [1913]	Yale	offers *Son*
TLS	to Cross, Wilbur	Dec. 18 [1916]	Yale	wants to submit fiction

*TLS	to Cross, Wilbur	Feb. 11 [1922]	Yale	solicits rev. of *Son* & *Daughter*
TLS	to Cross, Wilbur	July 7 [1919]	Yale	
ALS	to Cross, Wilbur	May 15 [1913]	Yale	$60 too little for Crane article
ALS	to Cross, Wilbur	Dec. 26 [1913]	Yale	negotiations for articles on Howells, Herne
*TLS	to Cross, Wilbur	April 25, 1913	Yale	Crane article
*TLS	to Cross, Wilbur	Jan. 13, 1913	Yale	re: mss submis.
*TLS	to Cross, Wilbur	Oct. 2, 1913	Yale	re: Crane poem in Herne's room
TLC	to Crowell, [Merle?]	Dec. 4	USC	possible use of diaries in book
ALS	to Cummings, Philip	June 30 [1929]	Middlebury	thanks for praise of Middle Border books
TLD	to Curry, Charles M.	Aug. 30, 1934	USC	re: use of "Martha's Fireplace"
TLD	to Curry, Charles M.	Aug. 30, 1934	USC	re: use of "Martha's Fireplace"
TLC	to Damron, Kenneth	May 23, 1913	USC	
TLS	to Darrow, Whitney	Feb. 2 [1933]	Princeton	arranges meeting
ALS	to Darrow, Whitney	Jan. 24 [1933]	Princeton	arranges meeting
ALS	to Davenport, Bruce	Feb. 11	Homestead	cannot meet
TLS	to Davis, Richard Harding	Feb. 15, 1915	Virginia	Author's League circular
ALD	to Davis [an editor]	[1915]	USC	evals "books of the year"
ALS	to Day, Fred Holland	Feb. 7, 1897	Indiana U	re: music version of Crane's poems
TLS	to De Ferron, Mlle.	March 2	Miami U	re: translations
TLC	to De Ferron, Mlle.	April 21	USC	does not think French interested in his work
TLC	to De Ferron, Mlle.	March 2	USC	re: translations
ALS	to De Vaux-Royer, Madame	Dec. 5	Morgan	arranges address for Authors' Relief Fund
ALS	to Dear Sir	March 24	Miami U	poems HG likes
TL	to Dear Sir	Sept. 30	Miami U	re: ambig. of baby's sex in "Branch"
TLC	to Defrees, Joesph H.	June 1, 1914	USC	
TLS	to Deland, Margaret	[1935]	Colby	tribute letter
ALS	to Dennis, Charles	Oct. 22	Newberry	praises Field book
TLC	to Denny, Thomas	Dec. 13 [1923]	USC	
TLC	to Derieux, Mary	May 29, 1927	USC	psychic
TLC	to Derieux, Mary	May 26 [1927]	USC	psychic
*ALS	to Derleth, August	Jan. 16, 1940	Wis HS	re: awareness of age
*TLS	to Derleth, August	April 8, 1938	Wis HS	doesn't like Derleth's poetry
*TLS	to Derleth, August	April 16 [1938]	Wis HS	porno rant; age

TLS	to Derleth, August	Dec. 5, 1939	Wis HS	
*TLS	to Derleth, August	Dec. 4, 1936	Wis HS	re: incl. in *Poetry Out of Wisconsin*
TLS	to Derleth, August	Nov. 27, 1939	Wis HS	re: Gale biography
TLS	to Derleth, August	April 29 [1937]	Wis HS	
ALS	to Derleth, August	Dec. 15, 1937	Wis HS	expresses delight w/ *Poetry Out of Wisconsin*
*ALS	to Derleth, August	Jan. 9, 1940	Wis HS	re: HG's return to critical favor
TLS	to Derleth, August	Nov. 18, 1936	Wis HS	
*TLS	to Derleth, August	July 2, 1939	Wis HS	offers to aid Gale biography
TLS	to Derleth, August	April 22, 1938	Wis HS	
ALS	to Derleth, August	April 23, 1938	USC	
TLS	to Derleth, August	Nov. 25, 1936	Wis HS	
TLS	to Derleth, August	Jan. 22, 1940	Wis HS	
ALS	to Derleth, August	March 2	Wis HS	
TLC	to Derleth, August	Jan. 22, 1940	USC	c. of Wis HS ltr
TLS	to Derleth, August	Nov. 10, 1936	Wis HS	
TLS	to Derleth, August	Jan. 29, 1940	Wis HS	commends *Wind Over Wisconsin*
TLC	to Derleth, August	[1940]	USC	
ALS	to Derleth, August	Dec. 29, 1939	Wis HS	sends 25 Gale letters
TLC	to Derleth, August	April 16 [1938]	USC	
TLS	to Dick, Miss	Sept. 19, 1937	USC	
ALS	to Dickey, John Marcus	Nov. 29 [1902]	Indiana U	
ALS	to Dickey, John Marcus	Jan. 2 [1923]	Indiana U	commends Riley book
TLC	to Dickinson, Thomas	March 24, 1913	USC	Chicago Thea Soc; encl. rev.
ALS	to Dickson, Edward	Nov. 10 [1934]	UCLA	sculpture museum
ALS	to Dickson, Edward	July 19 [1934]	UCLA	
ALS	to Dickson, Edward	Jan. 5	UCLA	Acad; good diction
TLS	to Dickson, Edward	Dec. 28 [1934]	UCLA	sculpture museum
ALC	to Dingwall, A. W.	Sept. 29 [1902]	USC LB 89	re: play adapt. of *Captain*
ALS	to Dodd	Sat. [1902]	Virginia	re: serial of unspec. ms
ALC	to Dodd, Anna M.	Feb. 9 [1904]	USC LB 193	dispute over payment for typing
ALC	to Dodd, Anna M.	Oct. 27 [1902]	USC LB 109	re: typing of ms
TLC	to Dodd, Anna M.	June 27, 1912	USC	
ALS	to Dodd, William E.	Oct. 14 [1922]	Clark	arranging lecture
ALS	to Dodd, William E.	Oct. [1922]	Clark	
TLS	to Dodd, William E.	Aug. 28 [1922]	Clark	
TLS	to Dodd, William E.	Oct. 8 [1922]	Clark	
TLC	to Doerflinger, William M.	Dec. 28, 1937	USC	

TLS	to Donaldson	Feb. 5 [1927]	U of Del	re: potential publ. in *Dearborn Independent*
ALS	to Donaldson	Feb. 8 [1927]	U of Del	send excerpt of *Trail Makers*
TLS	to Donaldson	Feb. 18 [1927]	U of Del	re: serial of *Westward March* in *Independent*
TLS	to Donaldson	Feb. 25 [1927]	U of Del	re: potential publ. in *Dearborn Independent*
ALS	to Donaldson	May 13 [1927]	U of Del	re: serial of *Westward March*
ALS	to Donaldson	May 22 [1927]	U of Del	re: serial of *Westward March*
TLS	to Donaldson	June 18 [1927]	U of Del	re: return of Wayside Inn article
ALS	to Donaldson	June 24 [1927]	U of Del	re: other pubs. in *Independent*
ALS	to Donaldson	July 19 [1927]	U of Del	receives copy of *Independent* pub. of *Westward*
TLS	to Donaldson	July 23 [1927]	U of Del	re: payment for *Westward March*
TLC	to Doran, George B.	June 16, 1914	USC	
AnS	to Dorfman, Joseph	[May 1930]	Columbia	
ALS	to Doubleday, Frank	Jan. 12, 1900	Harvard	arranging meeting
TLD	to Dounce, H. E.	n.d.	USC	deterioration of magazines
TLC	to Dow, Miss	Jan. 26	Miami U	arranges for Mary Isabel's lessons
TLC	to Dow, Miss	March 2	Miami U	advice about Mary Isabel
ALS	to Doyle, Arthur Conan	Aug. 11	USC	introd. Irving Bacheller
ALS	to Draa, Dr.	April 3 [1929]	USC	introd. Mary Isabel and Hardesty Johnso
ALD	to Drake, Colonel	n.d.	USC	re: selling mss
TLC	to Drane, Dora	March 11, 1935	USC	psychic
TLS	to Dreiser, Theodore	Jan. 16, 1913	U Penn	Little Room invite
TLS	to Dreiser, Theodore	Feb. 13, 1915	U Penn	Author's League circular
*ALS	to Dreiser, Theodore	Jan. 3 [1904]	U Penn	admires *Sister Carri*
*ALS	to Drinkwater, John	Dec. 27 [1919]	Yale	praises *Lincoln*
TLC	to Dudley, George W.	n.d.	USC	
TLC	to Dudley, George W.	Jan. 6, 1914	USC	
TLC	to Dudley, George W.	n.d.	USC	
TLC	to Dudley, George W.	April 22	USC	
TLC	to Dudley, George W.	Nov. 12, 1937	USC	selling Homestead

TLC	to Dudley, George W.	Feb. 22, 1913	USC	
TLC	to Dudley, George W.	Oct. 31 [1937]	USC	selling Homestead
TLC	to Dudley, George W.	April 14 [1938]	USC	sells Homestead to State
TLC	to Dudley, George W.	Jan. 20	USC	
TLC	to Dudley, George W.	n.d.	USC	
ALS	to Dudley, Mrs. C. Tarbell	Aug. 28	USC	
TLC	to Dudley, Mrs. C. Tarbell	June 21	USC	re: daughters' education
ALS	to Duneka, Frederick A.	Oct. 9 [1912]	Hunt	re: Homestead fire
ALS	to Duneka, Frederick A.	[1910?]	Hunt	re: proof of unspec. ms
TLC	to Duneka, Frederick A.	Dec. 8, 1913	USC	
ALC	to Duneka, Frederick A.	May 21 [1903]	USC LB 147	is revising *Hesper*
ALC	to Duneka, Frederick A.	Feb. 16 [1903]	USC LB 130-1	contract negotiations
TLC	to Duneka, Frederick A.	June 11	USC	
ALC	to Duneka, Frederick A.	June 25 [1903]	USC LB 166	re: publ. of *Hesper*
ALS	to Duneka, Frederick A.	April 9	Virginia	re: dispute over preface to unspec. book
ALS	to Duneka, Frederick A.	n.d.	Morgan	re: advance
ALC	to Duneka, Frederick A.	May 12 [1904]	USC LB 201	re: proposed serial of *Hesper*
TLC	to Duneka, Frederick A.	Dec. 13, 1913	USC	
*ALS	to Duneka, Frederick A.	Feb. 17 [1910]	Morgan	anger at Frederick Leigh
*ALC	to Duneka, Frederick A.	June 29 [1903]	USC LB 170-3	re: selling *Hesper*
TLC	to Duneka, Frederick A.	Aug. 5, 1912	USC	
TLC	to Durant	n.d.	Miami U	resp. to letter about NH Garland home-stead
TLC	to Durkee, Cara D.	Feb. 17, 1913	USC	
TLC	to Dwyer, Charles	Dec. 13, 1913	USC	
TLC	to Eastman, Charles A.	Jan. 2	USC	likes unspec. magazine prospectus
ALC	to Eaton	Oct. 8 [1902]	USC LB 97	no editorial to send
TLC	to Eaton, Allen	April 10 [1924]	USC	
ALS	to Eaton, Walter Prichard	Dec. 18 [1917]	Virginia	re: camping trip
ALS	to Eaton, Walter Prichard	Jan. 29 [1919]	Virginia	commends poems
TLS	to Eaton, Walter Prichard	June 7 [1916]	Virginia	
ALS	to Eaton, Walter Prichard	June 6 [1911]	Virginia	Chicago Thea Soc; worthwhile plays?
ALS	to Eaton, Walter Prichard	Sept. 16 [1933]	Virginia	
TLS	to Eaton, Walter Prichard	Sept. 16 [1916]	Virginia	
TLS	to Eaton, Walter Prichard	Jan. 6 [1919]	Virginia	Institute; E. elected; worthwhile plays?
ALS	to Eaton, Walter Prichard	June 28 [1916]	Virginia	
ALS	to Eaton, Walter Prichard	Oct. 25 [1917]	Virginia	Institute; nominates Eaton

ALS	to Eaton, Walter Prichard	Feb. 1, 1918	Virginia	Institute; election fails
TLS	to Eaton, Walter Prichard	March [2], 1917	Virginia	Com Lit Art circular
ALS	to Eaton, Walter Prichard	Jan. 7 [1916]	Virginia	
*TLS	to Eaton, Walter Prichard	Feb. 2 [1920]	Virginia	Pulitzer; dissatis. w plays
ALS	to Eaton, Walter Prichard	Dec. 31 [1921]	Virginia	
ALS	to Eaton, Walter Prichard	Jan. 8 [1916]	Virginia	Woodcraft League
*ALS	to Eaton, Walter Prichard	Feb. 2 [1922]	Virginia	req. to rev. Border edition
AnS	to Eaton, Walter Prichard	[April 20, 1920]	Virginia	play query on ltr to Fackenthal
*ALS	to Eaton, Walter Prichard	Nov. 17 [1921]	Virginia	resp. to praise of *Daughter*
*ALS	to Eddleman, Ora V.	Dec. 29 [1903]	U of OK	Indian; renaming
*TLS	to Edgett, Edwin F.	Dec. 18 [1928]	U of Del	re: Eggleston
ALS	to Editor, *Bookman*	July 6	U of Iowa	thanks for rev. of Middle Border
TLC	to Editor, *Boston Transcript*	Sept. 26, 1917	USC	re: lyrics of "Over t Hill in Legions"
ALS	to Editor, *Boston Transcript*	Sept. 26 [1917]	Hunt	re: lyrics of "Over t Hill in Legions"
ALS	to Editor, Century Co.	Aug. 12 [1908]	NYPL	sells "Night raid at Eagle River" for $55
ALS	to Editor, Century Co.	June 28 [1913?]	NYPL	submits *Son* as seria
TLC	to Editor, Educational Foundations	n.d.	USC	resp. to Julian Street patriotism
TLC	to Editor, *Era*	n.d.	USC	on value of hand-writing [incomplete]
TLD	to Editor, *Examiner*	Feb. 25, 1934	USC	re: Dickens
TLS	to Editor, *Golden Book*	May 24	Harvard	asks for payment
TLD	to Editor, *Leader Press*	n.d.	USC	approves flag campaign; patriotis
TLD	to Editor, *Los Angeles Examiner*	Dec. 11, 1933	USC	sculpture museum; dupl.
TLD	to Editor, *Los Angeles Times*	Dec. 11, 1933	USC	sculpture museum; dupl.
TLD	to Editor, *Los Angeles Times*	Dec. 11, 1933	USC	sculpture museum; dupl.
TLC	to Editor, *McClures Magazine*	Feb. 21, 1913	USC	
TLD	to Editor, *New York Times*	[1939]	USC	crosses; method - seance
TLD	to Editor, *New York Times*	n.d.	USC	resp. to rev. *Life & Letters of Howells*
ALD	to Editor, *New York Times*	[Dec. 1903]	USC	Indian; conditions; resp. to letter [in-complete]
TLD	to Editor, *New York Times*	June 19, 1937	Miami U	on death of Barrie

L	to Editor, *Nonpareil Magazine*	[after April 14, 1938]	USC	re: article about Homestead
LD	to Editor, *Post*	Dec. 6	USC	defends Ernest Seton Re; anarchism
LC	to Editor, *Saturday Review of Lit.*	June 27, 1939	USC	crosses; resp. to rev of book
LD	to Editor, *Saturday Review of Lit.*	[June 27, 1939]	USC	crosses; resp. to rev of book
LD	to Editor, *The Scholastic*	n.d.	USC	account of career
LS	to Editor, *West Salem Journal*	April 14, 1938	Homestead	re: article about homestead
LS	to Editor, [unknown]	[Dec. 1904]	NYPL	admitting ladies to Progress and Poverty dinner
LS	to Edwards, Thomas	June 4, 1931	Hunt	
LS	to Ehrman	April 22	DePauw	thanks for book
LC	to Eitel, Edmund Henry	March 2 [1925]	USC	
ALS	to Eitel, Edmund Henry	July 23 [1916]	Indiana U	re: death of Riley
LC	to Ellis, Don Carlos	March 3, 1913	USC	
LC	to Ellis, Don Carlos	Nov. 28, 1911	USC	
LC	to Ellis, Don Carlos	[March 1916]	USC	
LC	to Ellis, Don Carlos	Nov. 10, 1911	USC	
LC	to Ellis, Don Carlos	Feb. 24, 1913	USC	
LS	to Ellsworth	July 26 [1903]	Brown	can't subscribe to "fund"
LC	to Elson [William Harris?]	Nov. 14 [1922?]	Miami U	
LD	to Elwood, John W.	[1932]	USC	will record for NBC Acad; good diction
LD	to Elwood, John W.	June 4	USC	Acad; good diction
LD	to Elwood, John W.	n.d.	USC	Acad; good diction
LD	to Elwood, John W.	Jan. 6.	USC	Acad; good diction
LD	to Elwood, John W.	Sept. 18	USC	Acad; good diction
LD	to Elwood, John W.	n.d.	USC	Acad; good diction
ALS	to Ely	Feb. 17	U Texas	can't come to lunch
ALS	to Ely	Jan. 11	U Texas	asks to make address
ALS	to Ely, Richard	Aug. 25, 1894	Wis HS	re: free speech; stand w/ principles
LC	to Emerson, Guy	May 1 [1916]	USC	
TLS	to Erskine, John	Sept. 30	Columbia	
ALS	to Erskine, John	Aug. 18, 1939	Columbia	arranging meeting
ALS	to Erskine, John	Sept. 16 [1933]	Columbia	thanks for b-day greeting
ALS	to Erskine, John	July 20, 1939	Columbia	arranging meeting
ALS	to Erskine, John	Sept. 25	Columbia	wants daughters to take E's lectures
ALS	to Erskine, John	Jan. 17, 1903	Columbia	arranging talk at club
ALS	to Esch	Feb. 8	Homestead	Acad; charter bill
TLS	to Fackenthal, F. D.	Dec. 16 [1920]	Pulitzer	
TLS	to Fackenthal, F. D.	May 13	Pulitzer	
ALS	to Fackenthal, F. D.	Aug. 1 [1918]	Pulitzer	

TLS	to Fackenthal, F. D.	March 12 [1925]	Pulitzer	
TLS	to Fackenthal, F. D.	March 31 [1919]	Pulitzer	
ALS	to Fackenthal, F. D.	Oct. 14 [1921]	Pulitzer	
TLS	to Fackenthal, F. D.	May 20 [1921]	Pulitzer	
TLS	to Fackenthal, F. D.	Jan. 6 [1921]	Pulitzer	
TLS	to Fackenthal, F. D.	Feb. 9 [1920]	Pulitzer	
TLS	to Fackenthal, F. D.	May 6 [1920]	Pulitzer	
TLS	to Fackenthal, F. D.	Jan. 10 [1919]	Pulitzer	prize not to *Copperhead*
ALS	to Fackenthal, F. D.	Feb. 16 [1918]	Pulitzer	re: *Copperhead*
ALS	to Fackenthal, F. D.	March 13 [1925]	Pulitzer	
TLS	to Fackenthal, F. D.	Feb. 2 [1920]	Pulitzer	favors *Lincoln*
ALS	to Fackenthal, F. D.	April 26 [1920]	Pulitzer	votes for *Beyond the Horizon*
*TLS	to Fackenthal, F. D.	March 9 [1925]	Pulitzer	resigns from jury
TLS	to Fackenthal, F. D.	April 21 [1920]	Pulitzer	
*TLS	to Fackenthal, F. D.	May 22 [1921]	Pulitzer	award to *Miss Lulu Bett*
*TLS	to Fackenthal, F. D.	April 19 [1920]	Pulitzer	dislikes *Beyond the Horizon*
TLS	to Fackenthal, F. D.	April 30 [1920]	Pulitzer	votes for *Beyond the Horizon*
*TLS	to Fackenthal, F. D.	May 11 [1921]	Pulitzer	recommends no award for drama
*TLS	to Fackenthal, F. D.	March 22 [1919]	Pulitzer	no award
TLS	to Fackenthal, F. D.	Feb. 12 [1918]	Pulitzer	re: *Copperhead*
*TLS	to Fackenthal, F. D.	Nov. 11 [1924]	Pulitzer	out of sympathy w/ plays
*TLC	to Fackenthal, F. D.	May 11 [1921]	U of Ill	novel report
*TLS	to Fackenthal, F. D.	March 25 [1918]	Pulitzer	prize to *Why Marry*
TLC	to Fairbanks, Douglas	Nov. 29	Miami U	Fairbanks has declined membership ??
TLC	to Fairbanks, Douglas	March 27	USC	re: common interest Spencer
TLD	to Fairbanks, Douglas	March 15	USC	resp. to *Iron Mask*
TLC	to Falk, L.E.	June 20, 1936	USC	re: Dakota Homestead memorial
TLC	to Farran, Don	[Feb. 19 1934]	Miami U	likes Farran's work
TLC	to Farran, Don	Feb. 23, 1939	Hunt	
TLC	to Farrand, Max	Feb. 23, 1940	USC	crosses; disp. of mss Huntington
ALS	to Farrand, Max	Sept. 25, 1934	Hunt	what's in library at Santa Catalina Island?
TLC	to Farrar, John C.	Dec. 10, 1937	USC	crosses; submits ms
TLC	to Farrar, John C.	Sept. 20, 1923	USC	
TLC	to Farrar, John C.	Sunday 23	USC	

LC	to Farrar, John C.	April 8 [1921]	USC	praises *Bookman*; current rebels
LC	to Farrar, John C.	April 3. [1922]	USC	
LC	to Farrell, Mrs. Clinton	April 15, 1913	USC	
LC	to Feldmahn, L. E.	June 3, 1927	USC	
LC	to Ferris, Helen	April 27 [1928]	USC	okays rpt. of "The Prospector"
LS	to Ficke, Arther Davidson	April 20, 1931	Yale	arranging meeting
LC	to Field, Charles K.	Feb. 16, 1916	USC	
LS	to Field, Eugene	Feb. 5, 1895	NYPL	lunch at Attic Club
LS	to Field, Julia S.	Jan. 23, 1896	U Texas	expresses sympathy for death of Eugene
LS	to Field, Miss	Feb. 10	Harvard	okays rpt. of "Mrs. Ripley's Trip"
LS	to Finley, John H.	Dec. 17	NYPL	introd. Hardesty Johnson
LS	to Finley, John H.	April 13	NYPL	Acad; radio medal
LS	to Finley, John H.	June 15 [1926]	NYPL	re: missed meeting
LS	to Finley, John H.	March 25	NYPL	
LS	to Finley, John H.	Dec. 22	NYPL	
LS	to Finley, John H.	Wednesday	NYPL	
LS	to Finley, John H.	Nov. 19	NYPL	Acad
LS	to Finley, John H.	March 24 [1930]	NYPL	
LS	to Finley, John H.	July 30 [1921]	NYPL	
LS	to Finley, John H.	Sept. 26 [1921]	NYPL	wants F. to use Fuller for reviews
LC	to Finley, John H.	Feb. 27	NYPL	re: Turck
LS	to Finley, John H.	Jan. 2 [1927]	NYPL	asks if NYT is interested in Ford piece
LS	to Finley, John H.	Oct. 27 [1926]	NYPL	re: formation of Turck Institute
LS	to Finley, John H.	March 18	NYPL	Acad; radio medal
TLS	to Finley, John H.	Nov. 1	NYPL	describes Acad article he wants to do
LS	to Finley, John H.	March 26	NYPL	arranging meeting
LS	to Finley, John H.	April 6	NYPL	Acad; radio medal
LS	to Finley, John H.	Nov. 23	NYPL	arranging meeting
LS	to Finley, John H.	Nov. 13 [1927]	NYPL	congrats on election to Acad
ALS	to Finley, John H.	Sept. 25 [1921]	NYPL	
TLS	to Finley, John H.	March 9 [1922]	NYPL	to England
ALS	to Finley, John H.	Sunday	NYPL	arranging meeting
ALS	to Finley, John H.	April 10	NYPL	
ALS	to Finley, John H.	June 9 [1926]	NYPL	wants to borrow cap and gown
TLS	to Finley, John H.	Friday. 16	NYPL	arranging meeting; Acad. squabbles
ALS	to Finley, John H.	n.d.	NYPL	arranging meeting
ALS	to Finley, John H.	Sept. 6 [1930]	NYPL	

TLS	to Finley, John H.	July 19	NYPL	asks for "rewrite man" for Turck
ALS	to Finley, John H.	June 12 [1931]	NYPL	Acad: radio medal
ALS	to Finley, John H.	April 3	NYPL	
ALS	to Finley, John H.	Sept. 16 [1930]	NYPL	missed Finley at party
TLS	to Finley, John H.	May 18	NYPL	Acad; medal
TLS	to Finley, John H.	Aug. 28 [1930]	NYPL	Roadside near pub
ALS	to Finley, John H.	Monday. 13	NYPL	arranging meeting
ALS	to Finley, John H.	July 21 [1931]	NYPL	
ALS	to Finley, John H.	Sept. 5	NYPL	Fuller letters being collected
TLS	to Finley, John H.	Aug. 27, 1937	NYPL	asks for frank eval Crosses ms
TLS	to Finley, John H.	Nov. 7	NYPL	move to Calif. is permanent
ALS	to Finley, John H.	July 28	NYPL	
ALS	to Finley, John H.	Nov. 27 [1928]	NYPL	re: Life in Letters o Howells
ALS	to Finley, John H.	Sept. 22 [1930]	NYPL	arranging meeting
TLS	to Finley, John H.	March 17	NYPL	misses old friends
TLS	to Finley, John H.	July 4 [1931]	NYPL	re: article in Curren History on middle border
TLS	to Finley, John H.	Aug. 31, 1937	NYPL	re: ms of Crosses— asks Finley to read
TLS	to Finley, John H.	Aug. 15, 1937	NYPL	informs Finley abou Crosses
ALS	to Finley, John H.	Sept. 20 [1937]	NYPL	re: crosses
ALS	to Finley, John H.	July 31 [1931]	NYPL	
ALS	to Finley, John H.	Dec. 11	NYPL	Acad
ALS	to Finley, John H.	Aug. 24 [1937]	NYPL	crosses
ALS	to Finley, John H.	n.d.	NYPL	arranging meeting
ALS	to Finley, John H.	June 25 [1921]	NYPL	Acad
TLS	to Finley, John H.	Sept. 7 [1923]	NYPL	arranging meeting with Fuller
ALS	to Finley, John H.	Sept. 11, 1935	NYPL	encloses photo for NYT
ALS	to Finley, John H.	April 10	NYPL	enjoyed Finley's speech
ALS	to Finley, John H.	March 8, 1937	NYPL	arranging meeting
ALS	to Finley, John H.	[July?] 10, 1937	NYPL	asks if NYT will p for article on crosse
ALS	to Finley, John H.	Aug. 27	NYPL	
TLS	to Finley, John H.	Aug. 31 [1923]	NYPL	meeting with Fulle
TLS	to Finley, John H.	March 1, 1925	NYPL	sends protest about O'Neill for publ
TLS	to Finley, John H.	Jan. 27, 1925	NYPL	invite F. for Town Hall Club

TLS	to Finley, John H.	Oct. 20 [1924]	NYPL	re: Hutchinson letter to NYT
TLS	to Finley, John H.	Oct. 8 [1924]	NYPL	inquires about publ. Hutchinson letter
TLS	to Finley, John H.	March 13 [1923?]	NYPL	re: article on Turck
TLS	to Finley, John H.	Feb. 27 [1923?]	NYPL	wants to do signed article on Turck
ALS	to Finley, John H.	May 16	NYPL	is in town
ALS	to Finley, John H.	Sept. 11, 1935	NYPL	corrects b-day date
ALS	to Finley, John H.	Sept. 5, 1939	NYPL	re: "flippant" review of Crosses
ALS	to Finley, John H.	[after May 17, 1939]	NYPL	is sending a "protesting" article re: Crosses review
ALS	to Finley, John H.	Oct. 30	NYPL	
*ALS	to Finley, John H.	[Sept. 12, 1939]	NYPL	re: "Strange As It Seems" broadcast
TLS	to Finley, John H.	[1937?]	NYPL	re: ms of Crosses
TLS	to Finley, John H.	Nov. 30, 1938	NYPL	arranging meeting
TLS	to Finley, John H.	March 28, 1939	NYPL	announces publ. of Crosses
TLS	to Finley, John H.	[Aug.] 18 [1937]	NYPL	crosses
ALS	to Finley, John H.	Oct. 7	NYPL	letter gives pleasure
ALS	to Finley, John H.	Aug. 15 [1933]	NYPL	asks about nominating Stewart E. White to Acad
ALS	to Finley, John H.	Sept. 10 [1933]	NYPL	thanks for b-day letter
ALS	to Finley, John H.	Sept. 25	NYPL	responding to clipping—enjoyed it
ALS	to Finley, John H.	April 24	NYPL	congrats on becoming editor of NYT
ALS	to Finley, John H.	Aug. 2 [1935	NYPL	
TLS	to Finley, John H.	Nov. 13, 1925	NYPL	Town Hall Club circular
ALS	to Finley, John H.	Nov. 16	NYPL	arranging meeting
TLS	to Finley, John H.	Sunday	NYPL	
TLS	to Finley, John H.	Dec. 18 [1921]	NYPL	disappointed about no rev. of Daughter
TLS	to Finley, John H.	April 10 [1922]	NYPL	inquires about doing Grant article
TLS	to Finley, John H.	Sunday	NYPL	asks about doing Acad editorial—cornerstone
TLS	to Finley, John H.	Oct. 24, 1921	NYPL	invites to Burroughs meeting
ALS	to Finley, John H.	Saturday	NYPL	
ALS	to Finley, John H.	Feb. 7	NYPL	

TLS	to Finley, John H.	Nov. 19	NYPL	thanks for Acad editorial
TLS	to Finley, John H.	Dec. 20	NYPL	wants to know who literary editor is
TLS	to Finley, John H.	May 16	NYPL	re: insufficient pay
ALS	to Finley, John H.	Thursday	NYPL	arranging meeting
ALS	to Finley, John H.	Monday	NYPL	arranging meeting
ALS	to Finley, John H.	March 15	NYPL	Acad; radio medal
TLS	to Finley, John H.	Aug. 23 [1921]	NYPL	re: serial of *Daughter*
TLS	to Finley, John H.	Sept. 15 [1921]	NYPL	asks about syndication of *Daughter*
TLS	to Finley, John H.	April 17 [1922]	NYPL	re: Grant article
TLS	to Finley, John H.	April 16 [1922]	NYPL	re: Grant article
TLS	to Finley, John H.	March 4, 1925	NYPL	wants to write for NYT
TLS	to Finley, John H.	Oct. 30, 1924	NYPL	Acad; recog. of new members
ALS	to Finley, John H.	Dec. 4	NYPL	
ALS	to Finley, John H.	Mon.	NYPL	arranging meeting
ALS	to Finley, John H.	n.d.	NYPL	arranging meeting
TLC	to Finley, John H.	Aug. 31, 1937	USC	crosses; re: reaction to ms
ALS	to Finley, John H.	April 6 [1922]	USC	suggests centenniel Grant article
TLC	to Fiske, Horace Spencer	Jan. 25. 1912	USC	
ALD	to Flanagan, John T.	[Feb. 25, 1938]	USC	infl. of Minnesota on work
TLC	to Flude, Alfred L.	May 31, 1913	USC	
TLS	to Follette	June 6, 1925	Harvard	cannot meet
ALC	to Forbes, [James?]	March 7 [1904]	USC LB 195-6	scenario of *Captain*
TLC	to Forbes-Robertson, Johnston	Sept. 14, 1914	USC	
TLC	to Ford, Arthur	Nov. 2, 1939	USC	crosses
ALD	to Ford, Henry	June 26	USC	invites Ford to Bacheller Society
*ALD	to Ford, Henry	[June 27, 1939]	Hunt	offers mss to Ford museum
TLD	to Ford, Henry	Dec. 18	USC	thanks for visit; Americana
TLS	to Ford, J. A.	Aug. 11, 1936	Hunt	
*TLD	to Foster, Edward	Oct. 1 [1932]	USC	reply re: info Mary Wilkins
ALS	to Frechette, Achille	Feb. 15, 1899	Harvard	re: Archibald Lampman's death
ALS	to Frechette, Annie Howells	March 4 [1921]	Hunt	
*ALS	to Freeman, Mary Wilkins	Jan. 19, 1896	Knox	apprec. of work
trL	to Freeman, Mary Wilkins	April 12 [1926]	USC	Acad; gold medal address

*ALS	to Freeman, Mary Wilkins	March 31 [1926]	USC	Acad; gold medal address
*ALS	to Freeman, Mary Wilkins	April 12 [1926]	Miami U	sends draft of Howells Medal speech
ALS	to French, Alice	[Sept. 1894]	Newberry	describes visit west & work on homestead
*ALS	to French, Alice	Sept. 9, 1894	Newberry	re: summer's work; artistic aims
ALS	to French, Alice	Nov. 3, 1894	Newberry	re: lectures
TLC	to French, Major	Dec. 28, 1937	USC	crosses; asks permission to dig
TLC	to French, William M. R.	Aug. 2, 1913	USC	Institute: Chicago meeting
ALD	to French, William M. R.	Aug. 2 [1913]	USC	
TLS	to Freshman Class	Oct. 27, 1933	NY HS	thanks for praise of *Son*
TLC	to Friedman, Issac K.	June 6, 1912	USC	
TLC	to Frohman & Taubert	May 14 [1920]	USC	
ALD	to Frohman & Taubert	n.d.	USC	
TLC	to Frohman & Taubert	May 1 [1920]	USC	
TLC	to Frohman & Taubert	May 1 [1920]	USC	
ALS	to Fuller, Henry B.	Jan. 16 [1921?]	Miami U	help with *Daughter*
ApcS	to Fuller, Henry B.	Feb. 16, 1929	USC	
TLC	to Fuller, Henry B.	Oct. 3	USC	
trL	to Fuller, Henry B.	June 6, 1929	Newberry	
ApcS	to Fuller, Henry B.	Feb. 6, 1925	USC	
AnS	to Fuller, Henry B.	Sept. 17, 1926	Newberry	
TL	to Fuller, Henry B.	[Jan. 19, 1929]	Newberry	arranges lectures w/ Mary Isabel & Hardesty
TLC	to Fuller, Henry B.	Sept. 8	USC	
ApcS	to Fuller, Henry B.	Feb. 2, 1925	USC	
TLC	to Fuller, Henry B.	Jan. 15	USC	
TLS	to Fuller, Henry B.	Oct. 3 [1922]	Newberry	leaving England
ApcS	to Fuller, Henry B.	June 29	USC	
TLC	to Fuller, Henry B.	May 16	USC	sends copy of unspec. book
TLS	to Fuller, Henry B.	May 17 [1929]	Newberry	advice re: Knopf & royalties
ApcS	to Fuller, Henry B.	Feb. 18, 1925	USC	
ALS	to Fuller, Henry B.	May 3, 1899	USC	describes London
TLC	to Fuller, Henry B.	July 8	USC	
TLC	to Fuller, Henry B.	[1920]	USC	
TLS	to Fuller, Henry B.	April 13 [1918]	Newberry	
TL	to Fuller, Henry B.	Aug. 21 [1922]	Newberry	describes work, visits in England
ApcS	to Fuller, Henry B.	Jan. 3, 1929	USC	

*ALS	to Fuller, Henry B.	May 9, 1895	Newberry	re: *With the Procession*
*TLS	to Fuller, Henry B.	July 3, 1922	Newberry	describes London
*ALS	to Fuller, Henry B.	May 8, 1895	Newberry	commends *With the Procession*
*ALS	to Fuller, Henry B.	Nov. 6 [1918]	USC	resigns Players; in Century Club: "the top!"
*ALS	to Fuller, Henry B.	Jan. 17, 1894	Newberry	commends *Cliff Dwellers*
TLC	to Fuller, S. Richard	April 21, 1913	USC	
*ALS	to Fullerton, W. Morton	May 2, 1888	Virginia	re: review of lecture
ALS	to Gale, Zona	March 10 [1922]	Wis HS	thanks for praise of *Daughter*
TLS	to Gale, Zona	March 1, 1933	Virginia	re: Zulime's health
ALS	to Gale, Zona	May 24	Wis HS	resp. to essays/stories
ALS	to Galsworthy, John	March 10 [1922]	USC	thanks for nomin. to P.E.N.
TLS	to Garland, Constance	Tue	Hunt	crosses; stops digging
TL	to Garland, Constance	July 13 [1928]	Hunt	re: illus. for *Back-Trailers*
TL	to Garland, Constance	Sun.	Hunt	crosses; Macmillan declines book
*TLS	to Garland, Constance	Wed. [July 28, 1937]	Hunt	crosses; publicity ideas
TLS	to Garland, Constance	Thurs.	Hunt	*Roadside* outline
TLS	to Garland, Constance	n.d.	Hunt	re: illus. for *Roadside*
*TL	to Garland, Constance	Dec. 20 [1928]	Hunt	re: illus. for reissue of *Daughter*
*TL	to Garland, Constance	July 17 [1928]	Hunt	re: illus. for *Back-Trailers*; effort to finish
*TL	to Garland, Constance	[Aug. 11, 1937]	Hunt	crosses; title change
trL	to Garland, Franklin	Aug. 16. 1898	USC	
ALC	to Garland, Franklin	[Feb.-July 1905]	USC LB 217-8	re: farming
trL	to Garland, Franklin	July 22, 1906	USC	describes Venice
ALS	to Garland, Franklin	n.d.	USC	
trpc	to Garland, Franklin	June 14, 1906	USC	
trL	to Garland, Franklin	April 2, 1912	USC	
ALS	to Garland, Franklin	May 25, 1899	USC	describes London activities
ALS	to Garland, Franklin	n.d.	U Wis-LaCrosse	re: *Grant* research
trL	to Garland, Franklin	Aug. 27 [1898]	USC	
TLC	to Garland, Franklin	Nov. 21, 1915	USC	real estate transfer
TLC	to Garland, Franklin	n.d.	USC	[incomplete]
trL	to Garland, Franklin	Nov. 3, 1913	USC	
TLC	to Garland, Franklin	April 6	USC	
*ALS	to Garland, Franklin	Feb. 3, 1897	Hunt	re: death of Franklin's wife

TLC	to Garland, Franklin	June 11 [1915]	USC	real estate transfer
ALC	to Garland, Franklin	Feb. 21 [1905]	USC LB 212-3	
trL	to Garland, Franklin	July 26, 1906	USC	
ALS	to Garland, Franklin	March 17, 1897	USC	*Grant*; "Business" [play]
trL	to Garland, Franklin	July 9, 1906	USC	describes Rome
trpc	to Garland, Franklin	June 19, 1906	USC	
ALC	to Garland, Franklin	Feb. 22 [1905]	USC LB 214-6	re: Mexican mine
ALS	to Garland, Franklin	Feb. 6, 1897	USC	trouble w/ *Grant*; Appleton wants books
*ALS	to Garland, Franklin	[Oct. 25, 1899]	Hunt	re: marriage plans
*ALS	to Garland, Franklin	[Oct. 18, 1899]	Hunt	re: Zulime
TLC	to Garland, Franklin	June 1	USC	film interests; "Business"; *Daughter* serial
*trL	to Garland, Franklin	July 22, 1898	USC	in B. C.; to gold fields
ALS	to Garland, Isabelle M.	n.d.	USC	
trL	to Garland, Isabelle M.	May 1, 1898	USC	
trpc	to Garland, Isabelle M.	May 17, 1898	USC	
ApcS	to Garland, Isabelle M.	Fri.	Hunt	
ALS	to Garland, Isabelle M.	Wed.	USC	
ALS	to Garland, Isabelle M.	May 2, 1899	USC	
ALS	to Garland, Isabelle M.	April 25, 1899	USC	describes voyage to London
TLC	to Garland, Isabelle M.	April 30, 1899	Hunt	
ALS	to Garland, Isabelle M.	April 30, 1899	USC	describes London
ALS	to Garland, Isabelle M.	n.d.	U Wis-LaCrosse	re: Colo visit [incomplete]
ALS	to Garland, Isabelle M.	May 15, 1899	USC	
ApcS	to Garland, Mary Isabel	Aug. 11, 1906	USC	
*TL	to Garland, Mary Isabel	Dec. 25 [1936]	Hunt	Zulime's failing health
*TL	to Garland, Mary Isabel	[April 26, 1933]	Hunt	evals. Mary Isabel's novel
*TLS	to Garland, Mary Isabel	July 3 [1930]	Hunt	rev. suggestions for taxi story
ALS	to Garland, Mary Isabel	[Sept. 4, 1937]	Hunt	crosses
*ALS	to Garland, Mary Isabel	[Nov. 3, 1936]	Hunt	in Mexico; death of Lorado
*ALS	to Garland, Mary Isabel	Sept. 3 [1930[	Hunt	money to Mary Isabel; Zulime sick
TL	to Garland, Mary Isabel	Mon.	Hunt	brooding over daughters
*ALS	to Garland, Mary Isabel	June 10 [1924]	Hunt	closeness to Mary Isabel
ALS	to Garland, Mary Isabel	Nov. 2 [1936]	Hunt	in Mexico; death of Lorado
*ALS	to Garland, Mary Isabel	Nov. 24, 1936	Hunt	Zulime's worsening health

TL	to Garland, Mary Isabel	Tue.	Hunt	crosses; voices gone; Putnam as Constance's suitor
ALS	to Garland, Mary Isabel	n.d.	USC	
TL	to Garland, Mary Isabel	n.d.	Hunt	re: transcribing diaries for *Roadside*
TL	to Garland, Mary Isabel	[July 12, 1924]	USC	
ALS	to Garland, Mary Isabel	n.d.	USC	
ApcS	to Garland, Mary Isabel	June 14, 1906	USC	
ALS	to Garland, Mary Isabel	Feb. 12	Homestead	
ALS	to Garland, Mary Isabel	Wed.	Hunt	encourages to write
*TL	to Garland, Mary Isabel	May 24 [1930]	Hunt	re: rejection; publ. of *Roadside*
ALS	to Garland, Mary Isabel	Mon.	USC	
ALS	to Garland, Mary Isabel	April 23	Hunt	re: birthday tributes & Eldon Hill
TL	to Garland, Mary Isabel	Tue.	Hunt	reads Mary Isabel's first novel
TL	to Garland, Mary Isabel	Fri.	Hunt	takes Mary Isabel's ms to Latham
TL	to Garland, Mary Isabel	Thurs.	Hunt	crosses; placing ms
ALS	to Garland, Mary Isabel	May 13	Hunt	crosses; chides Mary Isabel for pawning items
ALS	to Garland, Mary Isabel	Mon.	Hunt	crosses; galleys
ALS	to Garland, Mary Isabel	[Sept. 4, 1937]	Hunt	crosses
TLS	to Garland, Mary Isabel	Oct. 8, 1937	Hunt	crosses; editing instruct; Putnam interested
TL	to Garland, Mary Isabel	Sat.	Hunt	crosses; G. Putnam interested
TL	to Garland, Mary Isabel	Sept. 16, 1934	Hunt	psychic; Aunt Dora; *Forty*
ApcS	to Garland, Mary Isabel	June 18, 1906	USC	
TL	to Garland, Mary Isabel	Sun.	USC	
TL	to Garland, Mary Isabel	Tue.	Hunt	crosses; placing ms
ALS	to Garland, Mary Isabel	Feb. 28	Homestead	
ALS	to Garland, Mary Isabel	July 16	Hunt	re: costuming for lectures
TL	to Garland, Mary Isabel	Wed. 9	Hunt	crosses
ALS	to Garland, Mary Isabel	April 30 [1931]	Hunt	re: rejection of "The Rehearsal"
TL	to Garland, Mary Isabel	Mon.	Hunt	re: Mary Isabel's ms & Z's health
TLS	to Garland, Mary Isabel	Sat.	Hunt	psychic; Aunt Dora; *Forty*
ALS	to Garland, Mary Isabel	Dec. 12, 1935	USC	re: HG's will
TL	to Garland, Mary Isabel	Jan. 30	Hunt	crosses
TLC	to Garland, Mary Isabel	Oct. 8, 1937	USC	crosses; rev. of ms

ALS	to Garland, Mary Isabel	May 5	Hunt	
TL	to Garland, Mary Isabel	Wed.	Hunt	crosses; Earhart; refusal of ms
TL	to Garland, Mary Isabel	May 24, 1937	Hunt	crosses; psychic article
TLS	to Garland, Mary Isabel & Constance	Sat.	Hunt	crosses; seance descr.
TLS	to Garland, Mary Isabel & Constance	July 26, 1937	Hunt	crosses; design
*ALS	to Garland, Mary Isabel & Constance	[Oct. 27, 1931]	Hunt	receives Roosevelt medal
ALS	to Garland, Mary Isabel & Constance	n.d.	Wis HS	
*TLS	to Garland, Mary Isabel & Constance	Fri. [Aug. 6, 1937]	Hunt	re: Earhart
TLC	to Garland, Richard	March 28, 1912	USC	
TLC	to Garland, Richard	Nov. 29, 1911	USC	
AnS	to Garland, Richard	n.d.	U Wis-LaCrosse	
ALS	to Garland, Richard & Isabelle	June 23, 1899	USC	
ALS	to Garland, Richard & Isabelle	n.d.	USC	
ALS	to Garland, Richard & Isabelle	May 21, 1899	USC	
ALS	to Garland, Richard Isabelle	May 6, 1899	USC	describes dinner & London
trL	to Garland, Richard & Isabelle	May 30, 1898	USC	
ALS	to Garland, Richard & Isabelle	n.d.	USC	
ALS	to Garland, Richard Isabelle	May 8, 1899	USC	plays cricket w/ Conan Doyle
trL	to Garland, Richard & Isabelle	June 10, 1898	USC	
*ALS	to Garland, Richard & Isabelle	June 10, 1899	USC	in Paris
*ALS	to Garland, Richard & Isabelle	May 30, 1899	USC	in Paris
*ALS	to Garland, Richard & Isabelle	June 4, 1899	USC	in Paris
*ALS	to Garland, Zulime	[April 19, 1904]	Hunt	meets President Diaz of Mexico
TL	to Garland, Zulime	[May 25, 1930?]	USC	cataloging books for sale
ApcS	to Garland, Zulime	June 6, 1906	USC	
ALS	to Garland, Zulime	Feb. 11	Homestead	
ALS	to Garland, Zulime	Sat.	Homestead	
ALS	to Garland, Zulime	Feb. 17	Homestead	
ALS	to Garland, Zulime	n.d.	U Wis-LaCrosse	

*ALS	to Garland, Zulime	Nov. 10 [1915]	Hunt	re: job offer and seria of *Son*
*ALS	to Garland, Zulime	[ca. June 7, 1900]	Hunt	typical "status report"
*AL	to Garland, Zulime	July 31 [1924]	Hunt	resp. to French art, people
TLS	to Garland, Zulime	Thur. 22 [May 22, 1930?]	USC	
ALS	to Garland, Zulime	[1906]	USC	
ALS	to Garland, Zulime	n.d.	USC	
ALS	to Garland, Zulime	June 2 [1906]	USC	
ALS	to Garland, Zulime	Aug. 7 [1906]	USC	
ALS	to Garland, Zulime	Aug. 3 [1906]	USC	
TL	to Garland, Zulime	Sat. [May 24, 1930?]	USC	
TL	to Garland, Zulime	June 3 [1930]	USC	
ALS	to Garland, Zulime	[July] 5, 1906	USC	
ALS	to Garland, Zulime	July 13 [1906]	USC	
ALS	to Garland, Zulime	[1906]	USC	
ALS	to Garland, Zulime	Aug. 16, 1906	USC	
ALS	to Garland, Zulime	[1906]	USC	
ALS	to Garland, Zulime	Aug. 12 [1906]	USC	
ALS	to Garland, Zulime	[1906]	USC	1906 letters = European trip
ALS	to Garland, Zulime	Sun.	Homestead	
*ALS	to Garland, Zulime	July 27 [1924]	USC	describes: meeting with Wharton
ALS	to Garland, Zulime	Jan. 22	Homestead	
TL	to Garland, Zulime	Mon. [May 19, 1930?]	USC	
ALS	to Garland, Zulime	Mon. [1906]	USC	
ALS	to Garland, Zulime	[1906]	USC	
TL	to Garland, Zulime	Nov. 3 [1931]	Hunt	
ALS	to Garland, Zulime	Fri. [1906]	USC	
ALS	to Garland, Zulime	[April 23, 1927]	USC	
ALS	to Garland, Zulime	Wed. [1906]	USC	
ALS	to Garland, Zulime	July 30, 1906	USC	
ALS	to Garland, Zulime	July 16 [1906]	USC	
ALS	to Garland, Zulime	Aug. 14	Hunt	
ALS	to Garland, Zulime	Sun. 17 [1906]	USC	
ALS	to Garland, Zulime	Fri.	Hunt	
ALS	to Garland, Zulime	July 20 [1906]	USC	
ALS	to Garland, Zulime	[1906]	USC	
ALS	to Garland, Zulime	Sun. [193-]	USC	
ALS	to Garland, Zulime	Thurs.	USC	
ALS	to Garland, Zulime	Aug. 5, 1906	USC	
ALS	to Garland, Zulime	July 9 [1906]	USC	
ALS	to Garland, Zulime	July 21, 1906	USC	
ALS	to Garland, Zulime	July 1 [1906]	USC	
ALS	to Garland, Zulime	July 13 [1906]	USC	

ALS	to Garland, Zulime	July 24, 1906	USC	
ALS	to Garland, Zulime	June 29 [1906]	USC	
ALS	to Garland, Zulime	Thurs. 14 [1906]	USC	
ALS	to Garland, Zulime	May 18	Hunt	Sullivan decides against add. install. of *Son*
ALS	to Garland, Zulime	[1906]	USC	
TL	to Garland, Zulime & family	[June 1930]	USC	book sale; "Ulizio is a crook"
TL	to Garland, Zulime & family	May 27 [1930]	USC	re: sale of books
ALS	to Garland [family]	Sun. [1924]	Homestead	
ALS	to Garnett, Edward	June 16 [1923]	U Texas	enjoyed meeting
ALD	to Garrett, Eileen J.	July 31 [1932]	USC	
ALS	to George, Henry	Nov. 10, 1896	NYPL	re: election
ALS	to George, Henry, Jr	July 23 [1904]	NYPL	re: death of George's mother
ALS	to George, Henry, Jr	[Dec. 1904]	NYPL	
ALS	to George, Henry, Jr	Dec. 21 [1904]	NYPL	
ALS	to George, Henry, Jr	Dec. 28 [1904]	NYPL	re: Progress and Poverty dinner
ALS	to George, Henry, Jr	[Dec. 1904]	NYPL	
ALS	to George, Henry, Jr	[Dec. 1904]	NYPL	
TLS	to Gerson, T. Perceval	Oct. 20, 1933	UCLA	
ALS	to Gerup, Inga	Sept. 16, 1936	USC	
ALS	to Gessler	Dec. 17	U of Iowa	wants copy of unspec. book
ALS	to Gessler	Dec. 2	U of Iowa	would like to meet
TLC	to Gigli, Benjamino	March 13 [1925]	USC	
TLC	to Gignilliat, Col. Leigh R.	Feb. 21, 1913	USC	
ALS	to Gilder, Richard Watson	May 5, 1894	NYPL	is giving commencement address at Kansas S C
ALS	to Gilder, Richard Watson	March 3	NYPL	promotes Taft's sculpture
ALS	to Gilder, Richard Watson	July 17, 1894	NYPL	asks for return of "Good Fellow's Wife"
ALS	to Gilder, Richard Watson	Feb. 27	Virginia	re: revision of "Quaker story"
ALS	to Gilder, Richard Watson	Sept. 23	NYPL	submits "novelette"
ALS	to Gilder, Richard Watson	April 20	NYPL	promotes Taft's sculpture
ALS	to Gilder, Richard Watson	[ca May 19, 1906]	NYPL	asks for letter to John Morley
ALS	to Gilder, Richard Watson	June 1 [1900]	NYPL	"Graven Image"
ALS	to Gilder, Richard Watson	March 2	NYPL	promotes Taft's sculpture

ALS	to Gilder, Richard Watson	Oct. 6	NYPL	encloses contract for unspec. work
ALS	to Gilder, Richard Watson	Sept. 26	NYPL	submits poems
ALS	to Gilder, Richard Watson	[1898]	NYPL	encloses rev. by Moulton of *Wayside*
ALS	to Gilder, Richard Watson	May 3 [1900]	NYPL	re: serial of "Plainsman"
*ALS	to Gilder, Richard Watson	[Oct. 1889]	NYPL	re: changes in "Flaxen"; Remington illus
ALS	to Gilder, Richard Watson	n.d.	Columbia	asks G. to read a "great ms" by Crane
ApcS	to Gilder, Richard Watson	[Oct. 20, 1905]	NYPL	re: sale of "Manhattan"
ALS	to Gilder, Richard Watson	n.d.	NYPL	re: "embargo on my writing"
ALS	to Gilder, Richard Watson	June 21 [1900]	NYPL	re: "Plainsman"
ALS	to Gilder, Richard Watson	May 1, 1899	NYPL	instructions re: "mss"
ALS	to Gilder, Richard Watson	June 19	NYPL	submits Indian story of "lighter vein"
ALS	to Gilder, Richard Watson	Sept. 7, 1900	NYPL	is returning to West Salem
ALS	to Gilder, Richard Watson	Friday night [1906]	NYPL	"Plainsman"; Mary Isabel's illness
ALS	to Gilder, Richard Watson	[Oct. 1900]	NYPL	re: title of *Her Mountain Lover*
ALS	to Gilder, Richard Watson	Jan. 15, 1900	NYPL	asks to consider Indian stories
ALS	to Gilder, Richard Watson	n.d.	NYPL	has returned from western trip
ALS	to Gilder, Richard Watson	n.d.	NYPL	wants to know status of "novelettes"
ALS	to Gilder, Richard Watson	Jan. 23	NYPL	submits "Quaker story"
ALS	to Gilder, Richard Watson	[Jan. 1901]	NYPL	offers *Captain* [incomplete]
ALS	to Gilder, Richard Watson	June 19, 1900	NYPL	
ALS	to Gilder, Richard Watson	Nov. 10, 1905	NYPL	"Manhattan" sells for $50
ALS	to Gilder, Richard Watson	Jan. 10, 1898	NYPL	when will *Century* use "Good Fellow's"?
*ALS	to Gilder, Richard Watson	Nov. 1, 1890	NYPL	"Member"; "Flaxen" proof
ALS	to Gilder, Richard Watson	April 15 [1900]	NYPL	re: serial of "Plainsman"
*ALS	to Gilder, Richard Watson	Oct. 30, 1889	NYPL	re: "Flaxen"; *Doll's House*
*ALS	to Gilder, Richard Watson	[after May 7, 1890]	NYPL	distinctions among dialects in "Girl Modern Tyre"

*ALS	to Gilder, Richard Watson	[after April 5, 1890]	NYPL	re: dialect
ALS	to Gilder, Richard Watson	[Dec. 1904]	NYPL	Progress and Poverty dinner
*ALS	to Gilder, Richard Watson	[Oct. 1889]	NYPL	re: "Flaxen"; "Ladrone"
*ALS	to Gilder, Richard Watson	Feb. 6, 1891	NYPL	"Widow at Alleys"
ALS	to Gilder, Richard Watson	Friday	NYPL	thanks for suggestions
*ALS	to Gilder, Richard Watson	[Aug. 29, 1900]	NYPL	re: *Her Mountain Lover*
*ALS	to Gilder, Richard Watson	[before March 1892]	NYPL	*Century* too slow; Appleton publ work
*ALS	to Gilder, Richard Watson	[ca. Jan. 1890]	NYPL	asks after "Jason Edwards"
*ALS	to Gilder, Richard Watson	April 19, 1895	NYPL	"Good Fellow's Wife"; based on true story
*ALS	to Gilder, Richard Watson	[after March 31, 1890]	NYPL	"Girl of Modern Tyre"
ALS	to Gilder, Richard Watson	Jan. 26 [1904]	NYPL	re: Gilder's illness
*ALS	to Gilder, Richard Watson	Nov. 12 [1905]	NYPL	re: MacDowell club
*ALS	to Gilder, Richard Watson	[before Sept. 1889]	NYPL	1st letter; sends stories
*ALS	to Gilder, Richard Watson	Oct. 10, 1889	NYPL	"Prairie Heroine"
*ALS	to Gilder, Richard Watson	Feb. 2, 1897	NYPL	dialect; "Corn Dance"
*ALS	to Gilder, Richard Watson	Sept. 7, 1889	NYPL	encloses stories; offers to soften language
*ALS	to Gilder, Richard Watson	Jan. 10, 1890	NYPL	encl. "Under the Wheel"
ALS	to Gilder, Richard Watson	July 11 [1904]	NYPL	re: Gilder's appendicitis
TLC	to Gillis, Mabel	August 31, 1937	USC	c. of Cal St ltr
TLS	to Gillis, Mabel	July 25, 1939	Cal St Lib	crosses; exhib
TLS	to Gillis, Mabel	Aug. 26, 1938	Cal St Lib	crosses; req. books on spirit photos
ALS	to Gillis, Mabel	Jan. 19, 1938	Cal St Lib	exhib
TLS	to Gillis, Mabel	Oct. 27, 1937	Cal St Lib	exhib; crosses; req. for books
TLS	to Gillis, Mabel	Sat. [Oct. 9, 1937]	Cal St Lib	exhib
ALS	to Gillis, Mabel	Feb. 8, 1938	Cal St Lib	exhib
ALS	to Gillis, Mabel	Dec. 3, 1939	Cal St Lib	crosses
ALS	to Gillis, Mabel	Nov. 10, 1936	Cal St Lib	exhib
TLS	to Gillis, Mabel	Aug. 31, 1937	Cal St Lib	exhib
TLS	to Gillis, Mabel	Aug. 25, 1937	Cal St Lib	exhib
ALS	to Gillis, Mabel	Sept. 18 [1933]	Cal St Lib	thanks for b-day letter
TLS	to Gillis, Mabel	Sept. 11, 1939	Cal St Lib	crosses; exhib
TLS	to Gillis, Mabel	Aug. 31, 1939	Cal St Lib	crosses; exhib
ALS	to Gillis, Mabel	Oct. 31, 1939	Cal St Lib	crosses; exhib
TLS	to Gillis, Mabel	Nov. 19, 1939	Cal St Lib	crosses; exhib

TLS	to Gillis, Mabel	[ca. Sept. 5, 1939]	Cal St Lib	crosses; exhib
TLS	to Gillis, Mabel	Sept. 19, 1939	Cal St Lib	crosses; exhib
ALS	to Gillis, Mabel	Sept. 28, 1939	Cal St Lib	crosses; exhib
ALS	to Gillis, Mabel	Aug. 20, 1939	Cal St Lib	crosses; exhib
TLS	to Gillis, Mabel	Aug. 25, 1939	Cal St Lib	crosses; exhib
ALS	to Gillis, Mabel	Dec. 9, 1939	Cal St Lib	crosses; exhib
TLS	to Gillis, Mabel	Aug. 4, 1939	Cal St Lib	crosses; exhib
TLS	to Gillis, Mabel	Nov. 14, 1939	Cal St Lib	crosses; exhib
TLC	to Gilman, Lawrence	June 22, 1912	USC	re: reading ms of "Middle Border"
ALS	to Gilman, Lawrence	Nov. 5	Yale	thanks for book; arranging meeting
TLS	to Gilman, Lawrence	March 1917	Yale	Com Lit Art circula
ALS	to Gilman, Lawrence	Feb. 14	Yale	re: MacDowell trib. in *Harpers*
TLC	to Gilson	Feb. 11	USC	re: lectures
ALC	to Glass, Miss	[Sept. 1904-May 1905]	USC LB 211	
ALC	to Glass, Miss	May 10 [1904]	USC LB 197	
ALC	to Glass, Miss	June 21 [1902]	USC LB 72	re: lectures
ALC	to Glass, Miss	Dec. 11 [1903]	USC LB 186	re: lectures: Indians, poems, trail
TLC	to Glass, William C.	June 24, 1914	USC	
TLC	to Glass, William C.	Oct. 25, 1911	USC	
TLC	to Glass, William C.	Oct. 8, 1913	USC	
TLC	to Glass, William C.	April 25, 1913	USC	
TLC	to Glass, William C.	April 23, 1914	USC	
TLC	to Glass, William C.	Oct. 2, 1914	USC	
TLC	to Glass, William C.	Sept. 30, 1913	USC	
TLC	to Glass, William C.	n.d.	USC	
TLC	to Glass, William C.	Nov. 9, 1914	USC	
ALD	to Glass, William C.	March 21	USC	
TLC	to Glass, William C.	April 30	USC	
TLC	to Glass, William C.	April 8, 1914	USC	re: lectures
ALS	to Godfrey, Marjory W.	[March 6, 1935]	Miami U	thanks for offer to index books
TLD	to Goethals, George W.	Oct. 30 [1921]	USC	had no part of unspe committee
TLD	to Goldwasser, David	Oct. 2 [1933]	USC	re: contribution to anthology
TLC	to Goodman, William O.	May 27, 1913	USC	
TLC	to Goodrich, Chester	Aug. 6, 1939	Hunt	
TLC	to Gordon, J. R.	June 30 [1927]	USC	
TLC	to Gordon, J. R.	June 20 [1927]	USC	psychic; Derieux, Crandon mediums
ALS	to Gorges, Raymond	Sept. 16, 1930	Virginia	thanks for present
ALS	to Gould, Elizabeth Porter	May 11, 1890	Boston PL	re: single-tax speech
*ALS	to Gould, Elizabeth Porter	Nov. 11, 1889	Boston PL	re: Gould's book and *Century* acceptance

ALS	to Gould, Elizabeth Porter	Dec. 1, 1899	Boston PL	thanks for "note"
TLC	to Grabill, E. W.	May 7, 1914	USC	
ALD	to Graham	April 4	USC	good diction
ALS	to Granberg, Fred	April 14 [1925]	U of Iowa	thanks for interest in work
ALS	to Grant, Jessie R.	Nov. 16, 1896	USC	re: *Grant* bio; interview
ALS	to Grant, Robert	Oct. 13 [1900?]	Harvard	thanks for copy of *Unleavened Bread*
TLC	to Graves, Henry S.	May 9, 1912	USC	asks for map of Glacier Park
ALS	to Gray, Clifton D.	Feb. 4 [1932]	USC	
ALS	to Gray, Edward	July 25 [1923?]	USC	Re: TR; HG's foreword to *Winning of the West*
TLC	to Great Northern Railway	May 29, 1912	USC	
ALS	to Green, Don	Jan. 13 [1932]	Hunt	re: visit
TLC	to Greenslet, Forris	May 19, 1913	USC	
ALS	to Griffith	Sept. 20	Virginia	likes Griffith's verses
TLS	to Griffith, Reginald H.	Feb. 4	U Texas	re: lectures
TLC	to Griffith, William	Feb. 17, 1913	USC	
TLC	to Griffith, William	Dec. 20, 1913	USC	
TLC	to Griffith, William	April 21, 1913	USC	
TLC	to Griffith, William	April 24 [1916]	USC	re: serial possibilities
ALS	to Griffith, William	Oct. 14	Bancroft	cannot attend unspec. event
TLC	to Griffith, William	Feb. 16, 1916	USC	
*TLC	to Grinnell, George Bird	July 29 [1902]	Southwest	Indian; renaming
TLC	to Grosset, Alexander	May 10 [1916]	USC	re: film adapt; serial *Hesper*
TLC	to Grosset, Alexander	April 8 [1916]	USC	re: film adaptation
ALS	to Grossman, Edwina Booth	Dec. 28 [1903]	Homestead	encloses Booth lecture for correction
ALS	to Grossman, Edwina Booth	April 2	Players	
ALS	to Grossman, Edwina Booth	April 1 [1904]	Players	
ALS	to Grosvenor, Gilbert	Dec. 2, 1895	UNC-CH	too busy to write for paper—*Rose*
ApcS	to Groves, John Stuart	[1932]	Hunt	re: authentic copy of *Wheel*
TLS	to Groves, John Stuart	May 2, 1938	Virginia	exhib; asks to borrow *Jason Edwards*
ALS	to Groves, John Stuart	Oct. 4, 1938	Virginia	exhib; returns *Jason Edwards*
TLS	to Guiney, Louise I.	Feb. 13, 1915	Princeton	invites Guiney to Author's League
TLC	to Gullickson	June 21	USC	
ALS	to Gunn	April 10	Miami U	about opera

TLC	to Hackett, Edmund	Feb. 10 [1917]	USC	
TLD	to Hackett, Francis	Dec. 18, 1938	USC	re: use of unspec. address
TLC	to Hackney, Louise	May 28, 1913	USC	okays rpt. of "Mrs Ripley's Trip"
TLC	to Hagedorn, Herman	Jan. 24 [1924-26]	Miami U	agrees to write of TI for TR's *Works*
ALD	to Hagedorn, Herman	June 1 [1931]	USC	re: Roosevelt award citation
ALS	to Hagedorn, Hermann	Aug. 21	USC	
ALS	to Hagedorn, Hermann	March 17	USC	
TLS	to Hagedorn, Hermann	March, 1917	USC	Com Lit Art circula
ALS	to Hagedorn, Hermann	Nov. 28	USC	
ALS	to Hagedorn, Hermann	June 10	USC	
ALS	to Hagedorn, Hermann	Sept. 17	USC	
ALS	to Hagedorn, Hermann	March 15, 1939	USC	
TLC	to Hagedorn, Hermann	Jan. 17. [1920]	USC	re: Max Ravage
*ALD	to Hagedorn, Hermann	[Feb. 4, 1919]	USC	suggests Roosevelt memorial volume
ALD	to Hagedorn, Hermann	Aug. 19 [1931]	USC	
*ALD	to Hagedorn, Hermann	Feb. 21, 1940	USC	re: HH's poem "Daddy" and loss of faith
TLS	to Hagedorn, Hermann	Aug. 31, 1937	USC	crosses; asks for addresses of historians
ALC	to Hagen	June 10 [1904]	USC LB 206	re: lectures
TLC	to Hahn, Herman	May 8, 1914	USC	invites to Cliff Dwellers
TLC	to Hahn, Herman	April 20, 1914	USC	
ALC	to Hallister Bros.	[March-April 1901]	USC LB 41	
ALC	to Hallister Bros.	[May, 1902]	USC LB 62	re: circular payment
ALS	to Halman	Nov. 10, 1894	U of Ill	
ALS	to Hamilton, Clayton	July 22	NYPL	re: Matthews' heal
ALS	to Hamilton, Clayton	June 28	NYPL	asks after Matthew health
TLS	to Hamilton, Clayton	[Aug. 27, 1923]	NYPL	thanks for aiding Mary Isabel's acting
ALS	to Hamilton, Clayton	Sept. 20	NYPL	re: production of *Cyrano*/Hampden Co.
TLC	to Hammond, Mrs.	May 30 [1919]	USC	re: restoration of TR birthplace
TLC	to Hamp, Seaford F.	March 10, 1913	USC	
TLC	to Hampden, Walter	March 18 [1923]	Miami U	arranges for Mary Isabel's acting
TLC	to Hampden, Walter	May 11	USC	good diction
TLC	to Hampden, Walter	n.d.	USC	good diction
ALS	to Hancher, John W.	June 23 [1931]	USC	

TLC	to Hansl, P. W.	April 8, 1914	USC	
TLC	to Hansl, P. W.	Dec. 20, 1912	USC	
TLC	to Hansl, P. W.	April 8, 1914	USC	
TLC	to Harben, Will N.	April 23, 1914	USC	
ALS	to Harford	Oct. 22	Princeton	re: lectures
TLC	to Harlan, Edgar R.	Oct. 9 [1915]	USC	
TLC	to Harlan, Edgar R.	Feb. 27 [1923]	USC	requests mementoes be sent to Am Acad
TLC	to Harned, Thomas B.	[1921?]	USC	Acad; request for Whitman material
ALS	to Harned, Thomas B.	June 24	U Penn	thanks for Whitman's *Selected Poems*
ALS	to Harper	July 14 [1913]	Congress	re: Roosevelt as speaker
ALS	to Harper	Tue., 28	Virginia	returns galley proof
TLC	to Harriman, Karl Edwin	March 9, 1912	USC	sends Middle Border ms
TLC	to Harriman, Karl Edwin	March 4, 1934	USC	doesn't like Peterson's *Trumpets*
TLC	to Harriman. Karl Edwin	May 8, 1912	USC	re: potential sale of "Prairie Mother"
ALS	to Harris, Fisher	Sept. 29 [1902]	Duke	asks whether Harris got unspec. book
ALS	to Harris, Joel Chandler	[ca 1890s]	Emory	wants to meet [incomplete]
ALS	to Harris, Joel Chandler	Jan. 3, 1902	Emory	re: autograph of *Uncle Remus*
ALS	to Harris, Joel Chandler	Dec. 7	Emory	Institute; plans to increase scope
ALC	to Harris, T. L.	Nov. 18 [1901]	USC LB 13	re: lectures
ALS	to Harrison	Feb. 19	U of Iowa	
ALS	to Harrison	Feb. 14	U of Iowa	re: lectures
ALS	to Harrison	Jan. 14	U of Iowa	
TLC	to Harrison, Bertram	April 29, 1912	USC	Chicago Thea Soc
ALS	to Harrison, Carter H., IV	Oct. 28	Newberry	thanks for encouragement of art in Chicago
ALD	to Harrison, Elizabeth	April 1917	USC	re: mother and "Mrs. Ripley's Trip"
ALS	to Harvey	Feb. 8, 1895	Virginia	re: lecture
*ALS	to Harvey, George B. M.	Feb. 5 [1902]	Ind HS	re: submission of "Redman's Present Needs"
*ALC	to Harvey, George B. M.	Oct. 7 [1902]	USC LB 94	promotes "Sitting Bull"
ALS	to Harvey, George B. M.	Oct. 24	Morgan	re: revision of Howells article
TLC	to Harvey, Roy L.	Feb. 26, 1913	USC	
TLC	to Harvey, Roy L.	Feb. 26, 1913	USC	

ApcS	to Haselton, Guy D.	[Dec. 1, 1939]	Hunt	re: dinner
ALS	to Haselton, Guy D.	Feb. 10, 1940	Hunt	no one pays for bio. film
AnS	to Haselton, Guy D.	n.d.	Hunt	re: enclosure [missing
TLS	to Hatfield, James Taft	Jan. 4 [1929]	Miami U	on Anna Morgan's book on Fuller
TLD	to Hawkinson, Roy E.	Nov. 9 [1939]	USC	HG posed for illus ir *MTR*
TLC	to Hawthorne, Julian	[June 1930]	USC	c. of June 10 [1931] ltr
ALS	to Hawthorne, Julian	April 5 [1930]	Bancroft	
ALS	to Hawthorne, Julian	March 24 [11930]	Bancroft	suggests univ. talks
ALS	to Hawthorne, Julian	July 15 [1931]	Bancroft	
ALS	to Hawthorne, Julian	July 24 [1933?]	Bancroft	
TLS	to Hawthorne, Julian	Aug. 17 [1933?]	Bancroft	
*ALS	to Hawthorne, Julian	Aug. 20 [1931]	Bancroft	encourages autobio
ALS	to Hawthorne, Julian	Sept. 18 [1933]	Bancroft	
ALS	to Hawthorne, Julian	Dec. 5	Bancroft	
*ALS	to Hawthorne, Julian	March 31 [1930]	Bancroft	has written to Univs on JH's behalf
*ALS	to Hawthorne, Julian	June 10 [1931]	Bancroft	b-day greeting
ALS	to Hawthorne, Mrs.	July 19 [1934]	Bancroft	re: Julian's death
TLC	to Hayes, Charles	March 5, 1913	USC	Chicago Thea Soc: review plays
TLD	to Hays, William Harrison	Aug. 29, 1936	USC	
TLC	to Hayward, Robert O.	May 31, 1913	USC	
TLC	to Hayward, Robert O.	Nov. 19, 1913	USC	
TLC	to Hendershot, Florence M.	Sept. 23	USC	
TLC	to Hendricks, Burton J.	Feb.18 [1925]	USC	can't find Walter Page letters
TLC	to Hening, H. B.	June 14, 1912	USC	writing "Threshing Day in Isleta"
TLC	to Henry, [Harold?]	Jan. 6, 1914	USC	
*trL	to Herne, James A.	[before Jan. 6, 1889]	Am Acad	praises *Drifting Apart*
*ALS	to Herne, James A.	Nov. 21, 1890	USC	re: B. O. Flower
ALS	to Herne, Julie	Nov. 10, 1936	USC	re: Lorado Taft's death
ALS	to Herne, Julie	April 9, 1937	USC	Zulime's health improved
ALS	to Herne, Julie	July 20 [1925]	USC	recommends Town Hall Club
ALS	to Herne, Julie	Aug. 1st [1914]	USC	reply to praise of Herne article
ALS	to Herne, Katharine	Dec. 2 [1938]	USC	
ALS	to Herne, Katharine	Sept. 26 [1929]	USC	*Roadside* serial to appear
ALS	to Herne, Katharine	Oct. 23 [1930]	USC	recommends book by William Gross
ALS	to Herne, Katharine	Dec. 19, 1937	USC	

ALS	to Herne, Katharine	Aug. 4 [1930]	USC	Zulime's health improved
ALS	to Herne, Katharine	May 12 [1914]	USC	in town; at work on *Son* serial
ALS	to Herne, Katharine	Dec. 23	USC	
TLS	to Herne, Katharine	May 10 [1937]	USC	Zulime's health improved; Haselton & film
ALS	to Herne, Katharine	Jan. 14 [1934]	USC	
ALS	to Herne, Katharine	Nov. 17 [1914]	USC	arranging meeting
ALS	to Herne, Katharine	June 6 [1927]	USC	come to Onteora tonight
*ALS	to Herne, Katharine	June 3 [1901]	USC	re: Herne's death
ALS	to Herne, Katharine	July 12 [1913]	USC	all is well
ALS	to Herne, Katharine	Feb. 8 [1913]	USC	re: first meeting
ALS	to Herrick, Robert	June 12 [1907]	U Chicago	reading *Real World*
ALS	to Herrick, Robert	[1897?]	U Chicago	invites membership in Little Room
ALS	to Herrick, Robert	June 18 [1907]	U Chicago	commends *The Real World*
ALS	to Herrick, Robert	Sept. 25 [1908]	U Chicago	commends *Together*
TLS	to Hickok	June 11	U of Iowa	re: fraternities
*ALS	to Higginson, Thomas W.	Dec. 15 [1908]	U of Iowa	re: org. of Cliff Dwellers
*ALS	to Higginson, Thomas W.	Oct. 16, 1897	Virginia	re: "Truth for Art's Sake"
ALC	to Hight, William A.	June 29 [1903]	USC LB 167	re: serial rights - *Captain*
ALS	to Hill	n.d.	Virginia	
TLC	to Hill, Charles S.	May 31 [1927]	USC	
ALS	to Hill, David Jayne	Nov. 29 [1921]	Rochester	Acad; req. books
ALS	to Hill, David Jayne	Nov. 18 [1920]	Rochester	Acad; Hill elected
TLS	to Hill, David Jayne	Nov. 22 [1921]	Rochester	Acad; req. books
TLS	to Hill, Eldon	Nov. 24, 1939	Miami U	about publ. of his material
ALS	to Hill, Eldon	[Jan. 10, 1940]	Miami U	re: 80th b-day plans
ALS	to Hill, Eldon	Dec. 6 [1933]	Miami U	arranging meeting
TLS	to Hill, Eldon	Feb. 9, 1934	Miami U	HG's influence upon others
ALS	to Hill, Eldon	[Jan. 10, 1940]	Miami U	re: 80th b-day plans
ALS	to Hill, Eldon	Nov. 9, 1934	Miami U	grants Hill permission to quote
TLS	to Hill, Eldon	[Feb. 1, 1940]	Miami U	another HG thesis: inc. Indian writings
ALS	to Hill, Eldon	Sept. 1 [1936]	Miami U	
TL	to Hill, Eldon	Oct. 11 [1939]	Miami U	crosses exhib.
TLS	to Hill, Eldon	Dec. 26, 1939	Miami U	crosses exhib. in Columbus

TL	to Hill, Eldon	Jan. 22, 1936	Miami U	asks about list of psychic writers
TLS	to Hill, Eldon	Sept. 12, 1939	Miami U	exhib; Hill's draft status
*TLS	to Hill, Eldon	Dec. 3, 1934	Miami U	HG on his verse
TLS	to Hill, Eldon	Feb. 8, 1937	Miami U	arranging details of bio film showings
ALS	to Hill, Eldon	[Feb. 5, 1937]	Miami U	grants perm. to use Howells info
ALS	to Hill, Eldon	Dec. 13, 1936	Miami U	encl. more material for exhib.
TLS	to Hill, Eldon	April 21 [1935]	Miami U	about Franklin in New Mexico
ALS	to Hill, Eldon	Feb. 4, 1935	Miami U	compares Chicago and NY world's fairs
TLS	to Hill, Eldon	Sept. 9 [1935]	Miami U	about his own manual labor
TLS	to Hill, Eldon	April 25 [1932]	Miami U	is interested in Hill's article on HG's verse
TLS	to Hill, Eldon	June 24, 1938	Miami U	sends thesis by "Miss Hill"
TLS	to Hill, Eldon	Jan. 19, 1937	Miami U	bio film; Zulime ill
ALS	to Hill, Eldon	Jan. 12, 1937	Miami U	
TLS	to Hill, Eldon	[Oct. 28, 1939]	Miami U	crosses exhib; Fuller letters
TLS	to Hill, Eldon	Oct. 4, 1939	Miami U	exhib. at Miami U
TLS	to Hill, Eldon	Nov. 26 [1939]	Miami U	HG's wishes about access to his material
TLS	to Hill, Eldon	Oct. 7, 1939	Miami U	encourages Hill to publish
TLS	to Hill, Eldon	Sept. 12 [1936]	Miami U	exhib
ALS	to Hill, Eldon	Dec. 13, 1936	Miami U	Hill is HG's rep. in exhib. at Deering
TLS	to Hill, Eldon	Dec. 3, 1935	Miami U	infl. of Olive Shriner and Wilkins
TL	to Hill, Eldon	July 23 [1938]	Miami U	arranging travel plans
TLS	to Hill, Eldon	Nov. 30, 1936	Miami U	exhib: Newberry, Harper, Madison
TLS	to Hill, Eldon	Oct. 19, 1939	Miami U	crosses exhib.; ad in NYT
TLS	to Hill, Eldon	June 10 [1938]	Miami U	influence of Russian writers
TLS	to Hill, Eldon	March 17 [1937]	Miami U	Zulime at cards scene filmed
ALS	to Hill, Eldon	Jan. 27, 1938	Miami U	recommends *High Trails* for bio info
TLS	to Hill, Eldon	July 28, 1935	Miami U	on his carpentry— mostly book shelves

*ALS	to Hill, Eldon	[ca. March 3, 1940]	Miami U	HG's last letter to Hill, re: psychic work
TLS	to Hill, Eldon	June 7, 1938	Miami U	note Jean Hill Parker has written thesis on him
TLS	to Hill, Eldon	July 10 [1939]	Miami U	on psychic work; wants Hill to classify letters
ALS	to Hill, Eldon	Dec. 29, 1936	Miami U	thanks for rev. of *Forty* in *Step Ladder*
ALS	to Hill, Eldon	Feb. 13, 1937	Miami U	exhib
ALS	to Hill, Eldon	June 20, 1939	Miami U	deciding placement of mss
TLS	to Hill, Eldon	Aug. 25, 1937	Miami U	exhib
ALS	to Hill, Eldon	Oct. 13, 1938	Miami U	arranging lecture
TLS	to Hill, Eldon	July 19, 1937	Miami U	exhib
TLS	to Hill, Eldon	April 28 [1937]	Miami U	exhib.
ALS	to Hill, Eldon	Nov. 27, 1938	Miami U	Thomas Bledsoe is writing a thesis on HG
TLS	to Hill, Eldon	Jan. 26 [1937]	Miami U	re: bio film—pleased w/ result; exhibit
TLS	to Hill, Eldon	June 28, 1937	Miami U	bio film
TLS	to Hill, Eldon	Dec. 15 [1934]	Miami U	about "Cry of the Age" and other verse
TLS	to Hill, Eldon	Feb. 27 [1933]	Miami U	re: Zulime's health
ALS	to Hill, Eldon	[Feb] 2, 1937	Miami U	exhib
ALS	to Hill, Eldon	July 12 [1932]	Miami U	admires Arthur H. Quinn
ALS	to Hill, Eldon	June 1 [1937]	Miami U	
TLS	to Hill, Eldon	[Dec. 5, 1939]	Miami U	encloses 2 unspec. letters
TLS	to Hill, Eldon	Jan. 2, 1940	Miami U	sends letters by Herne, Gillette & others
TL	to Hill, Eldon	[Dec. 14, 1939]	Miami U	encloses book plates
ALS	to Hill, Eldon	May 16, 1939	Miami U	
TLS	to Hill, Eldon	Feb. 19 [1937]	Miami U	exhib; bio film
TL	to Hill, Eldon	[Feb. 22, 1937]	Miami U	bio film not ready to ship
TLS	to Hill, Eldon	June 3, 1939	Miami U	waiting for Hill to publ; offers mss elsewhere
ALS	to Hill, Eldon	May 6, 1937	Miami U	film ready
TLS	to Hill, Eldon	[Sept. 7, 1938]	Miami U	arranges travel plans
ALS	to Hill, Eldon	Sept. 7 [1937]	Miami U	exhib; retake of Zulime film scene
ALS	to Hill, Eldon	Dec. 2, 1937	Miami U	exhib to Sacramento

TLS	to Hill, Eldon	[March 31, 1937]	Miami U	wants film to go to Madison
ALS	to Hill, Eldon	April 18 [1934]	Miami U	is visiting the Tafts
ALS	to Hill, Eldon	June 24, 1935	Miami U	directs Hill to Vanamee re: radio gold medal info
TLS	to Hill, Eldon	Jan. 15, 1934	Miami U	arranging lecture; title of *Afternoon*
TLS	to Hill, Eldon	June 6 [1935]	Miami U	declined Twain address because of is resemblance
TLS	to Hill, Eldon	Aug. 23 [1935]	Miami U	fears Hill is wasting his time on HG
TLS	to Hill, Eldon	Dec. 24 [1931]	Miami U	is interested in seeing Hill's article
TLS	to Hill, Eldon	Sept. 4 [1931]	Miami U	arranging a visit
TLS	to Hill, Eldon	Oct. 24 [1931]	Miami U	arranging a visit
TLS	to Hill, Eldon	Feb. 25 [1931]	Miami U	arranging lecture
TLS	to Hill, Eldon	Aug. 30 [1930]	Miami U	*Roadside* to be publ.; wonders effect of writing
ALS	to Hill, Eldon	April 8 [1935]	Miami U	directs Hill to middle border books for answers
ALS	to Hill, Eldon	April 19 [1934]	Miami U	arranging meeting
TLS	to Hill, Eldon	July 20 [1935]	Miami U	asks Hill to send poems to Mott [*Iowa, O Iowa*]
ALS	to Hill, Eldon	Sunday [May 7 1934]	Miami U	refers Hill to others for info
TL	to Hill, Eldon	May 9, 1939	Miami U	*Crosses* is published
TLS	to Hill, Eldon	Jan. 6, 1936	Miami U	lists writers of pyschic works he admires
ApcS	to Hill, Eldon	[April 16, 1936]	Miami U	is sending copy of *Forty*
TpcS	to Hill, Eldon	[Sept. 21, 1936]	Miami U	arranging exhibit shipment
TLS	to Hill, Eldon	Sept. 17, 1935	Miami U	thanks for b-day greeting
ALS	to Hill, Eldon	April 7, 1937	Miami U	re: bio film; exhib.
TLS	to Hill, Eldon	Oct. 7, 1936	Miami U	arranges shipment of ms. exhibit to Northwestern
TL	to Hill, Eldon	[March 13, 1937]	Miami U	coffee-making scene filmed
TLS	to Hill, Eldon	April 3 [1933]	Miami U	arranging lecture
ALS	to Hill, Eldon	Aug. 13 [1931]	Miami U	Zulime ill, so no dinner

TLS	to Hill, Eldon	April 6, 1937	Miami U	exhib
TLS	to Hill, Eldon	[March] 27, 1937	Miami U	wants film at Book-fellows exhibit
TLS	to Hill, Eldon	[March 7, 1937]	Miami U	re: bio film
ALS	to Hill, Eldon	June 20 [1937]	Miami U	encl. copy of Barrie letter sent to *NY Times*
ALS	to Hill, Eldon	April 6 [1930]	Miami U	thanks for review of Middle Border books
ALS	to Hill, Eldon	April 22 [1931]	Miami U	arranging lecture
TLS	to Hill, Eldon	March 24 [1931	Miami U	arranging lecture, fee
ALS	to Hill, Eldon	May 30 [1934]	Miami U	encloses an appreciative letter
TLS	to Hill, Eldon	Feb. 11 [1930]	Miami U	tells Hill to go ahead and write about *Roadside*
ALS	to Hill, Eldon	July 4 [1931]	Miami U	arranging meeting
TL	to Hill, Eldon	May 9 [1932]	Miami U	re: publ. of *Contemporaries*
ALS	to Hill, Eldon	Sept. 11 [1934]	Miami U	publ. of *Afternoon*; may meet
TLS	to Hill, Eldon	July 9 [1934]	Miami U	arranging meeting
ALS	to Hill, Eldon	Nov. 7, 1934	Miami U	is pleased by Hill's enthusiasm
*TLS	to Hill, Eldon	March 28, 1938	Miami U	re: composition of *Grant*
TLS	to Hill, Eldon	Feb. 23, 1938	Miami U	answers queries re: bio details: refers to clippings
ALS	to Hill, Eldon	May 30 [1928]	Miami U	is sending *Back-Trailers*
*TLS	to Hill, Eldon	Jan. 25 [1938]	Miami U	bored by Melville
*TLS	to Hill, Eldon	Dec. 18, 1937	Miami U	about literary influences
TLS	to Hill, Eldon	Oct. 22, 1936	Miami U	to Mexico; exhib. arrangements
TLS	to Hill, Eldon	Oct. 12 [1930]	Miami U	explains lecture dates
ALS	to Hill, Eldon	[June] 13 [1936]	Miami U	now ready for Hill's visit
ALS	to Hill, Eldon	Nov. 10, 1936	Miami U	exhib.
ALS	to Hill, Eldon	Dec. 22, 1938	Miami U	sends H. to Mac-millan to collect his letters
TLS	to Hill, Eldon	Nov. 22, 1933	Miami U	seeks lecture at Lake Forest
*TLS	to Hill, Eldon	Jan. 22, 1939	Miami U	Moody, work in drama
TLS	to Hill, Eldon	[April 10, 1938]	Miami U	Spencer's influence

TLS	to Hill, Eldon	May 4, 1938	Miami U	tired of Hill's collecting; wants him to write
TLS	to Hill, Eldon	[Feb. 15, 1940]	Miami U	extends loan of exhibs
TLS	to Hill, Eldon	n.d.	Miami U	re: additions to exhib.
TLS	to Hill, Eldon	Sept. 29, 1936	Miami U	exhibit shipment to Northwestern; bio film
TLS	to Hill, Eldon	April 5 [1929]	Miami U	asks for rec. of radio announcers
TLS	to Hill, Eldon	Oct. 13 [1929]	Miami U	announces lecture dates
TLS	to Hill, Eldon	Feb. 19 [1932]	Miami U	arranging lecture date
ALS	to Hill, Eldon	Feb. 20 [1929]	Miami U	[ink has run.— illeg.]
ALS	to Hill, Eldon	Jan. 19 [1929]	Miami U	thanks for enclosure —first letter to Hill?
ALS	to Hill, Eldon	Sept. 20 [1930]	Miami U	arranging meeting
TLS	to Hill, Eldon	Jan. 28, 1936	Miami U	arranging meeting
TLS	to Hill, Eldon	Jan. 10, 1935	Miami U	orig. of "Old Pap's Flaxen"
ALS	to Hill, Eldon	Nov. 22 [1936]	Miami U	Sacramento exhib.
ALS	to Hill, Eldon	May 28 [1936]	Miami U	visit arrangements
ALS	to Hill, Eldon	May 16 [1931]	Miami U	
ALS	to Hill, Eldon	June 4 [1936]	Miami U	
TLS	to Hill, Eldon	[April 5, 1937]	Miami U	encl. letter re: success of exhib/H's lecture at InU
TLS	to Hill, Eldon	Oct. 10 [1937]	Miami U	exhib; "Miller of Boscobel"
ALS	to Hill, Eldon	July 6 [1934]	Miami U	arranging meeting
TLS	to Hill, Eldon	May 4, 1936	Miami U	Hill coming to Calif.
ALS	to Hill, Eldon	March 3 [1935]	Miami U	encl. laudatory ltr from Paul Oeser re: *Afternoon*
ALS	to Hill, Eldon	Dec. 29, 1935	Miami U	encloses photo
TL	to Hill, Eldon	March 24, 1935	Miami U	thanks rev. *Afternoon* [mis-sign "Eldon C. Hill"]
ALS	to Hill, Eldon	March 1	Miami U	
*TLC	to Hill, Eldon	Feb. 14, 1939	USC	about veritism
ALS	to Hill, Eldon	April 28 [1931]	Miami U	
TLC	to Hill, Eldon	Oct. 4, 1939	Hunt	exhib
ALS	to Hill, Eldon	Feb. 18, 1935#1	Miami U	
TLS	to Hill, Eldon	June 9 [1932]	Miami U	
*ALS	to Hill, Eldon	Nov. 3 [1935]	Miami U	re: Hill's interest in HG
TLS	to Hill, Eldon	June 26 [1934]	Miami U	

TLC	to Hill, Eldon	Nov. 26	USC
ALS	to Hill, Eldon	Oct. 3, 1938	Miami U
AnS	to Hill, Eldon	[ca. March 26, 1935]	Miami U	re: n. re: poems on HG to Mott
TLS	to Hill, Eldon	Jan. 29, 1934	Miami U
TLS	to Hill, Eldon	June 23	Miami U
TLS	to Hill, Eldon	Dec. 26, 1934	Miami U
TL	to Hill, Eldon	Jan. 24, 1939	Miami U
TLS	to Hill, Eldon	Feb. 21 [1936]	Miami U
TLS	to Hill, Eldon	Sept. 21 [1939]	Miami U	crosses
ALS	to Hill, Eldon	Feb. 27, 1936	Miami U
TLC	to Hill, Eldon	[March 28, 1938]	USC	re: composition of *Grant*
TLC	to Hill, Eldon	Jan. 22, 1939	USC	about efforts in drama; Moody [incomplete]
*TLS	to Hill, Eldon	Aug. 2, 1938	Miami U	re: trip East
ALS	to Hill, Eldon	Sept. 28 [1934]	Miami U
TLS	to Hill, Eldon	Feb. 19 [1940]	Miami U
TL	to Hill, Eldon	May 1, 1935	Miami U
TLC	to Hill, Eldon	Dec. 26, 1939	USC	crosses; exhib.
TLC	to Hill, Eldon	Feb. 9, 1934	USC	re: birthday dinner and influence
TLS	to Hill, Eldon	May 29, 1935	Miami U	at work on *Forty*
ALS	to Hill, Eldon	Sept. 23 [1935]	Miami U	praises article (unidentified)
ALS	to Hill, Eldon	June 19 [1931]	Miami U
ALS	to Hill, Eldon	April 11 [1935]	Miami U
TLD	to Hill, Eldon	Jan. [2, 1940]	USC
TLS	to Hill, Eldon	March 10 [1931]	Miami U
ALS	to Hill, Eldon	Feb. 18, 1935#2	Miami U
TLS	to Hill, Eldon	Feb. 17	Miami U	crosses; exhib
TL	to Hill, Eldon	Feb. 21	Miami U
ALC	to Hill, R.V.	Nov. 27 [1901]	USC LB 16	re: lectures
ALS	to Hilliard	March 7, 1896	Rochester	doesn't advise starting unspec. magazine
TLC	to Hilton, Henry Hoyt	Oct. 1, 1934	USC	re: *Parade of the Living*, Bradley
TLC	to Himrod, James Lattimore	n.d.	USC
TLC	to Himrod, James Lattimore	[April 1921]	USC
TLC	to Hiscox, Mrs. Morton	May 12, 1913	USC
TLC	to Hiscox, Mrs. Morton	April 25, 1913	USC
ALS	to Hitchcock, Ripley	July 5	Indiana U
TLC	to Hitchcock, Ripley	June 1, 1914	USC	Institute; nominates Henry S. Harrison
trL	to Hitchcock, Ripley	June 19, 1897	Indiana U	re: English rights

TLC	to Hix, John	Aug. 18, 1939	USC	crosses; broadcast of
AL	to Hodge, Frederick Webb	April 7	Southwest	request reports for Cliff Dwellers
ALS	to Hodge, Frederick Webb	Oct. 26	Southwest	
ALS	to Hodge, Frederick Webb	Feb. 6 [1901]	Southwest	apprec. drawings/ report
ALS	to Hodge, Frederick Webb	Sept. 16 [1933]	Southwest	
ALS	to Hodge, Frederick Webb	March 28	Southwest	
ALS	to Hodge, Frederick Webb	Aug. 18, 1934	Southwest	condolences
ALS	to Hodge, Frederick Webb	Oct. 3, 1900	Southwest	request reports
TLS	to Hodge, Frederick Webb	Jan. 16 [1917]	Southwest	re: film of *Captain*
TLS	to Hodge, Frederick Webb	[Dec. 30, 1936]	Southwest	crosses; return from Mexico
ALS	to Hodge, Frederick Webb	Sept. 29, 1900	Southwest	c. of Ghost Dance for "Sitting"
TLC	to Hodge, Frederick Webb	Oct. 22, 1936	USC	crosses; exhib.
ALS	to Hodge, Frederick Webb	Sept. 28, 1900	Southwest	Indian; asks for Bureau reports
TLS	to Hodge, Frederick Webb	Oct. 16, 1936	Southwest	crosses; re: temp. housing
ALS	to Hodge, Frederick Webb	Oct. 7, 1936	Southwest	
ALC	to Hodges	June 29 [1903]	USC LB 168	re: serial of *Hesper*
*ALS	to Hodges, Harrison B.	Dec. 20 [1908?]	Players	wants to restrict Players membership
ALS	to Hodges, Harrison B.	Nov. 24 [1908]	Players	req. Players greeting for Cliff D's inaug.
ALS	to Hodges, Harrison B.	Dec. 17 [1908]	Players	
ALS	to Hodges, Harrison B.	Dec. 24 [1908]	Players	
ALS	to Hodges, Harrison B.	Dec. 31 [1908]	Players	
ALS	to Hodges, Harrison B.	[ca Dec. 31 1908]	Players	
TLC	to Hoffman, D.	May 7 [1919]]	USC	re: Vitagraph staff
TLC	to Hogan, Gertrude	March 15, 1912	USC	Chicago Thea Soc
ApcS	to Holmes, C. H.	[Nov. 4, 1894]	U of Ill	re: circulars
TLS	to Holmes, Fred L.	May 28 [1921]	Wis HS	notes *Daughter* will be publ.
ALS	to Holt, Dr.	Sun.	U of Iowa	arranging lectures at Rollins College
ALS	to Holt, Dr.	Sept. 20, 1939	Virginia	re: invitation to Bookseller/ Bacheller dinner
TLS	to Holt, Dr.	April 2	U of Iowa	declines lectures
ALS	to Holt, Hamilton	Sept. 29, 1898	U of Del	offers verse
TLS	to Holt, Henry	Sept. 13, 1918	Princeton	Com Lit Art; 2nd exhib
TLS	to Holt, Henry & Company	Oct. 15, 1918	Princeton	Com Lit Art; list of books
TLS	to Holt, Henry & Company	Oct. 25, 1919	Princeton	Com Lit Art; 3rd exhib

ALD	to Hoover, Herbert	[1933]	USC	suggests celebration of CA settlement
ALS	to Hopkins, Fred	March 5, 1896	Penn HS	re: Poe cottage preservation
TLS	to Horn, Andrew	April 28 [1935]	UCLA	declines lecture offer
TLS	to Hotchkiss, Thomas	June 24	Princeton	re: contribution to "monument"
TLC	to Houston, Herbert S.	March 24, 1913	USC	
*ALS	to Howe, Edgar W.	July 2, 1886	USC	appreciation and info req.
*AL	to Howe, Edgar W.	July 15, 1886	USC	resp. to *Country* [incomplete]
ALS	to Howe, F. C.	Feb. 4 [1915]	NYPL	
ALS	to Howe, F. C.	Feb. 12 [1915]	NYPL	re: lectures
TLC	to Howe, Mark Anthony DeWolfe	May 8, 1912	USC	asks if *Youth's Companion* wants *Son*
*TLS	to Howe, Mark Anthony DeWolfe	May 19 [1932]	Harvard	re: misident. of "Emily" Dickinson
ALS	to Howe, Will D.	Aug. 30 [1926]	USC	re: Roosevelt memorial edition
ALS	to Howell, Alfred C.	Nov. 29, 1934	USC	re: insurance
*ALS	to Howell, Alfred C.	April 15 [1936]	USC	re: Mary Isabel's separation & inheritance
ALS	to Howells, Elinor	Jan. 9, 1894	Harvard	offers to aid while WDH is away
ALS	to Howells, Joseph A.	Oct. 22, 1897	R.B.Hayes	
ALS	to Howells, Mildred	Dec. 14 [1921]	Harvard	dates a letter
ALS	to Howells, Mildred	Nov. 21 [1928]	Harvard	re: *Life and Letters*
ALS	to Howells, Mildred	Feb. 17 [1926?]	Harvard	dates a letter
ALS	to Howells, Mildred	May 17 [1921]	Harvard	sends part of letters
ALS	to Howells, Mildred	April 22 [1921]	Harvard	
TLS	to Howells, Mildred	Feb. 6 [1926]	Harvard	WD's praise of HG poem
ALS	to Howells, Mildred	Nov. 25 [1928]	Harvard	has received *Life in Letters*
ALS	to Howells, Mildred	Aug. 26 [1924]	Harvard	IDs context of letter
ALS	to Howells, Mildred	May 16 [1921]	Harvard	sends letters
ALS	to Howells, Mildred	Jan. 18 [1921]	Harvard	re: Howells exhib in LA
ALS	to Howells, Mildred	Nov. 12 [1928]	Harvard	suggests Fuller as reviewer of *Life in Letters*
ALS	to Howells, Mildred	Oct. 26 [1928]	Harvard	wants to aid *Life in Letters*
ALD	to Howells, Mildred	Feb. 6 [1926]	USC	re: WD's praise of HG's poem
ALS	to Howells, Mildred	April 28 [1921]	Harvard	suggests storing letters at Acad

ALS	to Howells, Mildred	June 13 [1921]	Harvard	finds more letters
TLS	to Howells, Mildred	Aug. 29 [1921]	Harvard	finds more letters
*ALS	to Howells, Mildred	Nov. 22 [1925]	Harvard	HG and WD on social issues
*ALS	to Howells, Mildred	Jan. 21 [1921]	Harvard	re: WD's visits and plans for letters
*ALS	to Howells, Mildred	Dec. 4 [1928]	Harvard	finishes *Life in Letters*
*TLS	to Howells, Mildred	Dec. 2 [1925]	Harvard	re: HG's influence on *Hazard*
*TLC	to Howells, William D.	Dec. 22 [1916]	Miami U	has ended all clubs but Century; other news
*TLC	to Howells, William D.	Jan. 12 [1919]	Miami U	writing about TR consumes him; lectures
*ALS	to Howells, William D.	[Jan. 1892?]	Brigham Young	re: "Salt Water Ditch"
*ALS	to Howells, William D.	[ca July 1893]	Wagner	introd. Markham
*ALS	to Howells, William D.	April 6 [1909]	Harvard	brief resp. to rev. of Herrick's *Together*
*TLC	to Howells, William D.	Feb. 7, 1913	USC	Chicago meeting of Institute
*ALS	to Howells, William D.	Oct. 29, 1890	Harvard	re: *Member*
*ALS	to Howells, William D.	March 29 [1910]	Harvard	resp. to letter re: *Cavanagh*
*TLC	to Howells, William D.	June 29, 1912	USC	advice re: *Son*
*ALS	to Howells, William D.	April 3 [1910]	Harvard	re: *Cavanagh* and limitations
*ALS	to Howells, William D.	[1890]	Harvard	re: *Career of a Nihilist*
*AL	to Howells, William D.	[before March 21, 1917]	USC	praises book; notes age
TLC	to Hoyns, Henry	May 6 [1916]	USC	
TLC	to Hoyns, Henry	June 22	USC	
TLC	to Hoyns, Henry	Dec. 16, 1913	USC	
TLC	to Hoyns, Henry	April 26, 1913	USC	
ALD	to Hoyns, Henry	Nov. 17	USC	
TLC	to Hoyns, Henry	Oct. 25, 1911	USC	
TLC	to Hoyns, Henry	May 26	USC	
TLC	to Hoyns, Henry	April 8	USC	
TLC	to Hoyns, Henry	June 2 [1929]	USC	re: reissue of *MTR*
TLC	to Hoyns, Henry	Sept. 23	USC	
TLC	to Hoyns, Henry	June 19 [1916]	USC	
TLC	to Hoyns, Henry	July 8 [1921]	USC	re: edition of works
TLC	to Hoyns, Henry	March 27 [1936]	USC	
TLC	to Hoyns, Henry	Oct. 3, 1914	USC	
TLC	to Hoyns, Henry	June 1 [1916]	USC	re: reissue of *MTR*

TLS	to Hoyns, Henry	Jan. 3 [1933]	Hunt	re: opinion of Zane Grey
ALS	to Hoyns, Henry	Aug. 11 [1937]	Hunt	
TLS	to Hoyns, Henry	Nov. 5 [1932]	Hunt	re: HG books in Honolulu
TLS	to Hoyns, Henry	Aug. 30, 1934	Hunt	re: rpt. rates
ALS	to Hoyns, Henry	May 19	Hunt	re: lunch meeting
TLS	to Hoyns, Henry	Nov. 1 [1937]	Hunt	re: photos and *Crosses*
TLS	to Hoyns, Henry	Oct. 26, 1937	Hunt	re: *Crosses*
TLS	to Hoyns, Henry	Oct. 15 [1937]	Hunt	offers *Crosses*
TLS	to Hoyns, Henry	Oct. 25	Hunt	re: *Crosses*
TLS	to Hoyns, Henry	Nov. 12, 1937	Hunt	re: *Crosses*
ALS	to Hoyt, Vance	Feb. 5	U of Oregon	
ALS	to Hoyt, Vance	July 22	U of Oregon	dinner invitation; film of *Malibu*
TLS	to Hoyt, Vance	Mon.	U of Oregon	
ALS	to Hoyt, Vance	Aug. 27	U of Oregon	likes *Malibu*
ALS	to Hoyt, Vance	Sept. 9	U of Oregon	dislikes H's ms: animals too humanized
TLS	to Hoyt, Vance	May 8	U of Oregon	suggests article re: *Sequoya*
ALS	to Hoyt, Vance	Dec. 20, 1939	U of Oregon	arranging meeting
TLS	to Hudson, Hoyt Hopewell	April 4 [1929]	Homestead	good diction
ALD	to Hudson, Hoyt Hopewell	April 4 [1929]	USC	good diction
ALS	to Hudson, Margerie Leigh	Jan. 20, 1935	USC	"an advocate"
TLS	to Hughes, Charles E.	Oct. 5, 1921	Nat'l Arch	Acad; req. State Dept. rep. for cornerstone
TLS	to Hughes, Charles E.	Feb. 24, 1919	Columbia	Roosevelt Mem vol: solicits stories; encl. circ
ALS	to Hughes, Rupert	July 9 [1933]	USC	declines membership in unspec. club
TLC	to Hughes, Sam T.	May 12, 1913	USC	
TLC	to Hughes, Sam T.	May 9, 1913	USC	
TLC	to Hull, Elsie (Mrs. Raymond Hull)	Sunday	USC	crosses; re: authentication
TLS	to Hull, Elsie and Raymond	June 27, 1938	USC	crosses; re: authentication
TLD	to Hull, Elsie and Raymond	[June 27, 1938]	USC	crosses; re: authentication
TLS	to Hull, Raymond	Wed. 17	USC	crosses; re: authentication
TLS	to Hull, Raymond	Nov. 12, 1936	USC	crosses; re: authentication
ALS	to Hume, Mae A.	June 18 [1931]	USC	re: play version of unspec. HG work
TLC	to Humphreys, Pauline A.	Sept. 29, 1934	USC	re: lecture

TLC	to Hunt, Jarvis	March 8, 1913	USC	re: "New Chicago"
TLC	to Hunt, W. R.	Feb. 9, 1912	USC	Cliff Dwellers: Hunt out
ALS	to Huntington, Anna Hyatt	Sunday	Syracuse	arranges to see home
TLC	to Huntington, Archer	Jan. 22 [1923]	Miami U	Acad; offers to collect items for H.
ALD	to Huntington, Archer M.	Sunday	USC	
TLC	to Huntington, Archer M.	March 31 [1923?]	USC	Acad; good diction
ALD	to Huntington, Archer M.	Nov. 15	USC	praises poems
*ALS	to Huntington, Archer M.	March 10 [1921]	Syracuse	Acad: gratitude for H's building
TLC	to Huntington, Archer M.	Nov. 29 [1923]	USC	Acad; suggests 20th anniv. celeb.
TLS	to Huntington, Archer M.	June 16	Syracuse	condolences on illness of Mrs H.
TLC	to Huntington, Archer M.	June 4 [1929]	USC	Acad; good diction, success of
TLC	to Huntington, Archer M.	June 29 [1929]	USC	Acad; re: goals
ALD	to Huntington, Archer M.	July 5	USC	Acad; good diction [incomplete]
TLC	to Huntington, Archer M.	Sept. 21	USC	Acad; desire to publicize
ALD	to Huntington, Archer M.	June 20	USC	Acad; good diction; Johnson's rule violation
ALS	to Huntington, Archer M.	Nov. 15	Syracuse	reads H's poems
ALS	to Huntington, Archer M.	Feb. 22	Syracuse	arranges visit
TLS	to Huntington, Archer M.	Nov. 29 [1923]	Syracuse	Acad: suggests 20 anniv. celeb.
ALS	to Huntington, Archer M.	May 31	Syracuse	arranges visit
*TLS	to Huntington, Archer M.	June 4 [1929]	Syracuse	Acad: Good Diction campaign
ALS	to Huntington, Archer M.	Feb. 17	Syracuse	reads H.'s poems
TLS	to Huntington, Archer M.	Feb. 12 [1921]	Syracuse	Howells Memorial; Valdes
ALS	to Huntington, Archer M.	May 18	Syracuse	Acad: sculpture show
*ALS	to Huntington, Archer M.	Nov. 14 [1926]	Syracuse	Acad: not in favor of women members
TLS	to Huntington, Archer M.	Jan. 30	Syracuse	Acad; promoting through Universities
*TLC	to Huntington, Archer M.	Oct. 7 [1923]	USC	Acad; 2nd version of Oct. ltr
TLC	to Huntington, Archer M.	Oct. 7	USC	Acad; "qualif. endorsement of my work"
ALS	to Hurd, Charles	July 17, 1894	Virginia	a "status report"
ALS	to Hurd, Charles	Nov. 18, 1893	NYPL	
TLC	to Husband, Joseph	June 15, 1914	USC	re: delight in HG's writing

TLC	to Hutchings, DeWitt V.	July 26, 1939	USC	crosses; exhib at Mission Inn
TLC	to Hutchinson, Charles L.	April 16, 1912	USC	
TLC	to Hutchinson, Charles L.	Oct. 3, 1914	USC	
TLC	to Hutchinson, Charles L.	Oct. 26, 1911	USC	
ALS	to Hutchinson, Charles L.	Nov. 21	Newberry	arranging meeting
TLC	to Hutchinson, Charles L.	Jan. 10, 1912	USC	
ALS	to Hutton, Lawrence	Tue. [Dec. 1885]	Princeton	re: missed meeting
ALS	to Hutton, William Holden	[1923]	USC	
TLD	to Ince, Thomas H.	Sept. 19 [1921]	USC	solicits film adapt: *Son, MTR, High Trails*
TLC	to International Press Bureau	Jan. 18, 1912	USC	
TLC	to IRS	Dec. 8, 1939	USC	
TLC	to Irvin, Will	Oct. 1, 1912	USC	
ALS	to Isaacs, Mrs.	April 20 [1927]	Syracuse	agrees to tribute to E. A. Robinson
ALD	to Jackson, Zeb	June 7	USC	
TLC	to Jensen, Jens	May 10, 1913	USC	
TLC	to Jerome, Jerome K.	Oct. 10, 1914	USC	
ALC	to Jessup, Alexander	[July-Nov. 1903]	USC LB 175	
TLC	to Johns	Jan. 12	Miami U	arranging English lectures, with daughter
TLC	to Johnson, Charles B.	Feb. 26 [1923]	USC	
ALS	to Johnson, Katharine M.	Feb. 24	U Texas	
ALS	to Johnson, Katharine M.	Nov. 16	U Texas	arranging meeting
TLS	to Johnson, Merle	Sat.	NYPL	re: sale of letters
ALD	to Johnson, Robert U.	Jan. 26, 1918	Miami U	accepts election to Academy
ALS	to Johnson, Robert Underwood	Friday 19 [1909]	NYPL	re: death of Gilder
ALS	to Johnson, Robert Underwood	[c 1908/09?]	Am Acad	Institute; fund raising ideas
ALS	to Johnson, Robert Underwood	Dec. 17	Am Acad	Institute; wants to "lose" Carnegie's name
ALS	to Johnson, Robert Underwood	June 8, 1900	NYPL	pushes for decision re: *Mountain*
ALS	to Johnson, Robert Underwood	Sept. 15, 1900	NYPL	re: editing *Mountain*
ALS	to Johnson, Robert Underwood	Sept. 8 [1926]	Am Acad	Acad; nominations; O'Neill et al
ALS	to Johnson, Robert Underwood	Aug. 22, [1917]	Am Acad	offers to write article (unfav) on German lit
ALS	to Johnson, Robert Underwood	March 17, [1923]	Am Acad	Acad; accepts election to board of directors

ALS	to Johnson, Robert Underwood	Dec. 30, 1900	NYPL	
TLC	to Johnson, Robert Underwood	Dec. 21, 1911	USC	
TLS	to Johnson, Robert Underwood	Jan. 22 [1924]	Am Acad	Acad; 20th anniv. celeb.
tel	to Johnson, Robert Underwood	Sept. 21, 1900	NYPL	re: titles for *Mounta*
ALS	to Johnson, Robert Underwood	March 11, 1925	Am Acad	Acad; wants to elect Booth to Hall of Fame
ALS	to Johnson, Robert Underwood	June 29	NYPL	
ApcS	to Johnson, Robert Underwood	Oct. 11 1900	NYPL	
ALS	to Johnson, Robert Underwood	Nov. 13 [1912]	NYPL	submits *Son* ms for serial/book
tel	to Johnson, Robert Underwood	Sept. 20, 1900	NYPL	re: titles for *Mounta*
ALS	to Johnson, Robert Underwood	[1904?]	Am Acad	Institute; re: organization of Academy
ALS	to Johnson, Robert Underwood	April 20 [1909]	NYPL	re: article on MacDowell farm
TLC	to Johnson, Robert Underwood	March 21, 1913	USC	
TLC	to Johnson, Robert Underwood	Jan. 22 [1924]	USC	c. of Am Acad letter
tel	to Johnson, Robert Underwood	Sept. 26, 1900	NYPL	re: titles for *Mounta*
ALS	to Johnson, Robert Underwood	April 19	NYPL	promotes Taft's sculpture; article
ALS	to Johnson, Robert Underwood	Sept. 20, 1900	NYPL	
TLC	to Johnson, Robert Underwood	Sept. 15, 1914	USC	
ALS	to Johnson, Robert Underwood	April 17, 1900	NYPL	submits *Mountain*
ALS	to Johnson, Robert Underwood	Oct. 18	NYPL	
tel	to Johnson, Robert Underwood	Aug. 26	NYPL	
TLS	to Johnson, Robert Underwood	Dec. 17 [1928]	Wis HS	re: radio address; H(hated it
ALS	to Johnson, Robert Underwood	n.d.	NYPL	
ALS	to Johnson, Robert Underwood	June 8 [1913]	Wis HS	resp to news RUJ resigns from *Century*

ALS	to Johnson, Robert Underwood	Feb. 14 [1920]	Wis HS	congrats J on appointment as ambassador to Italy
ALS	to Johnson, Robert Underwood	May 22, 1900	NYPL	re: *Mountain*
tel	to Johnson, Robert Underwood	Sept. 22, 1900	NYPL	re: titles for *Mountain*
ALS	to Johnson, Robert Underwood	n.d.	NYPL	
ALS	to Johnson, Robert Underwood	June 12, [1914]	Am Acad	Institute; possible presidents
ALS	to Johnson, Robert Underwood	Jan. 10	Wis HS	
ALS	to Johnson, Robert Underwood	Dec. 15 [1900]	NYPL	re: location accuracy in *Mountain*
ALS	to Johnson, Robert Underwood	March 10 [1910]	NYPL	offers Booth articles
ALS	to Johnson, Robert Underwood	March 8	NYPL	proof of "The Rooster"
ALS	to Johnson, Robert Underwood	n.d.	NYPL	
ALS	to Johnson, Robert Underwood	Aug. 12 [1900]	NYPL	re: titles of *Mountain*
ALS	to Johnson, Robert Underwood	Dec. 19 1901	NYPL	
ALS	to Johnson, Robert Underwood	n.d.	NYPL	
ALS	to Johnson, Robert Underwood	March 31 [1919]	U Texas	Roosevelt Mem vol: solicits story
ALS	to Johnson, Robert Underwood	June 19 [1909]	NYPL	asks to do article on MacDowell
ALS	to Johnson, Robert Underwood	Jan. 2 [1901]	Virginia	re: revision of *Mountain*
ALS	to Johnson, Robert Underwood	Nov. 1 [1931]	U Texas	
ALS	to Johnson, Robert Underwood	Nov. 2	U Texas	Com Lit Art; asks RUJ to read poem at dinner
ALS	to Johnson, Robert Underwood	Jan. 1 [1925?]	Bancroft	re: death of Mrs. R. U. Johnson
ALS	to Johnson, Robert Underwood	April 1	NYPL	
ALS	to Johnson, Robert Underwood	Oct. 28 [1909]	NYPL	re: article on MacDowell farm
ALS	to Johnson, Robert Underwood	Nov. 4	U Texas	has qualified to be a "Centurian"
*ALS	to Johnson, Robert Underwood	July 10 [1900]	NYPL	disc. terms of *Mountain*

*ALS	to Johnson, Robert Underwood	Sept. 7 [1937]	Am Acad	Acad; porno rant; Lewis
ALS	to Johnson, Robert Underwood	April 11 [1907]	Wis HS	evals (negatively) J verse
*ALS	to Johnson, Robert Underwood	May 13, 1895	NYPL	"Good Fellow's Wife"
ALS	to Johnson, Robert Underwood	April 30, 1900	NYPL	re: *Mountain*
*ALS	to Johnson, Robert Underwood	June 28, [1913]	Am Acad	re: Dreiser
*TLS	to Johnson, Robert Underwood	Feb. 20, 1913	Am Acad	solicits article on J. Miller; Institute
*ALS	to Johnson, Robert Underwood	Jan. 28, 1918	Am Acad	re: election to Acad.
TLC	to Jones, Howard Mumford	Dec. 22	USC	re: praise for *Son*
*ALS	to Jones, Howard Mumford	June 28, 1938	USC	porno rant
ALS	to Jones, Howard Mumford	June 11, 1939	Harvard	re: *Transcript*: Jones lit. ed.
ALS	to Jones, Mrs.	March 29 [1924]	Yale	arranges meeting w/ Wharton
ALC	to Jones, William A.	Nov. 3 [1902]	USC LB 112-6	re: Indian; renaming
*ALS	to Jones, William A.	Dec. 7 [1903]	Nat'l Arch	arguments & justif. for Eastman's work
AnS	to Jones, William A.	[April 23, 1903]	Nat'l Arch	endorses Grinnell's sugg. re: Stouch
ALS	to Jones, William A.	Dec. 22 [1903]	Nat'l Arch	praises Eastman's work
ALC	to Jones, William A.	March 14 [1903]	USC LB 138	re: Indian; renaming
ALC	to Jones, William A.	Dec. 7 [1903]	USC LB 180-5	re: Indian; renaming
*ALS	to Jones, William A.	Nov. 3 [1902]	Nat'l Arch	outlines renaming procedure
ALC	to Jones, William A.	March 12 [1903]	USC LB 137	re: Indian; renaming
ALS	to Jones, William A.	March 7 [1904]	Nat'l Arch	wants schools to use names on rolls
AnS	to Jones, William A.	[April 7, 1904]	Nat'l Arch	req. sick leave for Eastman
ALS	to Jones, William A.	July 11 [1903]	Nat'l Arch	rev. suggestions: tre like Polish names
AnS	to Jones, William A.	Feb. 3 [1904]	Nat'l Arch	req. granting leave for Eastman
ALS	to Jones, William A.	April 18 [1903]	Nat'l Arch	re: roll methodology
ALS	to Jones, William A.	[Feb. 22, 1901]	Nat'l Arch	re: preserving Indian arts
ALS	to Jones, William A.	Sept. 20, 1900	Nat'l Arch	req. Bur. reports; is writing "Sitting Bull"
ALS	to Jones, William A.	March 9 [1903]	Nat'l Arch	suggests new form for listing names
ALS	to Jones, William A.	April 15 [1903]	Nat'l Arch	req. transport., lette

ALS	to Jones, William A.	April 7 [1903]	Nat'l Arch	suggests sending circular to NY papers
ALS	to Jones, William A.	June 15 [1903]	Nat'l Arch	suggests keeping Eastman in field
ALS	to Jones, William A.	[Jan. 14, 1903]	Nat'l Arch	asks for Crow Creek roll
ALS	to Jones, William A.	Feb. 7 [1903]	Nat'l Arch	re: revising rolls
ALS	to Jones, William A.	March 2 [1903]	Nat'l Arch	Souix rolls; asks for letter of introd
ALS	to Jones, William A.	July 20 [1903]	Nat'l Arch	req. travel expenses for Eastman
*ALS	to Jones, William A.	Dec. 22 [1903]	Nat'l Arch	Indian; renaming
ALS	to Jones, William A.	Sept. 22 [1902]	Nat'l Arch	approves circular
ALS	to Jones, William A.	[Dec. 16, 1902]	Nat'l Arch	suggests renaming personnel
ALC	to Jones, William A.	Dec. 22 [1903]	USC LB 188-9	re: Indian; renaming; Eastern
AnS	to Jones, William A.	[March 14, 1903]	Nat'l Arch	req. Eastman remain at Crow Creek
ALS	to Jones, William A.	Dec. 29 [1902]	Nat'l Arch	req. for forms; Roosevelt approves circular
ALS	to Jones, William A.	Jan. 31 [1902]	Nat'l Arch	re: Indian stock-raising; rumor stop Indian song
ALS	to Jones, William A.	Oct. 14 [1903]	Nat'l Arch	req. travel expenses for Eastman
ALS	to Jordan, Elizabeth	Jan. 17	NYPL	arranging meeting
ALS	to Judah, John	June 10 [1930]	USC	
TLC	to Judson, Harry Pratt	Dec. 23, 1911	USC	
TLC	to Kauffman, W. H.	Oct. 26	USC	
*ALS	to Kauser, Alice	July 19 [1911]	Virginia	Chicago Thea Soc; req. for plays
ALS	to Kauser, Alice	Oct. 18 [1911]	USC	Chicago Thea Soc; Hunter's play
*TLS	to Kauser, Alice	Oct. 7, 1911	USC	Chicago Thea Soc; Hunter's play
TLS	to Kauser, Alice	Oct. 2, 1911	USC	Chicago Thea Soc
*ALS	to Kauser, Alice	Sept. 8 [1911]	Virginia	Chicago Thea Soc; re: Oppenheim plays
*ALS	to Kauser, Alice	Aug. 29 [1911]	Virginia	Chicago Thea Soc; non-commercial plays
TLC	to Kays, Victor C.	May 28, 1913	USC	
TLC	to Keith, Elva I.	Oct. 29, 1934	USC	
TLC	to Kellor, Frances B.	May 23, 1913	USC	
TLC	to Kelly, Alfred	April 10, 1913	USC	
ALC	to Kelso, Miss	Sept. 26 [1902]	USC LB 87	re: lectures
ALC	to Kelso, Miss	Sept. 30 [1902]	USC LB 91	
TLC	to Kennealy, J. F.	Dec. 13, 1939	USC	crosses; exhib

ALS	to Kent, Charles W.	Sept. 19, 1899	Virginia	regrets missing "unveiling"
ALS	to Kerby, Mrs.	Oct. 9	Yale	thanks for letter
TLC	to Kerr, Alva Milton	Feb. 17, 1912	USC	
TLS	to Kester, Paul	Nov. 5, 1917	NYPL	Com Lit Art: exhib. circular
ALS	to Kester, Paul	Jan. 2	NYPL	arranging meeting
ALS	to Kiernan, Reginald H.	June 20	USC	
TLC	to Kimball, Charles R., and Mrs.	May 4, 1938	USC	restoring the homestead
ApcS	to Kimball, Hannibal Ingalls	Aug. 12, 1896	Miami U	
ApcS	to Kimball, Hannibal Ingalls	[1896]	Miami U	
ApcS	to Kimball, Hannibal Ingalls	[Oct. 18, 1893]	Miami U	re: sending copies of books
ALS	to Kimball, Hannibal Ingalls	n.d.	Miami U	send books
ApcS	to Kimball, Hannibal Ingalls	[Nov. 30, 1896]	Miami U	
ALS	to Kimball, Hannibal Ingalls	May 12, 1896	Virginia	encloses letter from "Bailey"
ApcS	to Kimball, Hannibal Ingalls	April 6, 1897	Virginia	asks to see English reviews of Rose
AnS	to Kimball, Hannibal Ingalls	[ca May 4, 1895]	NYPL	recommends Markham story
ALS	to Kimball, Hannibal Ingalls	May 24, 1895	NYU	re: mailing books
ApcS	to Kimball, Hannibal Ingalls	[July 23, 1896]	Knox	send Rose to Edward Forsyth
ApcS	to Kimball, Hannibal Ingalls	May 19, 1896	Knox	arranging meeting
ApcS	to Kimball, Hannibal Ingalls	Sept. 19, 1896	Knox	enquires after "novelettes"
ApcS	to Kimball, Hannibal Ingalls	June 7, 1897	Knox	keep posted on English edition
*ALS	to Kimball, Hannibal Ingalls	Sept. 16, 1894	U of Ill	dispute re: lecture circulars
ALS	to Kimball, Hannibal Ingalls	June 15, 1895	Virginia	introd. Henry J. Brandon
*TLS	to Kimball, Hannibal Ingalls	Oct. 15, 1896	NYPL	re: contract: Rose, Spoil
*ALS	to Kimball, Hannibal Ingalls	March 12, 1897	Duke	dissatis. w/ advertising of Rose
TLS	to Kimberly, Clifford B.	June 17, 1826	Virginia	
TLC	to King, Florence	n.d.	USC	
ALS	to King, Grace	March 11	Louisiana St	re: missed lecture due to illness

ALS	to King, Miss	Jan. 20	Homestead	regrets can't help w/ thesis about self
ALS	to Kipling, Caroline	Sept. 25, 1899	Syracuse	condolences on health of Kipling
ALD	to Kipling, Rudyard	Sept. 16 [1933]	USC	thanks for b-day greeting
*ALS	to Kipling, Rudyard	Jan. 4. [1921]	USC	Acad; Howells memorial
TLC	to Kipling, Rudyard	May 28 [1920]	Am Acad	Howells memorial meeting
TLC	to Kirchway, Dean	April 24	USC	re: prisons
TLC	to Kirchway, Dean	May 8	USC	re: prisons
ALS	to Kirk	Sept. 30, 1896	Virginia	*Chapbook* not interested in K's poems
ALS	to Knight, Grant C.	Oct. 16, 1935	U of KY	re: request for photo
TLS	to Knight, Grant C.	Nov. 18 [1929]	U of KY	re: info about James Lane Allen
TLC	to Knight, Thomas D.	May 23, 1913	USC	
TLC	to Knight, Thomas D.	Oct. 2, 1913	USC	
TLC	to Knopf, Alfred A.	Jan. 10 [1924]	USC	want description of Crane for collected edition?
TLC	to Koch, Theodore	Jan. 2, 1939	USC	
TLS	to Koch, Theodore	Sept. 29 [1936]	Northwestern	arranging exhib
ALS	to Koch, Theodore	Dec. 22, 1938	U of Mich	asks if interested in "permanent loan" of ms
ALS	to Koch, Theodore	Dec. 12, 1936	U of Mich	
ALS	to Koch, Theodore	Jan. 20, 1940	U of Mich	crosses; exhib; encl. clipping, args
TLS	to Koch, Theodore	Nov. 30 [1936]	Northwestern	
TLS	to Koch, Theodore	Oct. 22, 1936	Northwestern	exhib; stresses signif
TLS	to Koch, Theodore	[Nov.] 22, 1936	Northwestern	
TLS	to Koch, Theodore	Jan. 3, 1939	Northwestern	exhib; describes contents
TLS	to Koch, Theodore	April 29, 1939	Northwestern	
ALS	to Koch, Theodore	May 9	Northwestern	
TLS	to Koch, Theodore	Oct. 20, 1936	Northwestern	exhib; re: bio film of HG
TLS	to Kunz, Mrs.	March 20, 1925	NY HS	re: membership in Town Hall Club
ALS	to Kyle	Dec. 30 [1917?]	USC	
TLS	to Kyle	Dec. 30 [1917]	Virginia	re: misreading of *Son*
ALC	to Labodie	June 13 [1904]	USC LB 207	
ALC	to Labodie	[May-June 1904]	USC LB 202-3	re: Booth, Joys of Trail lectures
TLC	to Lamb, Frederick S.	March 24, 1914	USC	

*TLS	to Lane, Franklin K.	Feb. 11 [1920]	Nat'l Arch	Roosevelt Mem. scholarship: Congres sional bill
TLC	to Lane, Franklin K.	Feb. 11 [1920]	USC	c. of Nat'l Arch; Roosevelt Mem. scholarship
*TLS	to Lane, Franklin K.	March 21, 1913	Nat'l Arch	Indian; renaming; summary
ALD	to Lane, William Arbuthnot	July 5	USC	re: Turck Foundation (on ltrhead)
ALS	to Lanier, Henry W.	March 21	Harvard	re: *Golden Book* publ.
TLC	to Lasky, Jesse L.	June 1, 1914	USC	
TL	to Latham, Harold	Oct. 7 [1924?]	Miami U	re: middle border pubs.
TLC	to Latham, Harold S.	Fri. [March 18, 1938]	USC	crosses; routing ms
TLC	to Latham, Harold S.	March 8 [1932]	USC	re: poor sales
ALD	to Latham, Harold S.	n.d.	USC	re: Bradley & *Parade of the Living*
TLC	to Latham, Harold S.	Nov. 28 [1921]	USC	re: L's interest in uniform ed.
TLC	to Latham, Harold S.	Sept. 7, 1939	Hunt	exhib; school price; crosses broadcast
TLC	to Latham, Harold S.	n.d.	USC	
TLC	to Latham, Harold S.	[Sept. 1932]	USC	suggests *Forty*
TLD	to Latham, Harold S.	June 1 [1930]	USC	re: sale of Crane, Riley books
TLC	to Latham, Harold S.	Aug. 10, 1937	USC	crosses; rev. of ms
TLC	to Latham, Harold S.	March 1 [1933]	USC	*Afternoon* completed
ALS	to Latham, Harold S.	Sept. 26, 1934	USC	re: presentation c. of *Contemporaries*
TLC	to Latham, Harold S.	May 14 [1920]	USC	
TLC	to Latham, Harold S.	April 19 [1932]	USC	re: design of *Contemporaries*
ALS	to Latham, Harold S.	Oct. 17 [193-]	USC	
TLC	to Latham, Harold S.	Aug. 13, 193[9]	Hunt	crosses; exhib; "Fortunate Exiles"
TLC	to Latham, Harold S.	April 7 [1932]	USC	
TLD	to Latham, Harold S.	April 29	USC	re: illustrations
TLC	to Latham, Harold S.	April 6 [1924]	USC	
TLC	to Latham, Harold S.	Jan. 15, 1926	USC	re: *Trail-Makers* & *Roadside*
TLC	to Latham, Harold S.	Jan. 29 [1926]	USC	*Trail-Makers*
TLC	to Latham, Harold S.	Aug. 18 [1927]	USC	
ALS	to Latham, Harold S.	June 10, 1939	Hunt	re: dumping books; school price
TLC	to Latham, Harold S.	n.d.	Hunt	
TLC	to Latham, Harold S.	Nov. 25, 1935	Hunt	re: *Forty*; incl. Drane in book

*TLS	to Latham, Harold S.	Aug. 7, 1937	USC	re: Earhart
TLS	to Latham, Harold S.	March 24 [1932]	USC	*Contemporaries*
TLC	to Latham, Harold S.	May 4 [1932]	USC	*Contemporaries*
ALS	to Latham, Harold S.	Aug. 21 [193-]	USC	re: juvenile ed. of *Trail-Makers*
ALS	to Latham, Harold S.	April 7 [1933?]	USC	
AL	to Latham, Harold S.	Oct. 1 [1939]	Hunt	exhib; school price/books
*TLC	to Latham, Harold S.	Nov. 25 [1923]	USC	re: dissatis. w/ treatment
*TLC	to Latham, Harold S.	Dec. 26 [1921]	USC	dissatis. w/ advert. *Daughter*
*ALS	to Latham, Harold S.	Aug. 5 [1937]	USC	Earhart seance transcript
TLC	to Latham, Harold S.	n.d.	USC	
*ALD	to Latham, Harold S.	Dec. 18 [1921]	USC	inc; dissatis. w/ advert. *Daughter*
*TLC	to Latham, Harold S.	April 11 [1932]	USC	re: HG's judgment of *Contemporaries*
TLC	to Latham, Harold S.	Nov. 25, 1933	Hunt	re: title of *Afternoon*
*TLC	to Latham, Harold S.	June 24 [1929]	USC	*Roadside*
ALS	to Lawrence, Josephine	Feb. 15, 1936	USC	porno rant; fav. resp. to "Four Apples"
*ALS	to Lawson, Victor	[June 6, 1896]	Brigham Young	re: "Hisses for HG"
TLC	to Lee, Catherine	March 13, 1914	USC	
ALC	to Leigh, Frederick T.	Oct. 6 [1902]	USC LB 93	submits "Sitting Bull"
ALC	to Leigh, Frederick T.	March 9 [1903]	USC LB 134-6	contract negotiations
ALC	to Leigh, Frederick T.	Oct. 8 [1902]	USC LB 96	re: advertising of *Captain* & lectures
ALC	to Leigh, Frederick T.	May 16 [1902]	USC LB 56	wishes to dramatize *Captain*
TLC	to Leonard, Miss	May 8, 1913	USC	
TLC	to Leonard, William Ellery	May 16 [1919]	USC	re: patriotism
TLC	to Leonard, William Ellery	June 26 [1919]	USC	re: Barbusse & War
ALS	to Leup, Francis	[ca April 22, 1904]	Nat'l Arch	re: schools not using lists
ALS	to Leup, Francis E.	Friday 14.	Miami U	re: Seger and Indian service
TLC	to Lewis, Edwin H.	June 12, 1912	USC	
TLC	to Lewis, John	Feb. 10, 1914	USC	
TLC	to Lewis, L. Leon	June 27, 1912	USC	
ALS	to Lewis, Mrs.	April 16	SE MO ST	condolence letter re: death of husband
*ALS	to Lewis, Sinclair	Feb. 5 [1921]	Yale	on *Main Street*
*ALS	to Lewis, Sinclair	Oct. 5 [1915]	USC	dislike of *Trail of the Hawk*
TLC	to Libby, D. M.	April 9, 1914	USC	
TLC	to Libby, D. M. [by sec'ty]	April 8, 1914	USC	

TLS	to Liberty National Bank	Nov. 20	USC	
*TLS	to Lilly, Josiah Kirby	May 28 [1930]	Indiana U	re: sale of Riley books
ALS	to Lincoln, Joseph C.	[1894]	Virginia	re: lecture management
ALS	to Lincoln, Joseph C.	March 20, 1894	Miami U	re: reading of poems
*ALS	to Lindsay, Nicholas Vachel	March 7. [1911]	USC	apprec. poetry & delivery
ALS	to Lindsay, Nicholas Vachel	Wed. [March 15, 1911]	USC	re: luncheon talk
*ALS	to Lindsay, Nicholas Vachel	March 30. [1911]	USC	advice re: publication
*ALS	to Lindsay, Nicholas Vachel	Oct. 26 [1931]	USC	resp. to L's resp. to *Companions*
*TLC	to Lindsay, Nicholas Vachel	Dec. 26, 1912	USC	advice re: ms
*TLC	to Lindsay, Nicholas Vachel	Oct. 21, 1911	USC	advice re: rev. of ms
*TLC	to Lindsay, Nicholas Vachel	May 20, 1912	USC	interested in L's 2-year tour of west
*TLS	to Lindsay, Nicholas Vachel	May 18 [1931]	USC	req. early letters returned
TLC	to Lindsay, Nicholas Vachel	May 10, 1913	USC	asks for verse for Friends of Native Landscape
TLC	to Lindsay, Nicholas Vachel	April 8, 1914	USC	exchange book for Cliff Dweller dues
TLC	to Lindsay, Samuel McCune	March 1, 1913	USC	
TLC	to Lindsay, Samuel McCune	May 23, 1913	USC	
TLC	to Linn, James Weber	April 20, 1914	USC	
ALS	to Literary Editor, *Sun*	Nov. 7 [1926?]	NYU	thanks for rev.
TLS	to Lithtig, Harry H.	Oct. 9, 1935	Newberry	re: film adapt.
TLC	to Livermore, R. L.	Aug. 5, 1914	USC	
ALS	to Lloyd	Oct. 19, 1897	Wis HS	re: George campaign
AnS	to Locke, W. J.	[Aug. 9, 1924]	USC	
*TLC	to Logan, Floyd	Feb. 5, 1934	USC	porno rant
ApcS	to Logan, Floyd	Oct. 28 [1938]	Indiana U	re: itinerary
TLC	to Logan, Floyd	Jan. 9, 1934	Hunt	re: indexes [incomplete]
TLC	to Logan, Frank E.	July 24, 1911	USC	Chicago Thea Soc; threatens to resign
telC	to London, Jack	May 24, 1916	Hunt	re: Roosevelt nomination
ALS	to London, Jack	Aug. 27 [1913]	Hunt	expresses sympathy for loss of Wolf house
ALS	to London, Joan	Sept. 10, 1937	Hunt	never knew Jack; wishes Joan success w/ book
TLC	to Long, Catherine S. [Mrs. J. H.]	Oct. 8, 1913	USC	

TLC	to Lorch, Fred. W.	[March 1938]	Hunt	re: Twain and politics; *Spoil*
TLC	to Lord, Forrest A.	Sept. 23 [1921]	USC	re: serial rights in *Business Farmer*
TLD	to Lord, Forrest A.	Sept. 27 [1921]	USC	re: serial rights in *Business Farmer*
TLS	to Lorimer, George H.	May 29, 1909	Penn HS	req. books for Cliff Dwellers
TLC	to Lorimer, George H.	Feb. 16, 1916	USC	asks for publ. date of "Steadfast Widow Delaney"
TLS	to Lorimer, George H.	July 23	Penn HS	solicits article on Turck
AnS	to Lorimer, George H.	March 6, 1906	Penn HS	inscription / New Year greeting
TLS	to Lorimer, George H.	May 21 [1932]	USC	re: excerpt of Shaw piece from *Contemporaries*
TLC	to Lorimer, George H.	Feb. 18, 1927	USC	approves *Post* editorials
ALS	to Lounsberry, Thomas	June 13 [1935]	Miami U	thanks for letter
ALS	to Lounsbury, Thomas R.	Dec. 1 [1903]	Yale	re: lecture date at Yale
ALS	to Lounsbury, Thomas R.	Dec. 3 [1903]	Yale	re: lecture postponement
ALS	to Lounsbury, Thomas R.	Feb. 6 [1904]	Yale	re: missed Institute dinner
ALS	to Lounsbury, Thomas R.	Dec. 12, 1900	Yale	re: autograph for *Cooper*
ALS	to Lounsbury, Thomas R.	Jan. 18 [1904]	Yale	will lecture on "Joys of the Trail"
ALS	to Lounsbury, Thomas R.	Jan. 26 [1904]	Yale	dinner invitation
ALS	to Lounsbury, Thomas R.	Dec. 30 [1903]	Yale	re: lectures
ALS	to Lounsbury, Thomas R.	Dec. 17 [1903]	Yale	re: lectures
TLC	to Lovett, Robert Morse	Jan. 17 [1919]	USC	solicits work from *Dial*
TLC	to Low, Will H.	Nov. 8, 1913	USC	
TLS	to Lowell, Amy	Nov. 9, 1917	Harvard	Com Lit Art
TLS	to Lowell, Amy	April 26, 1921	Harvard	MacDowell Club: lit. comm.
TLS	to Lowell, Amy	Oct. 25, 1917	Harvard	Com Lit Art
ALS	to Lowell, Amy	Nov. 2, 1917	Harvard	Com Lit Art
tel	to Lowell, Amy	[Nov. 1, 1917]	Harvard	Com Lit Art
ALS	to Lowell, Amy	Nov. 16, 1917	Harvard	Com Lit Art
TL	to Lummis, Charles F.	[ca. Nov. 19]	Southwest	NIAL form letter: invitation
ALS	to Lummis, Charles F.	May 9 [1903]	Southwest	Indian; renaming
TLS	to Lummis, Charles F.	March 1917	Southwest	Com Lit Art circular

TLC	to Lummis, Charles F.	Feb. 1 [1917]	USC	re: Vitagraph consultation
TLC	to Lummis, Charles F.	Dec. 3, 1902	USC	Indian; renaming
ALS	to Lummis, Charles F.	Oct. 21	Southwest	
ALS	to Lummis, Charles F.	Dec. 30	Bancroft	
ALS	to Lummis, Charles F.	[Feb. 1902]	Southwest	Indian; Sequoya; reservation
ALS	to Lummis, Charles F.	Feb. 25 [1902]	Southwest	Indian; Sequoya
*ALS	to Lummis, Charles F.	April 15, 1902	Southwest	Indian; Roosevelt's resp. to "Redman"
AnS	to Lummis, Charles F.	[ca. Dec. 1, 1902]	Southwest	Indian; renaming; circular from Jones
*ALS	to Lummis, Charles F.	Feb. 1 [1902]	Southwest	Indian; reservation conditions; Sequoya
ALS	to Lummis, Charles F.	Nov. 9	Southwest	
ALS	to Lummis, Charles F.	April 17	Southwest	
*TLS	to Lummis, Charles F.	Dec. 3, 1902	Southwest	Indian; renaming; orig of USC c.
*ALS	to Lummis, Charles F.	Dec. 24 [1901]	Southwest	Indian; suggests Sequoya principles
*TLS	to Lummis, Charles F.	Nov. 26, 1902	Southwest	Indian; renaming; c. of Seger ltr;
*ALS	to Lummis, Charles F.	Feb. 5 [1902]	Southwest	Indian; Sequoya
*ALS	to Lummis, Charles F.	[after April 1902]	Southwest	Indian; Grinnell for Indian Commissioner
ALS	to Lungren, Fernand	June 8 [1928]	Hunt	
ALS	to Lungsten (?)	Nov. 11, 1899	U Wis-Mil	postpones lecture
TLS	to Lytig & Englander	Sept. 5, 1936	USC	
TLC	to Maas, Waldo	Sept. 14, 1937	USC	re: offer to index logbooks
*TLC	to Mabee, F. Carelton, Jr.	March 19, 1938	USC	about Flower and *Arena*
TLC	to Mabie, Hamilton Wright	March 27, 1912	USC	
*ALS	to Mabie, Hamilton Wright	Jan. 25, [1903?]	Am Acad	Institute; suggests goals
ALS	to Mabie, Helen	Jan. 19, 1899	Brown	ms poem dedicated to Mabie
ALC	to MacArthur, James	Oct. 9 [1902]	USC LB 99	re: father's insurance policy
*ALC	to MacArthur, James	[Oct. 20-27, 1902]	USC LB 106-7	re: drama of *Captain*
*ALC	to MacArthur, James	Oct. 19 1902	USC LB 104-5	re: drama of *Captain*
ALC	to MacArthur, James	Sept. 29 [1902]	USC LB 90	re: drama of *Captain*
TLS	to MacDonald	May 20 [1923]	Morgan	re: sale of books
ALS	to MacDonald	Nov. 25, 1922	Morgan	arranges to send books
TLS	to MacDonald	Jan. 4 [1923]	Morgan	sends autographed books
ALS	to MacDonald	Oct. 3 [1922]	Morgan	re: receipt of photo
TLS	to MacDonald	Nov. 12 [1922]	Morgan	re: photo

TLC	to MacHarg, William Briggs	May 8, 1912	USC	
TLC	to MacKaye, Percy	Nov. 8, 1913	USC	Institute; glad M. coming to Chicago meeting
TLC	to MacKenzie, F. A.	June 22, 1912	USC	
TLC	to MacKenzie, Maurice	Friday	USC	
TLS	to MacKinnon, J. C.	Oct. 22 [193-]	USC	
ALC	to MacMillan, G. H.	Nov. 6 [1901]	USC LB 7	re: farm management
TLD	to Macrae, John	April 28 [1939]	USC	crosses; publicity campaign
TLC	to Macrae, John	April 8, 1939	USC	crosses
TLC	to Macrae, John	June 20, 1938	USC	crosses
TLD	to Macrae, John	March 29, 1938	USC	crosses
TLD	to Macrae, John	June 23, 1939	USC	crosses; resp. to poor sales
ALS	to Macrae, John	Jan. 13, 1938	USC	crosses
TLC	to Macrae, John	[Jan. 13, 1940]	USC	re: Brown and refusal to sign article
TLC	to Macrae, John	Aug. 15, 1937	USC	crosses; offers ms
TLC	to Macrae, John	May 14, 1938	USC	crosses
TLC	to Macrae, John	[April 28, 1939?]	USC	crosses
TLD	to Macrae, John	April 8 [1939]	USC	crosses; plans additional vols.
TLC	to Macrae, John	May 3, 1939	USC	crosses
TLC	to Macrae, John	Dec. 15, 1939	USC	crosses; exhib
TLC	to Macrae, John	[April 16, 1939?]	USC	crosses; publicity ideas
ALD	to Macrae, John	May 19 [1938]	USC	crosses; suggests book design
TLC	to Macrae, John	May 17, 1938	USC	crosses; accepts offer to publish
TLC	to Macrae, John	[Aug. 6, 1939?]	USC	crosses; reviews; exhib; HG article
TLC	to Macrae, John	April 21, 1939	USC	crosses; publicity campaign
ALS	to Macrae, John	Jan. 13, 1938	USC	crosses
TLC	to Macrae, John	June 5, 1938	USC	crosses
TLC	to Macrae, John	Jan. 12, 1940	USC	crosses; exhib; list of
TLD	to Macrae, John, Jr.	May 23, 1938	USC	crosses
ALS	to Magill	Jan. 23, 1930	Homestead	arranging meeting
TLC	to Mahin, John Lee	Feb. 6, 1912	USC	
TLC	to Mallock, Douglas	Oct. 3, 1913	USC	
ALC	to Mandel Bros Dept Store	[March-May, 1903]	USC LB 141	re: bill for furniture
ALC	to Mandel Bros Dept Store	[May 13-8, 1903]	USC LB 145	bill dispute
ALC	to Mandel Bros Dept Store	[May 21-3, 1903]	USC LB 148-9	
ALS	to Manny, Frank	Jan. 5, 1940	U of Mich	psychic
ALS	to Mansfield, Beatrice C.	Feb. 24 [1916]	NYPL	re: Melville Stone
TLS	to Marden, Mrs.	April 18	Wagner	buys 3 dinner tickets

ALS	to Marie, Sister Frances	April 11, 1936	St Mary C	thanks for remembrance
ALD	to Markham, Anna	Sept. 25, 1936	USC	d. of Wagner ltr; substantial difference
ALS	to Markham, Anna	Sept. 25, 1936	Wagner	re: reports of Markham's illness
TLS	to Markham, Edwin	Dec. 8	Wagner	
ALS	to Markham, Edwin	Sept. 13 [1921]	Wagner	Acad; nominates Markham
ALS	to Markham, Edwin	April 10 [1926]	Wagner	Acad; invites to Wilkins medal
TLS	to Markham, Edwin	Oct. 14, 1916	Wagner	Com Lit Art: guest of honor invitation
ALS	to Markham, Edwin	Aug. 13 [1929]	Wagner	Acad; re: Markham's election
TLS	to Markham, Edwin	July 2 [1917]	Wagner	
TLS	to Markham, Edwin	Nov. 3, 1916	Wagner	Com Lit Art: req. poem
ALS	to Markham, Edwin	April 4	Wagner	Institute; Markham elected
ALS	to Markham, Edwin	[Jan. 18, 1905]	Wagner	
ApcS	to Markham, Edwin	June 3, 1895	Wagner	
TLS	to Markham, Edwin	July 24 [1917]	Wagner	sends advance c. of *Son*
ALS	to Markham, Edwin	Sept. 15 [1921]	Wagner	Acad; nomination
ALS	to Markham, Edwin	Nov. 13	Wagner	
TLS	to Markham, Edwin	Nov. 6, 1916	Wagner	Com Lit Art: poems
ALS	to Markham, Edwin	March 9	Wagner	
ALS	to Markham, Edwin	Nov. 25 [1908]	Wagner	req. Cedars greeting for Cliff Dweller. inaug.
TLS	to Markham, Edwin	March 1917	Wagner	Com Lit Art circular
ALS	to Markham, Edwin	Sept. 16 [1933]	Wagner	thanks for b-day tribute
ALS	to Markham, Edwin	Oct. 2 [1909]	Wagner	thanks for notice of *Moccasin Ranch*
TLS	to Markham, Edwin	April 9	Wagner	
ALS	to Markham, Edwin	Oct. 23	Wagner	
ApcS	to Markham, Edwin	[July 27, 1917]	Wagner	
ALS	to Markham, Edwin	June 27 [1927]	Wagner	
ALS	to Markham, Edwin	Jan. 6	U Texas	
ALS	to Markham, Edwin	April 5 [1922]	Wagner	thanks for praise of *Daughter*
ALS	to Markham, Edwin	Jan. 15, 1900	Wagner	
ALS	to Markham, Edwin	July 21 [1903]	Wagner	announces birth of Mary Isabel
ALS	to Markham, Edwin	n.d.	U Texas	
ALS	to Markham, Edwin & Anna	Dec. 16, 1937	Wagner	

TLC	to Marks, Jeannette	March 26, 1913	USC	Chicago Thea Soc
ALS	to Marks, Jeannette	March 8 [1922]	Mt Holyoke	
TLS	to Marks, Jeannette	Dec. 15 [1922]	Mt Holyoke	
ALS	to Marks, Jeannette	Oct. 6 [1922]	Mt Holyoke	lectures; encl. photo-circular w/ Mary Isabel
TLS	to Marks, Jeannette	Jan. 1 [1923]	Mt Holyoke	
TLS	to Marks, Jeannette	Dec. 19 [1922]	Mt Holyoke	
AnS	to Marks, Jeannette	Mon. [Dec. 1922]	Mt Holyoke	
ALS	to Marks, Jeannette	Oct. 22 [1922]	Mt Holyoke	
ALS	to Marks, Jeannette	Oct. 15 [1922]	Mt Holyoke	
ALS	to Marks, Jeannette	Nov. 4 [1922]	Mt Holyoke	
ALS	to Marks, Jeannette	Jan. 16 [1923]	Mt Holyoke	
ALS	to Marquis, Don	July 2	Players	resp. to Marquis's poetry
ALS	to Marquis, Don	Nov. 13, 1924	Players	Town Hall Club; comm.
TLC	to Marquis, J. Clyde	June 14, 1912	USC	re: "A Day in Isleta"
TLS	to Marquis, Neeta	Nov. 13 [1932]	Hunt	
TLS	to Marquis, Neeta	Jan. 6 [1932]	Hunt	
TLS	to Marquis, Neeta	Feb. 1 [1932]	Hunt	
ALS	to Marquis, Neeta	Jan. 11 [1932]	Hunt	
TLS	to Marquis, Neeta	Feb. 18 [1932]	Hunt	
TLC	to Marsh, Edward	n.d.	USC	re: *Captain*
TLC	to Marsh, Edward	Jan. 10 [1917?]	USC	*Son*
TLC	to Marsh, Edward	Feb. 26, 1917	USC	*Son*; contract; advertising
TLC	to Marsh, Edward	March 13 [1917]	USC	*Son*
TLC	to Marsh, Edward	March 10 [1917]	USC	*Son*
TLC	to Marsh, Edward	March 9 [1917]	USC	*Son*
TLC	to Marsh, Edward	July 21, 1917	USC	*Son*
TLC	to Marsh, Edward	July 18 [1917]	USC	*Son*
TLC	to Marsh, Edward	March 4 [1917]	USC	*Son*
TLC	to Marsh, Edward	March 1 [1917]	USC	*Son*
TLC	to Marsh, Edward	June 24, 1917	USC	*Son*
TLC	to Mason, Miss	Oct. 2, 1913	USC	encl. photo for unspec. magazine
ALS	to Masters, Edgar Lee	Jan. 14	U Texas	arranges lunch after "Poetry dinner"
ALS	to Matthews, Brander	Sat.	Columbia	Acad; Burroughs Soc wants to use bldg
ALS	to Matthews, Brander	Thurs. [Dec. 1897]	Columbia	reads and reviews *Outlines in Local Color*
ALS	to Matthews, Brander	n.d.	Columbia	
ALS	to Matthews, Brander	Sun.	Columbia	Acad; re: Johnson's management, sec. squabble

ALS	to Matthews, Brander	Jan. 24	Columbia	re: death of M's mother
ALS	to Matthews, Brander	Jan. 19	Columbia	
ALS	to Matthews, Brander	n.d.	Columbia	
ALS	to Matthews, Brander	Wed.	Columbia	
ALS	to Matthews, Brander	Jan. 12 [1918?]	Columbia	Acad; re: election?
ALS	to Matthews, Brander	Jan. 18, 1900	Columbia	
ALS	to Matthews, Brander	Jan. 10	Columbia	
ALS	to Matthews, Brander	Jan. 6	Columbia	re: exhib at Newberry
ALS	to Matthews, Brander	Dec. 18	Columbia	Acad; nominates Bacheller
ALS	to Matthews, Brander	March 15, 1892	Columbia	thanks for praise of stories
ALS	to Matthews, Brander	Dec. 14	Columbia	Acad; proxy vote against by-law changes
TLS	to Matthews, Brander	Dec. 11	Columbia	Acad; Johnson squabble; HG's repo▶
TLS	to Matthews, Brander	April 13	Columbia	re: M's operation and HG's sciatica
ALS	to Matthews, Brander	Dec. 9	Columbia	Acad; squabble re: salaries, Johnson
ALS	to Matthews, Brander	Jan. 29, 1897	Columbia	re: Kemeys
ALS	to Matthews, Brander	[ca May-June 1925]	Columbia	Acad; re: Hergesheimer
ALS	to Matthews, Brander	Tue.	Columbia	re: M's wife's death
ALS	to Matthews, Brander	Dec. 25	Columbia	sees *Candida*
ALS	to Matthews, Brander	Dec. 5, 1896	Columbia	re: Kemeys as illus. for HG's books
ApcS	to Matthews, Brander	Oct. 17, 1896	Columbia	
ALS	to Matthews, Brander	Nov. 26	Columbia	Acad; Johnson's stat▶
ALS	to Matthews, Brander	Sun.	Columbia	Acad; ready to move to new bldg
ALS	to Matthews, Brander	Thurs.	Columbia	
ALS	to Matthews, Brander	n.d.	Columbia	
ALS	to Matthews, Brander	Mon.	Columbia	
ALS	to Matthews, Brander	May 28 [1911?]	Columbia	Chicago Thea Soc; req. list of plays
ALS	to Matthews, Brander	Jan. 26	Columbia	
ALS	to Matthews, Brander	n.d.	Columbia	
ALS	to Matthews, Brander	Nov. 4, 1896	Columbia	
ALS	to Matthews, Brander	Jan. 8	Columbia	
ALS	to Matthews, Brander	Sun. [1920]	Columbia	Acad; appeals to M. to become chancellor
ALS	to Matthews, Brander	n.d.	Columbia	
TL	to Matthews, Brander	Feb. 12 [1925?]	USC	Acad; nominations
TLC	to Matthews, Brander	n.d.	USC	c. of Columbia ltr
ALS	to Matthews, Brander	Jan. 8	Columbia	

ALS	to Matthews, Brander	May 8	NYPL	
ALS	to Matthews, Brander	Sept. 28 [1913]	Columbia	Institute; wishes Woodrow Wilson would come
ALS	to Matthews, Brander	Sept. 26	Columbia	
TLC	to Matthews, Brander	Feb. 20, 1913	USC	
TLC	to Matthews, Brander	May 19, 1913	USC	c. of Columbia ltr
TLC	to Matthews, Brander	March 21 [1917]	USC	going to Battle Creek sanitarium; c. of USC
TLC	to Matthews, Brander	May 23, 1913	USC	c. of Columbia ltr
ALS	to Matthews, Brander	Oct. 29 [1919?]	Columbia	learns he is a "Centurian"
TLS	to Matthews, Brander	March 20	Columbia	
ALS	to Matthews, Brander	Jan. 8	Columbia	
ALS	to Matthews, Brander	Sept. 13	Columbia	
ALS	to Matthews, Brander	Nov. 22	Columbia	re: HG's sciatica
ALS	to Matthews, Brander	Oct. 1	Columbia	spelling reform; presidential recommendation
ALS	to Matthews, Brander	Nov. 24 [1913]	Columbia	Institute; need for money
ALS	to Matthews, Brander	Oct. 19	Columbia	
ALS	to Matthews, Brander	Sept. 21 [1921]	Columbia	Acad; cornerstone ceremony
ALS	to Matthews, Brander	Sept. 20	Columbia	Acad; nominates Finley
TLS	to Matthews, Brander	Sept. 28	Columbia	Acad; slogan (see HG to Sloane)
ALS	to Matthews, Brander	Feb. 29	Columbia	Acad; nominations: prefers Mackaye to Robinson
ALS	to Matthews, Brander	Nov. 29 [1922]	Columbia	Acad; bldg filling; M's health
ALS	to Matthews, Brander	Nov. 4	Columbia	
TLS	to Matthews, Brander	Oct. 28	Columbia	Acad; plan to "preent" books
ALS	to Matthews, Brander	Oct. 26	Columbia	
TLS	to Matthews, Brander	Oct. 27	Columbia	Acad; Gosse; liaison for English Academy
ALS	to Matthews, Brander	Nov. 14	Columbia	Acad; re: nominations
ALS	to Matthews, Brander	Nov. 30	Columbia	Acad; Johnson troubles
ALS	to Matthews, Brander	Sept. 23 [1921]	Columbia	Acad; Pulitzer; c cornerstone
ALS	to Matthews, Brander	May 26	Columbia	Acad; reform. officer elections
ALS	to Matthews, Brander	May 15, 1905	Columbia	
ALS	to Matthews, Brander	March 22, [1912]	Columbia	
ALS	to Matthews, Brander	Oct. 25	Columbia	

TLS	to Matthews, Brander	May 23, 1913	Columbia	Institute; plan for Chicago meeting
TLS	to Matthews, Brander	May 19, 1913	Columbia	Institute; plan; affiliation on books
ALS	to Matthews, Brander	Sept. 26	Columbia	
TLS	to Matthews, Brander	Sept. 15, [1918]	Columbia	
ALS	to Matthews, Brander	Dec. 29	Columbia	xmas greeting; pho[encl of daughters
ALS	to Matthews, Brander	Dec. 5 [1923]	Columbia	Acad; M. asked to b chancellor
ALS	to Matthews, Brander	Sept. 29, 1897	Columbia	re: entrance into Players Club
ALS	to Matthews, Brander	Dec. 29	Columbia	req. M. to second application to Century C
TLS	to Matthews, Brander	Feb. 3, 1913	Columbia	Institute; plan for Chicago meeting
ALS	to Matthews, Brander	Oct. 20	Columbia	spelling reform; dif to remember
ALS	to Matthews, Brander	Jan. 30	Columbia	
ALS	to Matthews, Brander	Oct. 10	Columbia	
TLS	to Matthews, Brander	Feb. 11, 1913	Columbia	Institute; plan for Chicago meeting
ALS	to Matthews, Brander	May 1, 1897	Columbia	Grant; "cut to smithereens"
ALS	to Matthews, Brander	Feb. 16, 1897	Columbia	
ALS	to Matthews, Brander	April 13, 1899	Columbia	
ALS	to Matthews, Brander	Oct. 21	Columbia	
ALS	to Matthews, Brander	March 15, 1899	Columbia	re: meeting w/ William Archer
ALS	to Matthews, Brander	Oct. 12	Columbia	Acad; not cand. for VP
ALS	to Matthews, Brander	Oct. 19	Columbia	
ALS	to Matthews, Brander	Jan. 20, 1898	Columbia	re: HG's rev. of "Outlines in Local Color"
ALS	to Matthews, Brander	Aug. 6, 1897	Columbia	re: entrance into Players Club
ALS	to Matthews, Brander	Mon. /5, 1900	Columbia	halfway thru "A Confident Tomorrow
ALS	to Matthews, Brander	Feb. 28	Columbia	
ALS	to Matthews, Brander	Feb. 7 [1913]	Columbia	Institute; list of speakers
ALS	to Matthews, Brander	April 7	Columbia	
ALS	to Matthews, Brander	Feb. 6	Columbia	
ALS	to Matthews, Brander	Oct. 7 [1921]	Columbia	Acad; cornerstone; others displeased w HG
ALS	to Matthews, Brander	Feb. 23	Columbia	

ALS	to Matthews, Brander	Feb. 15	Columbia	
ALS	to Matthews, Brander	Dec. 6	Columbia	Acad; angry w/ Johnson
ALS	to Matthews, Brander	Wed.	Columbia	
ALS	to Matthews, Brander	May 2 [1924]	Columbia	Acad; nominations: Robinson, Hadley
ALS	to Matthews, Brander	Dec. 8 [1923]	Columbia	Acad; M. elected chancellor
ALS	to Matthews, Brander	April 19 [1924]	Columbia	Acad; nominations: Hadley, Van Doren, Marshall
ALS	to Matthews, Brander	Nov. 29 [1913?]	Columbia	Institute; lack of money
ALS	to Matthews, Brander	March 4 [1913]	Columbia	Institute; re: Roosevelt as speaker
ALS	to Matthews, Brander	April 3 [1922]	Columbia	
ALS	to Matthews, Brander	Feb. 19	Columbia	
TLS	to Matthews, Brander	May 22	Columbia	re: Constance's attendance at Columbia
TLS	to Matthews, Brander	May 25	Columbia	re: edition of Howells' works
ALS	to Matthews, Brander	Feb. 17	Columbia	
ALS	to Matthews, Brander	June 8	Columbia	
TLS	to Matthews, Brander	June 5 [1921]	Columbia	Acad; related w/ Institute; new bldg
ALS	to Matthews, Brander	Sept. 3	Columbia	
TLS	to Matthews, Brander	Aug. 9	Columbia	Acad; nominates Taft
ALS	to Matthews, Brander	Nov. 5 [1930?]	Columbia	re: Roadsides?
TLS	to Matthews, Brander	June 13, 1921	Columbia	Acad; related w/ Institute = host, not equals
ALS	to Matthews, Brander	Aug. 8	Columbia	
TLS	to Matthews, Brander	Oct. 29	Columbia	recommends Turck
ALS	to Matthews, Brander	Dec. 17,1896	Columbia	re: Kemeys and book venture
TLS	to Matthews, Brander	Sept. 8	Columbia	
*TLS	to Matthews, Brander	[ca. Oct. 7, 1921]	Columbia	Acad; funding trouble for cornerstone ceremony
*ALS	to Matthews, Brander	Oct. 14, 1896	Columbia	re: colonialism, Americanism
ALS	to Matthews, Brander	May 3	Columbia	re: spelling
*ALS	to Matthews, Brander	Jan. 27, 1918	Columbia	Institute; women barred from admission
*ALS	to Matthews, Brander	Sept. 22 [1921]	Columbia	Acad; wants to oust Johnson
*TLS	to Matthews, Brander	March 21 [1917]	Columbia	re: Battle Creek, sciatica treatment

*TLS	to Matthews, Brander	March 11 [1925]	Columbia	Pulitzer
*ALS	to Matthews, Brander	Jan. 29 [1918]	Columbia	Institute; re: election of women
*ALS	to Matthews, Brander	May 7 [1922]	Pulitzer	condemns Anna Christie
TLS	to Matthews, Brander	July 25 [1916]	Columbia	Author's League: no affil. w/ unions
ALS	to Matthews, Brander	Aug. 31	Columbia	
*ALS	to Matthews, Brander	July 12, 1897	Columbia	re: entrance into Players Club
*ALS	to Matthews, Brander	Dec. 29, 1889	Columbia	re: *Drifting Apart*
*TLS	to Matthews, Brander	Sept. 15 [1921]	Columbia	Acad; disc. of admin. Pulitzer prizes
TLC	to Matthison, Minna	April 4 [1916]	USC	
TLC	to Matthison, Minna	April 8 [1916]	USC	
TL	to Mau, B. A.	March 7	Homestead	
TLS	to Mau, B. A.	Feb. 12	Homestead	
TLS	to Mau, B. A.	March 3	Homestead	
TLS	to Mau, B. A.	Feb. 4	Homestead	
TLC	to Mau, B. A.	April 23 [1920]	USC	
ALS	to Mau, B. A.	April 24	Homestead	
TLS	to Mau, B. A.	March 9 [#2]	Homestead	
TLS	to Mau, B. A.	March 9	Homestead	
TLS	to Mau, B. A.	March 11	Homestead	re: property management
TLS	to Mau, B. A.	March 8	Homestead	
ALS	to Mau, B. A.	Sept. 27	Homestead	
ALS	to Mau, B. A.	April 21	Homestead	
TLS	to Mau, B. A.	n.d.	Homestead	
ALS	to Mau, B. A.	April 24 [#2]	Homestead	
TLS	to Mau, B. A.	March 2	Homestead	
TLS	to Maurice, Arthur B.	July 24 [1922]	Princeton	can't attend unspec. symposium
TLS	to Maurice, Arthur B.	Oct. 22 [1922]	Princeton	lecture tour
TLS	to Maurice, Arthur B.	Oct. 15 [1922]	Princeton	HG and MI will go on lecture tour
ALS	to Maurice, Arthur B.	Sept. 17 [1931]	Princeton	thanks for rev. of *Contemporaries*
TLS	to Maurice, Arthur B.	Dec. 19 [1922]	Princeton	encl. lecture circular
TLC	to Mawson, Harry	Oct. 18, 1912	USC	Chicago Thea Soc
*ALD	to Maxwell, Perriton	June 6 [1926]	USC	man's penchant for war
ALS	to May, Beulah	March 11, 1938	Hunt	
ALS	to May, Beulah	March 10, 1939	Hunt	
TLS	to May, Beulah	March 2, 1939	Hunt	
TLS	to May, Beulah	Feb. 15 [1938]	Hunt	
ALS	to Mayfield, John S.	April 10 [1929]	Syracuse	expresses interest in article on Lanier
TLS	to Mayfield, John S.	Jan. 25 [1933]	Syracuse	arranges lecture

TLS	to Mayfield, John S.	June 6, 1938	Syracuse	thanks for Lanier pamphlet
TLS	to Mayfield, John S.	March 18 [1929]	Syracuse	re: Lanier, Woodberry
ALS	to Maynard	Nov. 12, 1897	Morgan	re: missed meeting
ALS	to McAfee, Miss		Bancroft	[incomplete]
TLC	to McAtamney, Hugh	March 31, 1913	USC	
ALS	to McCarthy, John R.	May 18, 1935	USC	dislike of M's poetry
ALS	to McClintock	Aug. 28 [1937]	Yale	liked McC's article in *Master Key*
TLC	to McClure, Samuel S.	Dec. 3. [1921]	USC	re: prospective serial topics
*ALS	to McClure, Samuel S.	Jan. 8, 1894	Virginia	req. work for Crane
ALS	to McClure, Samuel S.	Sept. 17 [1933]	Indiana U	thanks for B-day letter
TLS	to McClure, Samuel S.	Dec. 3 [1921]	Indiana U	suggests article on Riley
TLS	to McClure, Samuel S.	Nov. 5, 1917	Indiana U	Com Lit Art: exhib.
ALS	to McClure, Samuel S.	n.d.	Indiana U	re: article on Hardy
TLC	to McCormick, Edith R.	May 15, 1912	USC	Chicago Thea Soc
*TLC	to McCormick, Edith R.	July 24, 1911	USC	Chicago Thea Soc; offers to resign
TLC	to McCormick, Edith R.	May 29, 1912	USC	Chicago Thea Soc
TLS	to McCormick, Joseph Medill	June 28, 1912	Newberry	agrees to sign unspec. declaration for TR
ALS	to McCormick, Joseph Medill	June 28 [1912]	Newberry	wants to help in TR campaign
TLC	to Mcdonald, Pirie	April 17 [1919]	USC	
TLC	to McGhee, J. K. G.	April 19 [1920]	USC	
ALC	to McIldowney,	Wed.[Oct. 1, 1902]	USC LB 92	
TLC	to McKee, Samuel L.	March 28, 1912	USC	
TLS	to McKeighan, John H.	Jan. 5, 1935	Miami U	thanks for appreciative letter
ALS	to McKeyan	Jan. 20, 1935	Miami U	re: Eldon Hill
TLC	to McKinney, Dr.	Nov. 6, 1939	USC	crosses; exhib; repository
ALS	to McMaster	April 26 [1932]	U Wis-Mil	re: arrangements for commencement address
TLS	to McMaster	March 1, 1934	U Wis-Mil	re: lecture
TLS	to McMasters	Feb. 25	Virginia	
TLS	to McQueen, Elizabeth L.	June 26.	USC	
ALD	to Means, Marion Graybill	Aug. 20 [1933]	USC	
ALS	to Meiklejohn, Alexander	Aug. 7,	Amherst	re: lectures
ALS	to Mertins, Marshall Louis	Sunday. 25 [1937]	USC	arranging meeting
ALS	to Meyer	March 22	U of Iowa	Com Lit Art; thanks for singing
ALS	to Meyer, Annie Nathan	Nov. 16	Morgan	can't meet

*ALS	to Meyer, Annie Nathan	Jan. 13, 1898	NYPL	re: praise and req. for help
ALS	to Meyer, Annie Nathan	[March 1898]	U of Iowa	re: *Hedda Gabler*
ALS	to Meyer, Annie Nathan	March 9	Virginia	
ALS	to Meyer, Annie Nathan	Feb. 10, 1898	Allegheny	resp. to praise
ALS	to Meyer, Rose D.	Aug. 25 [1926]	USC	
TLC	to Meynell, Wilfrid	July 29 [1923]	USC	
TLD	to Miles, Sam T.	Dec. 10 [1938]	USC	
ALS	to Millard, Bailey	Jan. 7	U of Oregon	
ALS	to Millard, Bailey	Nov. 24 [1906]	U of Oregon	
TLD	to Millard, Bailey	March 20	USC	good diction; Prof. advisors listed
ALS	to Millard, Bailey	Dec. 4 [1906]	U of Oregon	believes in corrective power of satire
ALS	to Millard, Bailey	Sept. 24	U of Oregon	
ALS	to Millard, Bailey	n.d.	U of Oregon	resp. to poem
ALS	to Millard, Bailey	Jan. 13,	U of Oregon	
TLC	to Millard, Bailey	Dec. 15, 1934	USC	re: California Lit.
ALS	to Millard, Bailey	Oct. 15 [1931]	U of Oregon	thanks for rev. of *Contemporaries* [incomplete]
TLC	to Miller, Carrie Reed	June 26, 1913	USC	
TLC	to Miller, Frank A.	Jan. 30 [1934]	USC	sculpture museum
TLC	to Miller, Wilhelm	Oct. 3, 1913	USC	
TLC	to Miller, Wilhelm	March 11, 1914	USC	
*TLS	to Millett, Fred B.	March 1, 1937	Yale	porno rant; HG's work's virtue; Vitagraph
TLC	to Millikan, Robert A.	March 11 [1933]	USC	psychic
ALD	to Millikan, Robert A.	Jan. 10 [1937]	USC	crosses; assay
TLC	to Mills	April 25	USC	requests cabin to rent
TLC	to Mills, Emma	Feb. 2	Miami U	prefers not to be guest of honor
ALS	to Mills, Emma	Feb. 1	NYPL	arranging meeting
TLC	to Mills, Enos	Dec. 6, 1915	USC	Woodcraft
ALS	to Mims, Edwin	Sept. 7	Tenn-Nash	re: book on Lanier
ALS	to Mims, Edwin	May 8	Tenn-Nash	re: book on Lanier
ALD	to Minnich, Harvey C.	April 2, 1936	Miami U	McGuffey Reader: indicates favorites
*TLD	to Minnich, Harvey C.	April 2, 1936	USC	McGuffey reader
TLC	to Mitchell, S. Weir	Feb. 3, 1913	USC	invites to Cliff Dwellers lunch
TLC	to Mitchell, S. Weir	Feb. 10, 1913	USC	invites to Cliff Dwellers lunch
TLD	to Moffat, W. D.	Oct. 14 [1919]	USC	re: Roosevelt article
TLC	to Molloy, J. E.	April 18	USC	
ALS	to Monroe, Harriet	May 5 [1922]	U Chicago	wants to visit *Poetry* offices
TLS	to Monroe, Harriet	Nov. 5, 1917	U Chicago	Com Lit Art: exhib.

ALS	to Monroe, Harriet	Nov. 18, 1895	U Chicago	declines Fortnightly invitation
ALS	to Monroe, Harriet	Aug. 22 [1911]	U Chicago	Chicago Thea Soc; "Oriental Sister"
TLS	to Monroe, Harriet	Feb. 1 [1917]	U Chicago	Com Lit Art: South American writers
*TLS	to Monroe, Harriet	[ca. Oct. 2, 1920]	U Chicago	Asks if A. Lowell is "vital figure"
*ALS	to Monroe, Harriet	Sept. 13 [1912]	U Chicago	subscribes; praises *Poetry*
ALS	to Monroe, Harriet	Nov. 30 [1913]	U Chicago	praises *Poetry*; enq. re: submission
TLC	to Moody, W. S.	n.d.	USC	
ALS	to Moore, Aubertine Woodward	Oct. 23, 1895	Homestead	resp. to "Songs of the North"
TLD	to Moorhead, Frank G.	Aug. 23 [1921]	USC	serials
TLC	to Moorhead, Frank G.	May 15 [1919]	USC	
TLC	to Moorhead, Frank G.	May 29 [1920?]	USC	serials
TLC	to Moorhead, Frank G.	Oct. 28	USC	serials
TLC	to Moorhead, Frank G.	June 9	USC	serials
TLC	to Moorhead, Frank G.	Nov. 14 [1919]	USC	serials
ALS	to Moorhead, Frank G.	Aug. 15	Virginia	
*TLS	to Morgan, Arthur E.	Feb. 26, 40	Harvard	re: Bellamy's influence
ALC	to Morgan, Frank A.	June 16 [1904]	USC LB 208	
ALC	to Morgan, Frank A.	June 10 [1904]	USC LB 205	re: lectures
*TLC	to Morgan, Frank A.	April 15, 1913	USC	Forest ranger lecture: description
ALS	to Morley, C. D.	[after Jan. 17, 1916]	USC	
ALS	to Morley, Christopher	Sept. 17 [1933]	U Texas	resp. to b-day tribute
TLS	to Morley, Christopher	March 23, 1928	U Texas	
ALC	to Morningstar, R. E.	[Nov. 18-27, 1901]	USC LB 14	re: lectures
ALC	to Morningstar, R. E.	Nov. [1901]	USC LB 5	re: lecture management-East
TLC	to Morris, Ira Nelson	June 14, 1912	USC	Chicago Thea Soc: elections
TLC	to Morris, Ira Nelson	Feb. 17, 1913	USC	
TLC	to Morse, Edward S.	Dec. 30, 1911	USC	
ALS	to Moses, Montrose J.	Oct. 24 [1925]	Duke	can't meet at Author's Club
*TLS	to Moses, Montrose J.	March 18 [1921]	Duke	Pulitzer; asks for plays
AnS	to Moses, Montrose J.	May 14, 1908	Duke	re: Herne; on MJM to HG, 5/8/08
TLS	to Moses, Montrose J.	March 23, 1925	Duke	Town Hall C; invitation
*TLS	to Moses, Montrose J.	April 22 [1920]	Duke	Pulitzer; asks for plays; M. suggests *Beyond*

*TLS	to Moses, Montrose J.	Jan. 10 [1919]	Duke	Pulitzer; asks for plays; dislikes *Copperhead*
TLC	to Mott, Frank L.	Jan. 11, 1935	USC	re: rpt poems
ApcS	to Moulton, Louise Chandler	[Feb. 22, 1890]	Congress	
*ALS	to Moulton, Louise Chandler	Nov. 17, 1893	Congress	resp. to praise of *Songs*
*ALS	to Moulton, Louise Chandler	[June 1, 1891]	Congress	re: rev. of MTR and "Spring"
*ALS	to Moulton, Louise Chandler	[Jan. 10. 1890]	Congress	eval. M's poetry
TLC	to Moyle, Seth	June 5, 1912	USC	
TLC	to Moyle, Seth	Feb. 11, 1914	USC	
TLC	to Moyle, Seth	Feb. 21, 1913	USC	
TLC	to Moyle, Seth	May 8, 1912	USC	
TLC	to Moyle, Seth	May 22, 1913	USC	
TLC	to Moyle, Seth	March 26, 1912	USC	
TLC	to Moyle, Seth	May 13, 1913	USC	
TLC	to Moyle, Seth	April 10, 1913	USC	
TLC	to Moyle, Seth	Nov. 28, 1911	USC	re: ms of "Berea"
TLS	to Muir, John	April 12, 1898	U Pacific	Trans-Miss circular
TL	to Muir, John	Nov. 6, 1913	U Pacific	Institute: Chicago meeting circular
ALS	to Mumford, Lewis	Dec. 26 [1931]	U Penn	thanks for praise of *Companions*; future plans
ALS	to Munro, David A.	Nov. 13 [1902]	NYPL	re: revision of "Sanity in Fiction"
ALS	to Munro, David A.	April 19	Ind HS	re: "Sitting Bull"
ALC	to Munro, David A.	Oct. 9 [1901]	USC LB 0	
ALS	to Munro, David A.	Dec. 21	Ind HS	"Redman's Present Needs"; req. copy
ALS	to Munro, David A.	n.d.	Morgan	rush unspec. galley
ALS	to Munro, David A.	April 21	Morgan	asks after unspec. article
*ALS	to Munro, David A.	[ca April 1902]	Virginia	Indian; "Redman"; Roosevelt
ALC	to Munro, David A.	Oct. 9 [1902]	USC LB 100	re: dispute over money
ALS	to Munsterberg, Hugo	Dec. 18 [1908]	Boston PL	
ALS	to Munsterberg, Hugo	Dec. 14 [1908]	Boston PL	
TLS	to Munsterberg, Hugo	Oct. 16, 1908	Boston PL	*Shadow* circular
*TLS	to Munsterberg, Hugo	Nov. 23, 1908	Boston PL	*Shadow*; req. use of M's ltr for advert.
ALS	to Munsterberg, Hugo	March 17 [1908]	Boston PL	
ALS	to Neale, Walter	Feb. 20 [1930]	USC	
ALS	to Nelson, J. A.	Feb. 26, 1940	USC	boyhood memory; HG's last ltr?

TLC	to Nicholson, Calvin	Feb. 25, 1912	USC	
TLC	to Nicholson, Meridith	Dec. 27. 1911	USC	
TLC	to Norris, Charles G.	Apr. 8, 1914	USC	req. photo of Frank; reads *Vandover*
ALS	to Norris, Edward Everett	Jan. 28 [1913?]	U of Iowa	re: lecture on forest ranger
TLC	to North, Wilfred	April 5	USC	re: scenes of *Hesper*
TLC	to North, Wilfred	April 19	USC	re: costumes of *Hesper*
TLC	to North, Wilfred	March 29	USC	solicits work for Franklin G.
TLC	to North, Wilfred	March 26.	USC	
TLC	to North, Wilfred	April 18	USC	
TLC	to North, Wilfred	April 10 [1916]	USC	re: film adapt. of *Hesper*
TLC	to North, Wilfred	May 8	USC	
ALS	to Norton, Charles P.	Aug. 7 [1920]	Smith	re: lectures
TLS	to O'Brien, Howard V.	Jan. 6, 1916	Newberry	solicits stories for *Collier's*
TLC	to O'Connor, T. P.	Monday [July 1923]	USC	
ALS	to O'Connor, T. P.	Sunday [July 1923]	USC	
TLC	to O'Connor, T. P.	July 5 [1923]	USC	
AnS	to O'Dell, Edith	[Dec. 3, 1928]	Harvard	re: rpt. "Wm Bacon's Man" in *Golden Book*
TLC	to Oakleaf, J. B.	Dec. 26, 1911	USC	
TLC	to Oakleaf, J. B.	April 6, 1912	USC	
ALC	to Oates, J. F.	Oct. 8 [1902]	USC LB 95	re: Joys of Trail lecture
ALS	to Ochs-Oakes, George W.	March 18 [1931]	NYPL	
ALS	to Ochs-Oakes, George W.	May 30 [1931]	NYPL	
TLS	to Ochs-Oakes, George W.	July 3 [1931]	NYPL	declines to write unspec. article
TLS	to Ochs-Oakes, George W.	Sept. 26 [1931]	NYPL	
ALS	to Ochs-Oakes, George W.	May 16 [1931]	NYPL	
ALS	to Oehser, Paul H.	March 2, 1935	USC	re: goal of logbooks
TLC	to Oehser, Paul H.	March 3, 1935	USC	
TLC	to Onteora Club, Secretary	Aug. 6, 1939	Hunt	
ALS	to Osborne	Oct. 23 [1913]	NYPL	
TLC	to Osborne, Duffield	March 5, 1912	USC	
TLS	to Overton, Grant	Nov. 17	Morgan	thanks for praise of *Son*
TLS	to Page, Curtis Hidden	March 9, 1910	Columbia	re: Cliff D's initiation fee
ALS	to Page, Thomas N.	Feb. 3, 1897	Duke	*Grant*; req. introd. to Cosmos Club
ALS	to Page, Thomas N.	May [30, 1897]	Duke	is now staying at Regent Hotel
ALS	to Page, Thomas N.	Jan. 22, 1897	Duke	asks whether any DC clubs

ALS	to Page, Walter Hines	March 20	Harvard	invites to MacDowell dinner
ALS	to Page, Walter Hines	Dec. 6, 1895	Harvard	leaving for NY and wants to meet
TLC	to Page, Walter Hines	March 25, 1912	USC	re: "Middle West— Heart of the Country"
ALS	to Page, Walter Hines	[ca July 1895]	Harvard	re: P's resignation from the *Forum*
*ALS	to Page, Walter Hines	Aug. 27, 1899	Harvard	re: *Eagle's* as epic
*ALS	to Page, Walter Hines	Nov. 24, 1896	Harvard	resp. to rej. of "The Healer"
TLS	to Paine, Albert B.	Oct. 23 [1933]	Miami U	re: Zulime's health
ApcS	to Paine, Albert B.	[Aprl 30, 1918]	Miami U	arranging meeting
ALS	to Paine, Albert B.	July 22, 1896	Miami U	arranging meeting
TLS	to Paine, Albert B.	Nov. 13, 1924	Miami U	Town Hall Club circular
ALS	to Paine, Albert B.	Nov. 14 [1919]	Miami U	congrats on "performance
TLS	to Paine, Albert B.	Nov. 11 [1933]	Miami U	thanks for books; feeling his age
ApcS	to Paine, Albert B.	[Nov. 21, 1896]	Miami U	thanks for the favor
ALS	to Paine, Albert B.	Dec. 10, 1893	Miami U	re: publ. of *Forum* article
ApcS	to Paine, Albert B.	[May 13, 1918]	Miami U	
ApcS	to Paine, Albert B.	[Dec. 28, 1895]	Miami U	
ALS	to Paine, Albert B.	MAy 18	Miami U	arranging meeting
ALS	to Paine, Albert B.	Nov. 7	Miami U	"where are you?"
ALS	to Paine, Albert B.	Sept. 17 [1930]	Miami U	re: missed meeting at party
TLS	to Paine, Albert B.	Sept. 25	Miami U	arranging meeting
ALS	to Paine, Albert B.	Sept 30	Miami U	
ALS	to Paine, Albert B.	Aug. 5	Miami U	arranging meeting
ApcS	to Paine, Albert B.	[May 15, 1915]	Miami U	
ApcS	to Paine, Albert B.	[Dec. 12, 1895]	Miami U	arranging work for Carpenter
ApcS	to Paine, Albert B.	[Dec. 9, 1895]	Miami U	
ApcS	to Paine, Albert B.	[April 18, 1918]	Miami U	arranging meeting
ApcS	to Paine, Albert B.	[Feb. 4, 1918]	Miami U	leaves copy of *Son* for Paine
tel	to Paine, Albert Bigelow	[1910]	USC	re: death of Clemens
TLC	to Paine, Albert Bigelow	May 8, 1912	USC	re: Clemens' portrait
TLC	to Paine, Albert Bigelow	Nov. 28 [1934]	USC	re: title of *Afternoon*
TLC	to Parker, Austin H.	Oct. 3, 1913	USC	
TLC	to Parker, Austin H.	Oct. 9, 1913	USC	
ALS	to Pattee, Fred Lewis	Jan. 10	Penn State	arranging meeting
ALS	to Pattee, Fred Lewis	Jan. 8	Penn State	arranging meeting
TLS	to Pattee, Fred Lewis	Feb. 7	Penn State	cancelling meeting: sick

tel	to Pattee, Fred Lewis	Nov. 21, 1917	Penn State	asks Pattee to speak at Nat Arts Club
TLS	to Pattee, Fred Lewis	Aug. 25	Penn State	asks about lecture possiblity
ALS	to Pattee, Fred Lewis	Aug. 13	Penn State	thanks for lectures
ALS	to Pattee, Fred Lewis	Feb. 3 [1923 ?]	Penn State	arranging meeting
TLS	to Pattee, Fred Lewis	Feb. 25 [1923?]	Penn State	arranging meeting
TLS	to Pattee, Fred Lewis	Feb. 4 [1923?]	Penn State	arranging meeting
TLS	to Pattee, Fred Lewis	Feb. 5 [1920]	Penn State	cancelling meeting: sick
ALS	to Pattee, Fred Lewis	Jan. 21	Penn State	arranging meeting
ALS	to Pattee, Fred Lewis	Jan. 23 [1923]	Penn State	re: P's *History of Short Story*
TLS	to Pattee, Fred Lewis	Jan. 6	Penn State	re: lectures, Mary Wilkins Freeman
TLS	to Pattee, Fred Lewis	April 11	Penn State	arranging meeting
ApcS	to Pattee, Fred Lewis	Feb. 9 [1922]	Penn State	change of lecture date
ApcS	to Pattee, Fred Lewis	Feb. 3 [1922]	Penn State	arranging lecture date
TLS	to Pattee, Fred Lewis	April 27	Penn State	re: reports of his lecture
ALS	to Pattee, Fred Lewis	Feb. 16 [1918]	Penn State	explains content of lectures
TLS	to Pattee, Fred Lewis	April 19 [1916]	Penn State	returns O. Henry piece
ALS	to Pattee, Fred Lewis	Feb. 11	Penn State	arranging meeting
TLS	to Pattee, Fred Lewis	April 24	Penn State	requests info for new lecture circular
TLS	to Pattee, Fred Lewis	May 2	Penn State	re: lecture circular
ALS	to Pattee, Fred Lewis	Nov. 22 [1919]	Penn State	reports on success of Com Lit Art
TLS	to Pattee, Fred Lewis	[1917]	Penn State	sends *Son*; "Martha's Fireplace" rpt
*TLS	to Pattee, Fred Lewis	Nov. 24 [1923]	Penn State	re: Cather, Crane, Whitlock
TLS	to Pattee, Fred Lewis	June 23 [1920]	Penn State	
ALS	to Pattee, Fred Lewis	Feb. 23	Penn State	
ALS	to Pattee, Fred Lewis	[Feb. 23, 1920]	Penn State	
*ALS	to Pattee, Fred Lewis	Dec. 4 [1915]	Penn State	rereads *Hist of Am Lit 1870*; HG's influence
*ALS	to Pattee, Fred Lewis	Oct. 29 [1915]	Penn State	resp. to *Hist of Am Lit 1870*
ALS	to Pattee, Fred Lewis	Dec. 17	Penn State	arranging meeting
ALS	to Pattee, Fred Lewis	Dec. 24 [1922]	Penn State	re: HG's works
TLS	to Pattee, Fred Lewis	Jan. 11	Penn State	
*ALS	to Pattee, Fred Lewis	Dec. 30 [1914]	Penn State	resp. for bio. info; influences

TLS	to Pattee, Fred Lewis	Nov. 12 [1924]	Penn State	flooded w / rpt requests
TLS	to Pattee, Fred Lewis	March 27 [1916]	Penn State	re: O. Henry
ALS	to Pattee, Fred Lewis	Oct. 26 [1922]	Penn State	thanks for book
ALS	to Pattee, Fred Lewis	March 5, 1920	Penn State	arranging meeting
ALS	to Pattee, Fred Lewis	March 4, 1920	Penn State	arranging meeting
ALS	to Pattee, Fred Lewis	March 9	Penn State	evals a Pattee story
TLS	to Pattee, Fred Lewis	Nov. 21, 1917	Penn State	Com Lit Art: book exhib circular
ALS	to Pattee, Fred Lewis	Jan. 3	Penn State	re: story rpt
TLS	to Pattee, Fred Lewis	May 25 [1916]	Penn State	re: NYTM piece
TLS	to Pattee, Fred Lewis	Jan. 29 [1921]	Penn State	
TLS	to Pattee, Fred Lewis	Jan. 11	Penn State	
TLS	to Pattee, Fred Lewis	July 17 [1916]	Penn State	resp. to req. for anthology inclusion
TLC	to Patten, Mrs. Henry J.	Feb. 7, 1912	USC	Chicago Thea Soc: solicits funds
ALC	to Payne,	[March-May 1903]	USC LB 139-40	re: Booth lectures
TLS	to Payne, Leonidas W.	Oct. 3 [1924]	U Texas	re: rpt of *High Trails* stories
TLS	to Payne, Leonidas W.	Aug. 2 [1924]	U Texas	re: rpt of stories
ALS	to Payne, Leonidas W.	Sept. 27 [1924]	U Texas	will be in Texas in Spring
TLS	to Payne, Leonidas W.	Oct. 11 [1924]	U Texas	re: lectures
TLS	to Payne, Leonidas W.	Jan. 23, 1925	U Texas	
ALS	to Payne, Lesley	Dec. 21 [1923]	Indiana U	
TLC	to Payne, William Morton	May 5, 1914	USC	
TLC	to Payot & Co.	March 17 [1919]	USC	
ALS	to Pease	March 7	Knox	no serial available; "Plainsman Abroad"
ALD	to Peattie, Donald C.	Dec. 29, 1939	USC	
ApcS	to Peck, Harry Thurston	[Dec. 9, 1895]	Knox	reads proof
*ALS	to Peck, Harry Thurston	July 11, 1895	Virginia	re: Crane
ALS	to Peck, Harry Thurston	n.d.	Virginia	resp. to solicitation for articles
TLC	to Pelham, Laura Dainty	Feb. 21, 1913	USC	
ALS	to Perkins	Feb. 23, 1899	U of Iowa	Institute; P. elected treasurer
TLC	to Perkins, P. D.	March 2, 1936	USC	re: Japan lectures; introd.
ALS	to Perry, Lilla C.	Jan. 2, 1923	Colby	re: loss of Howells' portrait; praise for book
ALS	to Perry, Thomas S.	Dec. 1 [1917]	Colby	resp. to *Son* letter
ALS	to Perry, Thomas S.	Dec. 6 [1917]	Colby	wants to meet; is eager to read rev. of *Son*
TL	to Perry, Thomas S.	[Nov. 6, 1913]	Colby	Institute: Chicago meeting circular

TLS	to Perry, Thomas S.	Feb. 27, 1917	Colby	Com Lit Art: Howells meeting
TLS	to Perry, Thomas S.	May 20 [1920]	Colby	re: Howells
TLS	to Perry, Thomas S.	March 1 [1917]	Colby	urges P. to come to Howells meeting
TLC	to Phelps, H. L.	Sept. 13, 1937	USC	re: rpt. & publication advice
ALS	to Phelps, William Lyon	May 27,	Yale	Institute; nominates Dorothy Canfield Fisher
ALS	to Phelps, William Lyon	Aug. 13 [1930]	Yale	*Roadside*; agrees w/ estimate of current lit
ALS	to Phelps, William Lyon	May 4	Yale	
ALS	to Phelps, William Lyon	March 30,	Yale	appreciates rev. of poetry and Indian material
TLS	to Phelps, William Lyon	Nov. 19	Yale	Institute; congrats on election as president
ALD	to Phelps, William Lyon	Nov. 2	USC	
ALS	to Phelps, William Lyon	Nov. 26 [1931]	Yale	Institute
*TLS	to Phelps, William Lyon	April 28 [1922]	USC	Pulitzer; against *Anna Christie*
ALS	to Phelps, William Lyon	Jan. 25 [1931]	Yale	finishing *Companions*
TLC	to Phelps, William Lyon	Dec. 2	USC	disagrees w/ review
ALS	to Phelps, William Lyon	April 29, 1939	Yale	crosses; interested in reaction
*TLC	to Phelps, William Lyon	March 31 [1930]	USC	Institute; suggests nomin. J. Hawthorne
*ALS	to Phelps, William Lyon	Dec. 12 [1925]	Yale	porno rant; HG not precursor
*ALS	to Phelps, William Lyon	Nov. 3 [1930]	Yale	thanks for praise of *Roadside*
*TLC	to Phelps, William Lyon	March 27 [1917]	USC	Institute; incl. women
ALC	to Philipps	Nov. 13 [1901]	USC LB 8	re: Grant excerpts for lecture
TLC	to Phillips, Harry A.	March 25, 1912	USC	
ALC	to Phillips, Mrs. H. A.	May 23 [1903]	USC LB 150	re: lectures
TLD	to Pierce, Dante M.	May 26 [1922]	USC	
TLD	to Pierce, Dante M.	May 26 [1922]	USC	
ALS	to Pierces Weeklies	Sept. 17, 1921	Brown	aim of "Marshall Henry of Cripple Creek"
ALS	to Piercy, Josephine K.	[Feb. 24, 1929]	Indiana U	descr. method of composition
ALS	to Piercy, Josephine K.	Feb. 21 [1929]	Indiana U	will send pg of ms
ALS	to Piercy, Josephine K.	Feb. 19 [1925]	Indiana U	re: lectures
TLC	to Pierson, Jocelyn	Feb. 15 [1940]	USC	crosses; introd. to article
TLC	to Pierson, Jocelyn	June 14 [1939]	USC	crosses; Parent ms

TLC	to Pierson, Jocelyn	[June 22, 1939]	USC	crosses
TLC	to Pierson, Jocelyn	Sept. 11, 1939	Hunt	
TLD	to Pierson, Jocelyn	Feb. 15 [1940]	USC	crosses; Parent ms
TLC	to Pinchot, Amos E.	n.d.	USC	re: war finance
TLC	to Pinchot, Amos E.	n.d.	USC	re: war finance
TLC	to Pinchot, Gifford	April 10 (?), 1913	USC	
TLC	to Pitts	June 27, 1912	USC	
AnS	to Pond, Irving K.	[1915]	U of Mich	regrets can't attend Chicago Little Theatre
ALS	to Pond, Irving K.	Jan. 27	U of Mich	introd. Burnett
ALS	to Pond, Irving K.	May 6	U of Mich	
ALC	to Pond, J. H.	Oct. 8, 1902	USC LB 98	re: selling land
ALC	to Pond, James Burton	May 14 [1902]	USC LB 54	re: excessive bills
ALC	to Pond, James Burton	May 1 [1902]	USC LB 45	send copy of lecture list
ALS	to Pond, James Burton	n.d.	Homestead	
ALC	to Pond, James Burton	Nov. 27 [1901]	USC LB 15	re: lectures
ALC	to Pond, James Burton	Oct. 29 [1902]	USC LB 110	
ALC	to Pond, James Burton	Oct. 31 [1901]	USC LB 4	re: lecture management
ALC	to Pond, James Burton	Aug. 8 [1902]	USC LB 78	re: lectures
TLC	to Pond, James Burton [by sec'ty]	Sept. 10, 1913	USC	
ALC	to Pond, James Burton, Jr.	Feb. 2 [1903]	USC LB 121	
ALC	to Pond, James Burton, Jr.	[Feb-Mar, 1903]	USC LB 132	
ALC	to Pond, James Burton, Jr.	Feb. 14 [1903]	USC LB 127	
TLC	to Pond, James Burton, Jr.	Oct. 3, 1914	USC	
TLC	to Poole, Ernest	April 6 [1917]	USC	
TLS	to Poole, Ernest	March 23, 1928	USC	campaigns for election of Hoover
ALS	to Post, C. W.	[ca Aug. 20, 1914]	USC	
ALC	to Pottle, Emery	April 30 [1902]	USC LB 44	thanks for praise of *Captain*
ALS	to Pottle, Juliet W. Tompkins	Dec. 8 [1921]	Homestead	re: *Daughter*, intentions
TLC	to Pottle, Juliet W. Tompkins	[1923]	USC	re: English visit
TLC	to Pouncy	n.d.	USC	re: Thomas Hardy
TLS	to Poundstone, Leon H.	June 28, 1938	USC	crosses; permission
TLD	to Poundstone, Leon H.	Jan. 14, 1938	USC	crosses; testimony
TLC	to Powell, Mrs. I. N.	May 13, 1913	USC	
ALD	to Powers, James A.	Jan. 30 [1932?]	USC	
TLC	to Powers, James A.	May 5, 1935	USC	re: investments, real estate
TLS	to Poynton, John A.	March 15, 1926	USC	Town Hall Club: committee
TLC	to Pratt, Harry Noyes	Dec. 6, 1939	USC	crosses; repository
TLC	to Pringle, Rosa	April 21, 1939	USC	

TLC	to Pringle, Rosa	April 24, 1939	USC	sketch of MacDowell
ALS	to Pullman Co.	April 29 [1933]	Knox	re: ticket refund
ALS	to Putnam, George H.	June 28 [1928]	NYPL	re: copyright bill
TLS	to Putnam, George H.	April 26 [1928]	NYPL	re: copyright bill
*TLC	to Putnam, George P.	[Aug. 6, 1937]	USC	psychic; Amelia Earhart
ALD	to Putnam, Herbert	[Dec. 6, 1938]	USC	
*TLC	to Putnam, Herbert	Dec. 6, 1938	USC	re: depositing mss
TLC	to Putnam, Herbert	Feb. 6 [1922]	USC	
TLC	to Putnam, James	n.d.	USC	crosses
ALS	to Quick, John H.	April 18, 1900	Iowa HS	puts off reading Marshall's poetry
ALS	to Quick, John H.	March 13	Iowa HS	advice re: contracts
ALS	to Quick, John H.	Nov. 3	Iowa HS	thanks for unspec. book; "Joys of Trail" lecture
ALS	to Quick, John H.	Aug. 31	Iowa HS	re: Bobbs-Merrill as publ.
ALS	to Quick, John H.	June 18 [1900]	Iowa HS	disagrees w/ est. of Marshall's poetry
ALS	to Quick, John H.	Oct. 7	Iowa HS	thanks for criticism
ALS	to Quick, John H.	n.d.	Iowa HS	
ALS	to Quick, John H.	Tue.	Iowa HS	likes unspec. poem
ALS	to Quick, John H.	Oct. 31	Iowa HS	praises "The Good Ship"
TLS	to Quick, John H.	April 20, 1912	Iowa HS	thanks for sending "Leonard's play"
ALS	to Quick, John H.	n.d.	Iowa HS	
ALS	to Quinn, Arthur Hobson	March 11	U Penn	invites to League for Political Education lunch
TLS	to Quinn, Arthur Hobson	March 8	U Penn	re: lectures; suggests seeing unspec. O'Neill play
ALS	to Quinn, Arthur Hobson	March 20 [1930]	U Penn	re: praise of work; at work on *Roadside*
*ALS	to Quinn, Arthur Hobson	July 4 [1927]	USC	re: *Rip Van Winkle*
ALS	to Quinn, Arthur Hobson	Oct. 25 [1927]	U Penn	wants to copy *Rip*
ALS	to Quinn, Arthur Hobson	March 10	U Penn	
ALD	to Rager, Nora	Jan. 6, 1938	USC	crosses; testing Williams
TLD	to Rager, Nora	Dec. 26, 1937	USC	crosses; testing Williams
TLC	to Rager, Nora	Jan. 11, 1938	USC	crosses; testing Williams
TLC	to Rager, Nora	Sept. 20	USC	crosses
TLC	to Rager, Nora	Dec. 30, 1937	USC	crosses; testing Williams

TLC	to Rager, Nora	Jan. 18, 1938	USC	crosses; testing Williams
TLD	to Rager, Nora	n.d.	USC	crosses; testing Williams
TLD	to Rager, Nora	n.d.	USC	crosses; project history
TLC	to Rager, Nora	n.d.	USC	crosses; testing Williams
TLC	to Rager, Nora	Dec. 20, 1937	USC	crosses; tests will convince publisher
TLC	to Rager, Nora	Aug. 7, 1937	USC	crosses; testing Williams
TLD	to Rager, Nora	Jan. 18, 1938	USC	crosses
ALS	to Rainey, Halsey	Jan. 30, 1939	Hunt	re: "perm. loan" of mss
TLC	to Rainey, Halsey	Jan. 11, 1939	Hunt	re: "perm. loan" of mss
TLS	to Ranney, Louise	Dec. 28, 1938	Newberry	Williams as medium to find letters
ALS	to Ranney, Louise	n.d.	Newberry	
TLS	to Ranney, Louise	Sept. 7 [1938]	Newberry	enquires about his letters to Fuller
ALS	to Ranney, Louise	Oct. 29 [1938]	Newberry	
ALS	to Ranney, Louise	Nov. 8 [1938]	Newberry	
TLS	to Ranney, Louise	Jan. 4, 1939	Newberry	re: Williams
TLS	to Ranney, Louise	Sept. 13, 1938	Newberry	enquires about letter
*ALS	to Ranney, Louise	Nov. 3 [1938]	Newberry	finding letters to Fuller as test of psychic
ALD	to Ranney, Louise	Dec. 28, 1938	USC	crosses
TLS	to Rascoe, Burton	May 27	U Penn	too busy to write review
TLC	to Raue, Carl [by sec'ty]	Aug. 28, 1912	USC	
TLS	to Ray, Henry Russell	n.d.	U of Iowa	
ALS	to Raymond	Jan. 27	USC	
ALC	to Raymond	[May-June 1904]	USC LB 204	Booth/ Joys of Trail lectures
ALS	to Raymond	June 10	USC	
ALS	to Redding, Judge	Oct. 19, 1897	U of Iowa	
TLS	to Redding, Judge	Nov. 20, 1897	U of Iowa	req. Indian photos fc *McClures*
ALS	to Redding, Judge	Sept. 6 [1897]	U of Iowa	wants to buy moccasins
ALS	to Redding, Judge	Feb. 2, 1898	U of Iowa	invites to lunch to talk about Crow Agency
ALS	to Redding, Judge	Nov. 10, 1897	U of Iowa	
AnS	to Reed, Lois A.	[April 24, 1925]	Bryn Mawr	can't help finding *Crumbling Idols*

*TLC	to Reel, Estelle	Dec. 2, 1902	USC	Indian; renaming
*ALC	to Reel, Estelle	[June 15, 1903]	USC LB 152-62	Indian; education
*ALC	to Reel, Estelle	June 15 [1903]	USC LB 163	cover letter for previous
ALS	to Reel, Estelle	[June 2, 1902]	Nat'l Arch	HG's opinions re: Indian instruction
AnS	to Reel, Estelle	March 14 [1903]	Nat'l Arch	can't make Indian Educ. meet, but will send ltr
ALC	to Reel, Estelle	March 9 [1903]	USC LB 133	Indian; renaming
ALS	to Reel, Estelle	March 9 [1903]	Nat'l Arch	re: rolls, names, Cheyenne, Arapahoe
TLC	to Reese, Lisle	Oct. 3, 1938	USC	re: S. D. HG memorial: pamphlet
TLC	to Reese, Lisle	Jan. 2, 1939	USC	
ALD	to Reese, Lisle	Oct. 3, 1938	USC	
TLC	to Reese, Lisle	Aug. 18, 1939	Hunt	re: HG memorial pamphlet
TLC	to Reis, Alvin C.	April 9, 1913	USC	re: lectures: Forest Ranger
ALS	to Reynolds, Paul	June 4	Columbia	wants list of period. "Howling," "Red Man" sent
ALS	to Reynolds, Paul	April 26	Columbia	
ALS	to Reynolds, Paul	July 29	Columbia	
ApcS	to Reynolds, Paul	Sept. 5, 1897	Columbia	
ALS	to Reynolds, Paul	March 25	Columbia	
ALS	to Reynolds, Paul	July 26	Columbia	
ApcS	to Reynolds, Paul	[April 3, 1897]	Columbia	
ALS	to Reynolds, Paul	Dec. 11	Columbia	
ALS	to Reynolds, Paul	Aug. 3	Columbia	"Special Duty"; prej. against Indian stories
ALS	to Reynolds, Paul	May 1, 1901	Columbia	
ALS	to Reynolds, Paul	June 8	Columbia	re: sale of Indian stories
ALS	to Reynolds, Paul	July 7	Columbia	
ALS	to Reynolds, Paul	June 22	Columbia	re: Indian stories
ALS	to Reynolds, Paul	March 15	Columbia	
ALS	to Reynolds, Paul	Sept. 23	Columbia	
ALS	to Reynolds, Paul	Thurs. 26	Columbia	
ALS	to Reynolds, Paul	n.d.	Columbia	
ALS	to Reynolds, Paul	Feb. 26	Columbia	can sell "Howling Wolf" himself
ALC	to Reynolds, Paul	June 29 [1903]	USC LB 169	re: *Hesper*
ApcS	to Reynolds, Paul	[July 22, 1901]	Columbia	
ALS	to Reynolds, Paul	April 15	Columbia	"Howling Wolf"; still angry
ALS	to Reynolds, Paul	n.d.	Columbia	
ALS	to Reynolds, Paul	Oct. 1	Columbia	

ALS	to Reynolds, Paul	n.d.	Columbia	
*ALS	to Reynolds, Paul	March 1 [1903]	Columbia	Indian stories; HG's anger re: sales of work
ALS	to Reynolds, Paul	Nov. 4, 1898	Columbia	
*ALS	to Reynolds, Paul	[ca Nov. 25, 1898]	Columbia	angrily instructs R. how to sell
TLC	to Rhine, J. B.	July 5 [1936]	USC	psychic; *Forty*
ALS	to Rice, Wallace	n.d.	Newberry	
ALS	to Rice, Wallace	Feb. 4	Newberry	suggestions for Cliff D library
ALS	to Rice, Wallace	June 16	Newberry	
ApcS	to Rice, Wallace	Oct. 7 [1907]	Newberry	
ALS	to Rice, Wallace	Jan. 22	Newberry	suggestions re: Cliff library
ALS	to Rice, Wallace	April 26	Newberry	reminds R. of Cliff Dwellers librarian's duties
ALS	to Rice, Wallace	Oct. 30	Newberry	
ALS	to Rice, Wallace	Jan. 7	Newberry	re: Little Room
ALS	to Rice, Wallace	Jan. 7, 1901	Newberry	
ALS	to Rice, Wallace	Feb. 18	Newberry	beware a thief is at Cliff Dwellers
ALS	to Rice, Wallace	June 29	Newberry	
ALS	to Richards, Grant	June 2, 1899	U Texas	apologizes for forgetting "Puritans
ALS	to Richards, Grant	May 26, 1899	U Texas	arranging meeting
ALC	to Richards, Grant	Jan. 18 [1902]	USC LB 30-1	*Captain* contractural matters
ALC	to Richards, Grant	[Dec. 1901]	USC LB 24-5	offers *Captain*
ALS	to Richards, Grant	Thurs. [May 1899]	U Texas	accepts invitation to visit
ALS	to Richards, Grant	May 24, 1899	U Texas	arranging meeting
ALC	to Richards, Grant	Sept. 27, 1902	USC LB 86	re: English publ. of *Captain*
ALC	to Richards, Grant	Jan. 31 [1902]	USC LB 36	rev. proofs mailed
TLC	to Richardson, Frederick R.	March 4, 1912	USC	
ALS	to Riggs, Mrs. Kate D. Wiggin	Dec. 18, 1895	Indiana U	
ALS	to Riley, James Whitcomb	March 16 [1913]	Indiana U	wishes for improved health
ALS	to Riley, James Whitcomb	[Nov. 19, 1894]	Indiana U	praises unspec. R. book
TLS	to Riley, James Whitcomb	April 12, 1898	Indiana U	Trans-Miss circular
ALS	to Riley, James Whitcomb	[June 26, 1889]	Indiana U	is "into Chautauqua business"
ALS	to Riley, James Whitcomb	Sept. 20 [1915]	Indiana U	cannot attend Riley dinner
ALS	to Riley, James Whitcomb	[1888]	Indiana U	sends lecture circular

ALS	to Riley, James Whitcomb	Nov. 9, 1888	Indiana U	asks after "Ladrone"
ALS	to Riley, James Whitcomb	Feb. 8, 1890	Indiana U	advises R. to write, not lecture
ALS	to Riley, James Whitcomb	Nov. 16, 1895	Indiana U	invites to Field memorial reading
ApcS	to Riley, James Whitcomb	Aug. 18, 1893	Indiana U	re: "Real Conversations"
ALS	to Riley, James Whitcomb	Feb. 18, 1895	Indiana U	invites R. to joint lecture
ALS	to Riley, James Whitcomb	Aug. 23, 1893	Indiana U	re: "Real Conversations"
ALS	to Riley, James Whitcomb	Sept. 14 [1893]	Indiana U	encloses address of photographer
ALS	to Riley, James Whitcomb	Oct. 4 [1915]	Indiana U	sends affection
ALS	to Riley, James Whitcomb	188-?	Indiana U	arranging meeting
ALS	to Riley, James Whitcomb	May 13, 1895	Indiana U	at work on *Rose*
ALS	to Riley, James Whitcomb	Nov. 14 [1893]	Indiana U	sends "Real Conversations"
ALS	to Riley, James Whitcomb	Aug. 8 [1909]	Indiana U	reads R.'s verse to daughters
ALS	to Riley, James Whitcomb	Sept. 29 [1908]	Indiana U	nostalgia letter
ALS	to Riley, James Whitcomb	Oct. 20, 1897	Indiana U	re: George campaign
ALS	to Riley, James Whitcomb	Oct. 18 [1901]	Indiana U	may stop in Indianapolis
'ALS	to Riley, James Whitcomb	Oct. 25, 1887	Indiana U	praises "Nothin' at All to Say"
'ALS	to Riley, James Whitcomb	[Feb. 17, 1889]	Indiana U	invites R. to lecture in Boston
ALS	to Riley, James Whitcomb	June 21, 1888	Indiana U	wants to meet
'ALS	to Riley, James Whitcomb	April 15, 1891	Indiana U	encloses rev. of *Rhymes of Childhood*
'ALS	to Riley, James Whitcomb	Dec. 19, 1888	Indiana U	asks for name of agent
'ALS	to Riley, James Whitcomb	Aug. 5, 1888	Indiana U	sends draft of Riley article
'ALS	to Riley, James Whitcomb	Dec. 21, 1887	Indiana U	reads R. poems to farmers
'ALS	to Riley, James Whitcomb	[July 31, 1888]	Indiana U	sends "Ladrone" for eval.
'ALS	to Riley, James Whitcomb	Dec. 17, 1887	Indiana U	at work on *Transcript* Riley article
ALS	to Riley, James Whitcomb	July 13 [1914]	Indiana U	is still lecturing about R.
'ALS	to Riley, James Whitcomb	Sept. 4, 1888	Indiana U	re: Riley article; asks for return of "Ladrone"
'ALS	to Riley, James Whitcomb	Aug. 28, 1888	Indiana U	proposes collab. on play

*ALS	to Riley, James Whitcomb	[Jan. 5, 1890]	Indiana U	advises to see *Drifting Apart*
*ALS	to Riley, James Whitcomb	Oct. 11, 1888	Indiana U	reminds R. to return ms
*ALS	to Riley, James Whitcomb	Feb. 11, 1888	Indiana U	about HG's acting; poetry
TLC	to Riley, P. M.	June 10, 1912	USC	
TLC	to Riley, P. M.	June 14, 1912	USC	
TLC	to Riley, P. M.	April 1, 1912	USC	
TLC	to Riley, P. M.	Dec. 1, 1911	USC	
TLC	to Riley, P. M.	May 31, 1912	USC	photos to illus. "Middle West—Heart of Country"
ALS	to Risser, Miss	Sunday. Morning.	Miami U	arranges meeting
ALS	to Robb, Ellis	Oct. 20 [1930]	U Wis-Mil	thanks for praise o *Roadside*
TLC	to Roberts, Mary Fanton	March 24, 1913	USC	
TLC	to Roberts, Mary Fanton	March 8, 1913	USC	
TLC	to Roberts, Mary Fanton	April 9, 1913	USC	
*ALS	to Robertson, Donald	Feb. 6, 1909	Northwestern	re: "Miller of Boscobel"
*TLC	to Robertson, Donald	July 24, 1911	USC	Chicago Thea Soc; list
TLC	to Robins, Raymond	Aug. 26, 1924	Harvard	is opposed to LaFollette; will vo for Coolidge
TLS	to Robinson, Corinne Roosevelt	Nov. 27	Harvard	thanks for praise o *Companions*
ALS	to Robinson, Corinne Roosevelt	Nov. 11	Harvard	thanks for address
ALS	to Robinson, Corinne Roosevelt	March 31	Harvard	pleasure to meet
ALS	to Robinson, Corinne Roosevelt	March 6	Harvard	well wishes for recovery
ALS	to Robinson, Corinne Roosevelt	May 8	Harvard	praises R's book of verses
ALS	to Robinson, Corinne Roosevelt	Oct. 10 [1921]	Harvard	praises R's *Scribner* article on TR
TLS	to Robinson, Corinne Roosevelt	Nov. 12, 1916	Harvard	thanks for contrib. Nat. Arts Club program
ALS	to Robinson, Corinne Roosevelt	April 14	Harvard	resp. to "lines" at unspec. program
ALS	to Robinson, Corinne Roosevelt	Jan. 27 [1916]	Harvard	resp to speech: best "by a woman"
ALS	to Robinson, Doane	July 29 [1908]	S Dak HS	Indian stories; resp. to req. for info
*ALS	to Robinson, Doane	Feb. 2 [1897]	U of Iowa	western dialect

ALS	to Robinson, Edwin Arlington	Sept. 16 [1933]	Colby	thanks for b-day greeting
ALC	to Roe	Feb. 1 [1902]	USC LB 37	re: land management
ALC	to Roe	Jan. 23 [1902]	USC LB 34	establ. PO on Kansas land
ALS	to Rogers, John	Feb. 27 [1898]	NY HS	resp to art: "Checker Players"
ALD	to Rogers, Will	April 3	USC	thanks for "guarantee" for Hardesty Johnson
*ALD	to Rogers, Will	[ca. Sept. 1932]	USC	criticizes acting roles
ALD	to Rogers, Will	Nov. 20, 1934	USC	sends *Afternoon*
TLC	to Romer, F.	Sept. 19.	USC	
ALS	to Roosevelt, Edith K.	Feb. 14 [1918]	Congress	re: TR's health
*ALD	to Roosevelt, Edith K.	Jan. 7 [1919]	USC	upon TR's death
ALS	to Roosevelt, Edith K.	[ca April 29, 1902]	Congress	expresses pleasure at meeting
TLC	to Roosevelt, Theodore	April 12, 1913	USC	
ALS	to Roosevelt, Theodore	April 1 [1901]	Congress	re: *Mountain, Captain*, life on trail
ALS	to Roosevelt, Theodore	Jan. 22 [1904]	Congress	
ALS	to Roosevelt, Theodore	March 5 [1918]	Congress	re: TR's health
TLS	to Roosevelt, Theodore	June 3 [1918]	Congress	
ALS	to Roosevelt, Theodore	Nov. 28 [1914]	Congress	
ALS	to Roosevelt, Theodore	Saturday [1914]	Congress	Institute
ALS	to Roosevelt, Theodore	May 19 [1914]	Congress	
ALS	to Roosevelt, Theodore	Oct. 30 [1917]	Congress	re: R's b-day, recent speech
ALS	to Roosevelt, Theodore	April 9 [1913]	Congress	re: Progressive Club
*ALS	to Roosevelt, Theodore	[ca Aug. 6, 1905]	Congress	sends letter to Colo papers re: National Park
ALS	to Roosevelt, Theodore	June 30 [1913]	Congress	Institute; descr. program
TLS	to Roosevelt, Theodore	March 10, 1913	Congress	Institute; accepts; Author's League
ALS	to Roosevelt, Theodore	March 17, 1902	Congress	sends *Captain*; Indian; "Redman"
TLS	to Roosevelt, Theodore	April 12, 1913	Congress	re: Progressive Club
ALS	to Roosevelt, Theodore	Jan. 24 [1912]	Congress	
TLS	to Roosevelt, Theodore	Dec. 22 [1916]	Congress	Woodcraft, Boy Scouts: HG now favors jr militia
TLC	to Roosevelt, Theodore	May 8, 1913	USC	
ALS	to Roosevelt, Theodore	Dec. 4 [1916]	Congress	
TLS	to Roosevelt, Theodore	May 14 [1917]	Congress	re: Battle Creek, film of *Captain*
TLD	to Roosevelt, Theodore	n.d.	USC	supporting election
ALS	to Roosevelt, Theodore	[April 20, 1916]	Congress	

ALS	to Roosevelt, Theodore	Jan. 7 [1918]	Congress	re: Darrow, "Bolsheviki" in N\
ALS	to Roosevelt, Theodore	May 1 [1902]	Congress	approves order re: cattle barons, publi\ lands
ALD	to Roosevelt, Theodore	Sept. 14	USC	
ALS	to Roosevelt, Theodore	March 6 [1916]	Congress	
TLD	to Roosevelt, Theodore	Nov. 20 [1916]	USC	TD of Nov. 21, 1916
TLC	to Roosevelt, Theodore	Dec. 10	USC	re: film adapt.
TLS	to Roosevelt, Theodore	Sept. 26 [1917]	Congress	
ALS	to Roosevelt, Theodore	Aug. 28 [1916]	Congress	
TLC	to Roosevelt, Theodore	Oct. 12 [1916]	USC	re: praise of Middle\ Border
TLD	to Roosevelt, Theodore	Nov. 21 [1918]	USC	proposes Q. Roosev\ memorial
ALS	to Roosevelt, Theodore	May 5, 1911	Congress	
*ALS	to Roosevelt, Theodore	July 16 [1903]	Congress	announces birth of Mary Isabel
TLS	to Roosevelt, Theodore	Feb. 14 [1916]	Congress	
ALS	to Roosevelt, Theodore	[Aug. 4, 1903]	Congress	req. talk re: forest preserv; Shaw, Setc\
TLC	to Roosevelt, Theodore	April 10, 1913	USC	
ALS	to Roosevelt, Theodore	Dec. 18 [1912]	Congress	
TLS	to Roosevelt, Theodore	Jan. 31, 1913	Congress	Institute; urges R. to\ accept as speaker
TLS	to Roosevelt, Theodore	March 26 [1916]	Congress	
ALS	to Roosevelt, Theodore	Feb. 8 [1917]	Congress	re: R's letters as introd. to *Son*
ALS	to Roosevelt, Theodore	[April 8, 1901]	Congress	sends *Mountain*; discusses hunting
TLS	to Roosevelt, Theodore	[Oct. 27, 1918]	Congress	
*TLS	to Roosevelt, Theodore	Dec. 10 [1916]	Congress	re: film adaptation;\ Vitagraph
*ALS	to Roosevelt, Theodore	[June 16, 1906]	Congress	re: R's fight w/ oil, beef, mining interes\
*TLS	to Roosevelt, Theodore	Aug. 7, 1912	Congress	offers to help w/ 19\ campaign
*TLS	to Roosevelt, Theodore	Oct. 14 [1918]	Congress	Vigilantes; still needed
*TLS	to Roosevelt, Theodore	March 4, 1913	Congress	Institute; again urge\ TR as speaker
ALS	to Roosevelt, Theodore	Feb. 16 [1916]	Congress	
*TLS	to Roosevelt, Theodore	Dec. 20 [1916]	Congress	Com Lit Art: S. American writers
*ALS	to Roosevelt, Theodore	Aug. 1 [1917]	Congress	R's eval of *Son*; dis-approves father/ "silken rag"
*ALS	to Roosevelt, Theodore	April 22 [1913]	Congress	proposes law re: illegitimate childr\

*ALS	to Roosevelt, Theodore	April 1 [1902]	USC	Indian; proposes replacing Jones
*ALS	to Roosevelt, Theodore	July 17 [1917]	Congress	sends advance c. *Son*; rereads *Holidays*
*TLS	to Roosevelt, Theodore	May 8 [1918]	Congress	favors univ. service; suspension of German press
*TLS	to Roosevelt, Theodore	May 8, 1913	Congress	re: women's rights bill
*ALS	to Roosevelt, Theodore	July 22 [1918]	Congress	re: death of Quentin
*ALS	to Roosevelt, Theodore	Nov. 24 [1916]	Congress	resp. to *Through the Brazilian Wilderness*
*ALS	to Roosevelt, Theodore	[after April 28, 1913]	Congress	advocates women's rights bill
*ALD	to Roosevelt, Theodore	Nov. 21 [1916]	USC	re: Roosevelt introd. to *Son*
*ALS	to Roosevelt, Theodore	Jan. 22 [1913]	Congress	Institute; re: R. as speaker
*ALS	to Roosevelt, Theodore	Sept. 24 [1901]	Congress	re: TR's assumption of presidency
*ALS	to Roosevelt, Theodore	Aug. 15 [1905]	Congress	re: forest preservation; *Tyranny*
*ALS	to Roosevelt, Theodore	July 22 [1903]	Congress	disputes role of women
*TLC	to Roosevelt, Theodore	Nov. 22 [1918]	USC	Quentin memorial proposal
*ALS	to Roosevelt, Theodore	[July 29, 1902]	Nat'l Arch	suggests appointing renaming committee
TLC	to Rose	Feb. 16	Miami U	arranging meeting
TLC	to Rose, Edward	March 4, 1913	USC	Chicago Thea Soc; rej. play
ALC	to Rosenquist, J. W.	May 16 [1902]	USC LB 57	re: dramatization of *Captain*
ALS	to Rossiter, Alfred	April 14 [1923]	NYPL	
ALS	to Rouland, Minnie D.	July 14	U of AZ	
ALS	to Rouland, Minnie D.	July 25	U of AZ	
ALS	to Rouland, Minnie D.	Dec. 8	U of AZ	
ALS	to Rouland, Minnie D.	Jan. 7	U of AZ	
ALS	to Rouland, Minnie D.	May 2	U of AZ	
ALS	to Rouland, Minnie D.	Fri.	U of AZ	
ALS	to Rouland, Minnie D.	Nov. 2	U of AZ	
ALS	to Rouland, Minnie D.	Nov. 22	U of AZ	
ALS	to Rouland, Orlando	Dec. 15	U of AZ	
ALS	to Rouland, Orlando	Oct. 25	U of AZ	
ApcS	to Rouland, Orlando	Oct. 8 [1910]	U of AZ	
ALS	to Rouland, Orlando	March 15	U of AZ	
ALS	to Rouland, Orlando	Jan. 13	U of AZ	
ALS	to Rouland, Orlando	April 1	U of AZ	re: portrait; swollen eye

ALS	to Rouland, Orlando	Dec. 7	U of AZ	Woodcraft; invitation to join
ALS	to Rouland, Orlando	Sat.	U of AZ	
ALS	to Rouland, Orlando	April 25	U of AZ	
ALS	to Rouland, Orlando	Dec. 22	U of AZ	
ALS	to Rouland, Orlando	Jan. 27	U of AZ	
ALS	to Rouland, Orlando	March 28	U of AZ	re: portrait sitting
ALS	to Rouland, Orlando	May 30	U of AZ	
ALS	to Rouland, Orlando	May 12	U of AZ	normal eyes
ALS	to Rouland, Orlando	Nov. 15	U of AZ	
ALS	to Rouland, Orlando	Oct. 24	U of AZ	
ALS	to Rouland, Orlando	Dec. 11	U of AZ	
ALS	to Rouland, Orlando	Feb. 23	U of AZ	
ALS	to Rouland, Orlando	March 22	U of AZ	
TLS	to Rouland, Orlando	March 23, 1917	U of AZ	thanks for portrait
TLC	to Row, Mrs. R. K.	April 28, 1913	USC	
ALS	to Roz, Firmin	July 26 [1924]	Miami U	arranging translations
TLS	to Rugg, Harold Goddard	Nov. 17, 1938	Dartmouth	exhib
TLS	to Rugg, Harold Goddard	Feb. 15, 1939	Dartmouth	exhib
trL	to Russell, J. Almus	June 3, 1939	USC	exhib
TLC	to Sabine, Lillian	Nov. 28 [1919?]	USC	drama of Howells novel; Theatre Guild
ALS	to Salmon, Lucy M.	April 7 [1922]	U Texas	thanks for note
TLC	to Sanders, Franklyn B.	Oct. 26, 1911	USC	
TLS	to Sandford [or Sanford]	Nov. 5	U Wis-LaCrosse	re: lectures w/ Mary Isabel
TLS	to Sandford [or Sanford]	Oct. 26	U Wis-LaCrosse	re: lectures w/ Mary Isabel
ALD	to Sargent, John Singer	Thursday [July 1923?]	USC	Acad; seeks donation
ALD	to Sargent, John Singer	June 23	USC	
TLC	to Sargent, John Singer	July 29 [1923]	USC	Acad; seeks donation
ALD	to Sargent, John Singer	Monday [July 1923?]	USC	re: Middle Border saga
ALS	to Savage, Ruth	April 5 [1931]	USC	
TLC	to Saxton, Eugene F.	April 8, 1914	USC	
TLC	to Saxton, Eugene F.	July 3	USC	
ALD	to Scales, Jane	July 20 [1931]	USC	
ALS	to Schad, Robert	March 22 [1928]	Hunt	
ALS	to Schad, Robert	May 12, 1936	Hunt	
ALS	to Schad, Robert O.	July 27 [1936]	Miami U	introd. Hill to Huntington Lib.
TLD	to Schafer, Joseph	April 4, 1937	USC	exhib.
TLC	to Schuler, Eric	May 9	USC	
TLC	to Schuler, Eric	Sept. 16, 1914	USC	
TLC	to Schuler, Eric	Nov. 26	USC	
TLC	to Schulte, F. J.	Dec. 2, 1913	USC	film rights
TLC	to Schultz, James W.	March 26, 1914	USC	

ApcS	to Schuster, Sylvia	Nov. 11, 1936	Virginia	
TLC	to Scorer, John G.	Nov. 28, 1911	USC	
TLC	to Scorer, John G.	Nov. 9, 1914	USC	
TLC	to Scorer, John G.	Oct. 21, 1911	USC	
TLC	to Scorer, John G.	Jan. 31, 1912	USC	
TLC	to Scorer, John G.	Jan. 24, 1912	USC	re: lectures
TLS	to Scott, Catharine A. Dawson	Mon. [1922]	U Texas	asks why dropped as honorary member of P.E.N.
ALS	to Scott, Catharine A. Dawson	June 19 [1922]	U Texas	invites to tea
ALS	to Scott, Catharine A. Dawson	June 28 [1922]	U Texas	accepts invitation
AnS	to Scott, Catharine A. Dawson	June 26 [1922]	U Texas	
*TLS	to Scott, Catharine A. Dawson	Sat. [June 24, 1922]	U Texas	reasons why dinners bore him
ALC	to Scott, Frank H.	Nov. 1 [1901]	USC LB 1	"Red Pioneer"
TLC	to Scott, Leroy	May 26, 1916	USC	
ALS	to Scott, William	n.d.	NYPL	
ALS	to Scott, William	March 28, 1920	NYPL	
TLS	to Scribner, Arthur	Dec. 1, 1904	Princeton	invites to Progress and Poverty dinner
ALS	to Scribner, Arthur	April 6, 1900	Princeton	thanks for sending "Enoch Willoughby"
TLC	to Seaman, William G.	June 18, 1914	USC	pay is too little for unspec. work
ALS	to Sears, Joseph Hamblen	Sept. 22	NYPL	
ALS	to Sears, Joseph Hamblen	Feb. 19, 1909	Indiana U	re: plates of *Eagle's*
ALS	to Sears, Joseph Hamblen	Feb. 12, 1909	Indiana U	re: plates of *Eagle's*
ALC	to Sebastian, John	Nov. 1 [1901]	USC LB 2	re: "Red Pioneer"
TLC	to Sedgwick, Henry D.	March 31, 1913	USC	
TLC	to Sedgwick, Henry D.	March 16, 1914	USC	
TLC	to Sedgwick, Henry D.	April 28, 1913	USC	
TLC	to Sedgwick, Henry D.	March 26, 1914	USC	
ALS	to Sedgwick, Henry D.	Jan. 31, 1913	Am Acad	Institute; nominates Dreiser, Whitlock, Steele
TLC	to Sedgwick, Henry D.	April 21, 1913	USC	Institute; Chicago meeting
TLC	to Sedgwick, Henry D.	Oct. 3, 1914	USC	
ALC	to Seger, Jesse	[March-April 1901]	USC LB 42	re: land purchase
TLC	to Seger, Jesse	Jan. 24 [1924]	USC	re: farm management
ALC	to Seger, Jesse	July 11 [1905]	USC LB 219-20	re: land
ALC	to Seger, Jesse	May 19 [1902]	USC LB 58	sends money for land purchase
ALC	to Seger, Jesse	Sept. 6 [1902]	USC LB 82	land sale
ALC	to Seger, Jesse	May 19 [1902]	USC LB 59	re: land sale

ALC	to Seger, Jesse	Nov. 3 [1902]	USC LB 117	deed arrives; editing Seger's ms
ALC	to Seger, Jesse	June 3 [1902]	USC LB 67-8	land management expenses
TLC	to Seger, John H.	June 19	USC	re: farm management
ALC	to Seger, John H.	Jan. 20 [1902]	USC LB 32-3	re: land purchase
TLC	to Seger, John H.	Nov. 26, 1902	USC	Indian; renaming
TLC	to Seger, John H.	May 10 [1917]	USC	re: farm management
TLC	to Seger, John H.	June 25	USC	re: farm management
ALS	to Seger, John H.	April 29	USC	re: farm management
TLC	to Seger, John H.	Nov. 22	USC	re: farm management
TLC	to Seger, John H.	July 21	USC	re: farm management
ALC	to Seger, John H.	May 14 [1902]	USC LB 55	re: land purchase
ALC	to Seger, John H.	[June, 1902]	USC LB 73	re: land
TLC	to Seger, John H.	May	USC	re: farm management [incomplete]
ALC	to Seger, John H.	Sept. 22 [1902]	USC LB 83	sends money for land purchase
ALC	to Seger, John H.	May 13 [1903]	USC LB 144	wants to know status of farms
TLC	to Seger, John H.	March 29 [1917]	USC	re: farm management
ALC	to Seger, John H.	Sept. 22, 1902	USC LB 85	re: lease
TLC	to Seger, John H.	May 17	USC	re: farm management
ALC	to Seger, John H.	Dec. 28 [1901]	USC LB 27	re: land purchase
TLC	to Seger, John H.	May 9	USC	re: farm management
TLC	to Seger, John H.	June 6	USC	re: farm management
ALC	to Seger, John H.	[Feb. 14-June 1903]	USC LB 129	re: Seger's ms
ALC	to Seger, Neatha	Jan. 3 [1903]	USC LB 119	copy Seger's ms
TLS	to Seitz, Don C.	March 18, 1915	Miami U	sends Author's League application
TLC	to Selden	March 30, 1912	USC	thanks for letting father move into old house
TLC	to Selig, William N.	June 3, 1914	USC	solicits film adapt. of novels
TLC	to Seton, Ernest Thompson	May 31, 1913	USC	arranging meeting
ALD	to Seubert, E. E.	Aug. 7, 1939	USC	psychic
ALS	to Seymour, Flora	May 25, 1939	Knox	crosses; F.S.'s letter to *Time* re: rev. of book
TLS	to Seymour, Flora	Nov. 7 [1928]	Knox	pleased Bookfellows will rev. *Back-Trailers*
TLS	to Seymour, Flora	Nov. 7	Knox	
TLS	to Seymour, Flora	Oct. 30 [1922]	Knox	
TLS	to Seymour, Flora	Feb. 3 [1920]	Knox	praises *Step Ladder*
TLS	to Seymour, Flora	Oct. 13	Knox	
ALS	to Seymour, Flora	Jan. 17, 1940	Knox	crosses; exhib: "more requests than we can fill"

TLS	to Seymour, Flora	Feb. 16	Knox	
ALS	to Seymour, Flora	March 7, 1938	Knox	
TLS	to Seymour, Flora	Jan. 4 [1940]	Knox	crosses; exhib: Chicago Public Lib
TLS	to Seymour, Flora	Nov. 9, 1928	Knox	resp. to ltr. re: *Back-Trailers*; Seger
*TLS	to Seymour, Flora	Nov. 26, 1927	Knox	re: radio, reading; accepts chair advisory board
ALS	to Seymour, Flora	Jan. 21, 1937	Knox	
ALS	to Seymour, George & Flora	Oct. 23 [1929]	Knox	
TLS	to Seymour, George Steele	June 2, 1935	Knox	
TL	to Seymour, George Steele	July 20, 1935	Knox	re: *Joys of the Trail*; encl. poem
TLS	to Seymour, George Steele	Jan. 13, 1935	Knox	re: 1899 essay on "Joys"; future publ.
ALS	to Seymour, George Steele	Sept. 13 [1935]	Knox	re: *Joys of the Trail*
ApcS	to Seymour, George Steele	[Oct. 9, 1935]	Knox	
ALS	to Seymour, George Steele	Dec. 7	NYPL	
*TLS	to Seymour, George Steele	March 22, 1937	Knox	re: bio film: "most complete of man of letters"
*TLS	to Seymour, George Steele	May 22 [1938]	Knox	*Crosses*; Dutton postpones; importance of book
*TLS	to Seymour, George Steele	March 16, 1936	Knox	porno rant; drop from advisory council
*ALS	to Seymour, George Steele	Feb. 21, 1940	Knox	re: three warnings of death
ALS	to Seymour, George Steele	April 6 [1927]	Knox	
ALS	to Seymour, George Steele	July 24 [1936]	Knox	
TLS	to Seymour, George Steele	Sept. 10 [1937]	Knox	
ALS	to Seymour, George Steele	May 5 [1937]	Knox	
AnS	to Seymour, George Steele	n.d.	Knox	
ALS	to Seymour, George Steele	Feb. 25	Knox	re: possible ed. of "Silent Eaters"
ALS	to Seymour, George Steele	May 18 [1938]	Knox	*Crosses*; Dutton accepts ms
TLS	to Seymour, George Steele	Dec. 16, 1935	Knox	pleased with *Joys of the Trail*
TLS	to Seymour, George Steele	[Oct. 13, 1935]	Knox	evals. proof of *Joys of the Trail*
ALS	to Seymour, George Steele	May 16 [1936]	Knox	
ALS	to Seymour, George Steele	Oct. 11, 1935	Knox	
ALS	to Seymour, George Steele	May 25 [1936]	Knox	
TL	to Seymour, George Steele	May 10 [1932]	Knox	
AnS	to Seymour, George Steele	May 18, 1935	Knox	
TLS	to Seymour, George Steele	Feb. 7, 1935	Knox	re: *Joys of the Trail*
ALS	to Seymour, George Steele	[Dec. 23, 1934]	Knox	

TLS	to Seymour, George Steele	Feb. 19 [1927]	Knox	concert by Mary Isabel, Hardesty; encl. circular
ALS	to Seymour, George Steele	April 8, 1935	Knox	
ALS	to Seymour, George Steele	March 7, 1939	Knox	
TLS	to Seymour, George Steele	Feb. 21 [1923]	Knox	suggests advisory board for Book-fellows
ALS	to Seymour, George Steele	Nov. 7 [1922]	Knox	asks could Constance illus 2nd ed. *Pioneer*
ALS	to Seymour, George Steele	Oct. 14, 1939	Knox	
ALS	to Seymour, George Steele	Nov. 15 [1920]	Knox	
ALS	to Seymour, George Steele	[Dec. 12, 1926]	Knox	
TLS	to Seymour, George Steele	Jan. 26, 1935	Knox	re: *Joys of the Trail*
TLS	to Seymour, George Steele	Jan. 31 [1936]	Knox	
*TLS	to Seymour, George Steele	April 22, 1938	Knox	re: disposition of mss; West Salem memorial
AnS	to Seymour, George Steele	July 9 [1935]	Knox	
TLS	to Seymour, George Steele	Dec. 21, 1935	Knox	shocked at cost of *Joys of the Trail*
TLS	to Seymour, George Steele	Dec. 7, 1935	Knox	
ALS	to Seymour, George Steele	March 25 [1922]	Knox	
ALD	to Seymour, George Steele	Nov. 26, 1939	USC	c. Dec. 3, 1939 ltr—Knox
TL	to Seymour, George Steele	Aug. 4, 1936	Knox	
TL	to Seymour, George Steele	Jan. 23, 1935	Knox	re: *Joys of the Trail*
AnS	to Seymour, George Steele	n.d.	Knox	
TL	to Seymour, George Steele	Nov. 15, 1935	Knox	evals. Neihardt's "latest book"—Indian
An	to Seymour, George Steele	[ca. March 6, 1923]	Knox	
TLS	to Seymour, George Steele	Oct. 12 [1934]	Knox	
ALS	to Seymour, George Steele	May 22 [1933]	Knox	
ALS	to Seymour, George Steele	Dec. 6 [1933]	Knox	
TLS	to Seymour, George Steele	Sept. 16, 1934	Knox	
TLS	to Seymour, George Steele	May 30 [1921]	Knox	
ALS	to Seymour, George Steele	March 25, 1936	Knox	suggests advisory board
TLS	to Seymour, George Steele	March 2 [1936]	Knox	asks to have subsc. w/drawn: porno publ in *Step*
ALS	to Seymour, George Steele	March 23, 1936	Knox	
TLS	to Seymour, George Steele	Feb. 9	Knox	
ALS	to Seymour, George Steele	[June 2, 1933]	Knox	
TLS	to Seymour, George Steele	March 1 [1933]	Knox	
ApcS	to Seymour, George Steele	[Oct. 20, 1936]	Knox	
ALS	to Seymour, George Steele	April 23 [1934]	Knox	
Tpc	to Seymour, George Steele	[March 28, 1933]	Knox	

ALS	to Seymour, George Steele	March 26 [1934]	Knox	
TLS	to Seymour, George Steele	Dec. 4 [1933]	Knox	
TLS	to Seymour, George Steele	April 18 [1933]	Knox	
*TLS	to Seymour, George Steele	[Feb. 26, 1940]	Knox	re: correct d o b (Sept. 14); another "warning"
TLS	to Seymour, George Steele	June 13 [1937]	Knox	re: stolen book offered for sale to S.
TLS	to Seymour, George Steele	Jan. 7 [1931]	Knox	
ALS	to Seymour, George Steele	Feb. 5, 1940	Knox	too old, tired, for b-day parties
ALS	to Seymour, George Steele	Jan. 2 [1934]	Knox	
TLS	to Seymour, George Steele	April 3 [1936]	Knox	re: Mexico trip
ALS	to Seymour, George Steele	May 4 [1936]	Knox	
ALS	to Seymour, George Steele	Jan. 4, 1935	Knox	
ALS	to Seymour, George Steele	Feb. 16	Knox	
ALS	to Seymour, George Steele	[Jan. 22, 1940]	Knox	crosses; exhib: Chicago
TLS	to Seymour, George Steele	Oct. 29, 1934	Knox	prefers Harper ed. of *Rose* for rpt.
TLS	to Seymour, George Steele	June 28, 1937	Knox	bio film; crosses
ALS	to Seymour, George Steele	Oct. 29 [1937]	Knox	
ALS	to Seymour, George Steele	[April 29, 1937]	Knox	rev of Eisenschiml, *Why Was Lincoln Murdered?*
ApcS	to Seymour, George Steele	[Aug. 25, 1937]	Knox	
ALS	to Seymour, George Steele	Sept. 5	Knox	re: location of McClintock house
ALS	to Seymour, George Steele	Aril 4, 1937	Knox	
TLS	to Seymour, George Steele	[Dec. 14, 1939]	Knox	
ALS	to Seymour, George Steele	Sept. 25, 1934	Knox	
ALS	to Seymour, George Steele	Jan. 25, 1940	Knox	crosses; exhib; Columbus; encl. args, descr
TLS	to Seymour, George Steele	Jan. 24, 1940	Knox	crosses; exhib; Chicago, Columbus; encl. args
TLS	to Seymour, George Steele	Feb. 15	Knox	accepts honary chairmanship
TLS	to Seymour, George Steele	Oct. 29 [1937]	Knox	resp. to Rhine's psychic studies
ALS	to Seymour, George Steele	Jan. 3, 1940	Knox	crosses; exhib: Chicago Public lib
TLS	to Seymour, George Steele	Dec. 6, 1934	Knox	
ALS	to Seymour, George Steele	April 26 [1938]	Knox	
ALS	to Seymour, George Steele	Oct. 5 [1932]	Knox	
ALS	to Seymour, George Steele	Jan. 10, 1940	Knox	crosses; exhib: Chicago Public lib
TLS	to Seymour, George Steele	June 13	Knox	

*TLS	to Seymour, George Steele	Dec. 3, 1939	Knox	history of early books: Barta, Arena
ALS	to Seymour, George Steele	April 25, 1938	Knox	re: Ranney, Fuller's letters; send to E. Hill
ALS	to Seymour, George Steele	April 15 [1938]	Knox	enq. re: Louise Ranney; Fuller's letters
TLS	to Seymour, George Steele	March 4 [1937]	Knox	re: bio film; exhib
ALS	to Seymour, George Steele	[Sept. 20, 1937]	Knox	crosses; req. check Nora Rager's credentials
AnS	to Seymour, George Steele	[May 16, 1938]	Knox	
ALS	to Seymour, George Steele	Sept. 7, 1938	Knox	
ALS	to Seymour, George Steele	[May 10, 1938]	Knox	
TLS	to Seymour, George Steele	July 25, 1938	Knox	re: bio film: color, voice
ALS	to Seymour, George Steele	Dec. 20, 1937	Knox	
TLS	to Seymour, George Steele	July 23 [1938]	Knox	will give Acad Blashfield address Nov. 10, 1938
ALS	to Seymour, George Steele	Nov. 11, 1936	Knox	
ALS	to Seymour, George Steele	Nov. 3 [1936]	Knox	Zulime shaken by Lorado's death
ALS	to Seymour, George Steele	Dec. 15, 1936	Knox	exhib: Harper Lib, Madison
ALS	to Seymour, George Steele	Feb. 23, 1939	Knox	
TLS	to Seymour, George Steele	[Nov. 28, 1938]	Knox	
ALS	to Seymour, George Steele	April [14, 1927]	Knox	
ALS	to Seymour, George Steele	Jan. 12, 1937	Knox	exhib
ALS	to Seymour, George Steele	Oct. 1, 1937	Knox	
TLS	to Seymour, George Steele	[May 8, 1938]	Knox	
ALS	to Seymour, George Steele	Nov. 5, 1937	Knox	
ALS	to Seymour, George Steele	[Dec. 6, 1937]	Knox	
ApcS	to Seymour, George Steele	July 8 [1938]	Knox	
ALS	to Seymour, George Steele	Feb. 21, 1938	Knox	re: depositing mss at Bookfellows
ALS	to Seymour, George Steele	Jan. 9, 1938	Knox	
ALS	to Seymour, George Steele	Oct. 1, 1938	Knox	
AL	to Seymour, George Steele	Nov. 2, 1936	Knox	in Mexico [incomplete]
TLS	to Seymour, George Steele	Jan. 26, 1937	Knox	re: bio film
ALS	to Seymour, George Steele	[March 30, 1937]	Knox	
TLS	to Seymour, George Steele	Dec. 16 [1931]	Knox	
TLS	to Seymour, George Steele	July 24 [1932]	Knox	
ApcS	to Seymour, George Steele	[May 7, 1938]	Knox	
TLS	to Seymour, George Steele	Oct. 25 [1932]	Knox	
TLS	to Seymour, George Steele	Dec. 16 [1931]	Knox	

TLS	to Seymour, George Steele	Oct. 9 [1932]	Knox	encl. photos of grandkids
TLS	to Seymour, George Steele	[March 18, 1937]	Knox	re: bio film
ALS	to Seymour, George Steele	Oct. 28 [1938]	Knox	
AL	to Seymour, George Steele	Dec. 29 [1931]	Knox	
AnS	to Seymour, George Steele	[Oct. 21, 1926]	Knox	
TLS	to Seymour, George Steele	Oct. 6 [1931]	Knox	
TLS	to Seymour, George Steele	Sept. 4 [1931]	Knox	
ALS	to Seymour, George Steele	Aug. 12 [1925]	Knox	
TLS	to Seymour, George Steele	Sept. 30 [1932]	Knox	
TLS	to Seymour, George Steele	Jan. 26 [1924]	Knox	
TLS	to Seymour, George Steele	April 13 [1924]	Knox	
ALS	to Seymour, George Steele	Oct. 18 [1932]	Knox	re: value of books
ALS	to Seymour, George Steele	Oct. [22, 1925]	Knox	
TLS	to Seymour, George Steele	Sept. 28 [1925]	Knox	
TLS	to Seymour, George Steele	Oct. 14 [1923]	Knox	
ALS	to Seymour, George Steele	Oct. 7, 1938	Knox	
ALS	to Seymour, George Steele	Sept. 22, 1939	Knox	
TLS	to Seymour, George Steele	[Oct. 8, 1939]	Knox	sends only photo of HG in evening dress
TLS	to Seymour, George Steele	Oct. 11, 1938	Knox	
TLS	to Seymour, George Steele	Oct. 8 [1938]	Knox	
ALS	to Seymour, George Steele	Oct. 13 [1938]	Knox	
ALD	to Seymour, George Steele	Monday [193-]	USC	crosses; seeks credentials of medium
TLS	to Seymour, George Steele	Jan. 19 [1920]	Knox	
TLC	to Seymour, George Steele	Aug. 14, 1937	USC	crosses; Calif. history research
TLC	to Seymour, George Steele	Oct. 10 [1921]	USC	
TL	to Seymour, George Steele	June 15 [1920]	Knox	
ALS	to Seymour, George Steele	Nov. 5 [1932]	Knox	resp. to S's "Piony" rhymes
ALS	to Seymour, George Steele	Oct. 11, 1936	Knox	exhib: Doheny, Northwestern
TLS	to Seymour, George Steele	Dec. 12 [1921]	Knox	
TL	to Seymour, George Steele	[Oct. 1, 1920]	Knox	
An	to Seymour, George Steele	[ca. Feb. 25, 1923]	Knox	
TLS	to Seymour, George Steele	March 11 [1922]	Knox	
TLS	to Seymour, George Steele	Nov. 12 [1917]	Knox	
AnS	to Seymour, George Steele	[ca. Sept. 8, 1919]	Knox	
TLS	to Seymour, George Steele	Sept. 18 [1919]	Knox	
TLS	to Seymour, George Steele	Oct. 10 [1921]	Knox	
TLS	to Seymour, George Steele	March 17 [1921]	Knox	
TLS	to Seymour, George Steele	[Oct. 17, 1938]	Knox	
*TLS	to Seymour, George Steele	Feb. 11, 1937	Knox	re: bio film, HG's hopes for
ALS	to Seymour, George Steele	Nov. 6, 1938	Knox	
ALS	to Seymour, George Steele	Oct. 21, 1939	Knox	

ALS	to Seymour, George Steele	Dec. 17, 1938	Knox	re: origin of HG's name
TLS	to Seymour, George Steele	[Feb. 19, 1939]	Knox	
TLS	to Seymour, George Steele	April 10 [1939]	Knox	
TLS	to Seymour, George Steele	[April 22, 1939]	Knox	
ALS	to Seymour, George Steele	April 11 [1927]	Knox	
ALS	to Seymour, George Steele	Dec. 6 [1922]	Knox	
ALS	to Seymour, George Steele	[Nov. 9, 1938]	Knox	
ApcS	to Seymour, George Steele	[Oct. 6, 1938]	Knox	
ALS	to Seymour, George Steele	[Nov. 8, 1938]	Knox	
TL	to Seymour, George Steele	Feb. 2 [1935]	Knox	re: *Joys of the Trail*
TLS	to Seymour, George Steele	Aug. 3 [1920]	Knox	
ALS	to Seymour, George Steele	March 30 [1932]	Knox	
ALS	to Seymour, George Steele	May 17, 1939	Knox	
TLC	to Seymour, George Steele	Dec. 14 [1935]	USC	distrib. copies of *Joy of the Trail*
TLS	to Seymour, George Steele	April 15 [1932]	Knox	
ALS	to Seymour, George Steele	Dec. 7 [1920]	Knox	
ALS	to Seymour, George Steele	Jan. 19 [1931]	Knox	
ALS	to Seymour, George Steele	April 4 [1927]	Knox	resp. to req. to issue book of verse
TLS	to Seymour, George Steele	Sept. 4, 1936	Knox	re: Emerson Hough a western writer
ALS	to Seymour, George Steele	April 29 [1933]	Knox	
TLC	to Shafer, Joseph	April 4, 1937	USC	reply to offer to hou mss—Wis HS
TLC	to Shannon, Angus Roy	March 9, 1938	Hunt	
TLC	to Shannon, Angus Roy	May 24	USC	film adapt. of *Witches Gold*
TLS	to Shaw, Albert	June 27	NYPL	wants Finley to be mayor of NYC
ALS	to Shaw, Albert	Aug. 24	NYPL	re: Roosevelt, LaFollett
ALS	to Shaw, Albert	Jan. 1	NYPL	
ALS	to Shaw, Albert	March 25	NYPL	
TLS	to Shaw, Albert	Jan. 23 [1922]	NYPL	solicits rev. of *Daughter*
TLS	to Shaw, Albert	[Jan. 13, 1902]	NYPL	
ALS	to Shaw, Albert	Dec. 12 [1928]	NYPL	
ALS	to Shaw, Albert	n.d.	NYPL	
ALS	to Shaw, Albert	Feb. 17	NYPL	
ALS	to Shaw, Albert	Aug. 10	NYPL	
TLS	to Shaw, Albert	Oct. 14, 1916	NYPL	Com Lit Art: invite 1916 exhib
TLS	to Shaw, Albert	March 1917	NYPL	Com Lit Art circular
ALS	to Shaw, Albert	March 25	NYPL	commends Thomas V Stevens' pageantry
ALS	to Shaw, Albert	Dec. 5 [1916]	NYPL	Woodcraft; Boy Scouts as ext. of arm

ALS	to Shaw, Albert	Dec. 8 [1916]	NYPL	Boy Scouts; Seton; Roosevelt
TLS	to Shaw, Albert	July 14, 1937	NYPL	complains about type size in *Lit Digest*
TLS	to Shaw, Albert	June 23, 1936	NYPL	
ALS	to Shaw, Albert	Jan. 31	NYPL	
ApcS	to Shaw, Albert	[Dec. 14, 1893]	NYPL	
TLS	to Shaw, Albert	April 16	NYPL	asks to do piece on IL gov. Frank Lowden
TLS	to Shaw, Albert	Jan. 25 [1922]	NYPL	repeats req. to rev. *Daughter*
ApcS	to Shaw, Albert	Jan. 9, 1894	NYPL	
ALS	to Shaw, Albert	[Feb. 27, 1902]	NYPL	
ALS	to Shaw, Albert	[Feb. 20, 1902]	NYPL	Mexican land
ALS	to Shaw, Albert	Jan. 26 [1929]	NYPL	thanks for rev. (of 4 vols Middle Border)
ALS	to Shaw, Albert	April 3 [1919]	NYPL	Roosevelt Mem vol: solicits poss. authors
ALS	to Shaw, Albert	April 4 [1893]	NYPL	
ALS	to Shaw, Albert	April 12, 1898	NYPL	Trans-Miss circular
ALS	to Shaw, Albert	Jan. 3, 1936	NYPL	
ALS	to Shaw, Albert	Feb. 25 [1902]	NYPL	Mexican land
ALS	to Shaw, Albert	Dec. 15 [1926]	NYPL	resigns from Town Hall Club
TLS	to Shaw, Albert	Nov. 13, 1924	NYPL	re: Town Hall Club circular
ALS	to Shaw, Albert	June 4, 1936	NYPL	re: Mary Isabel's separation
ALS	to Shaw, Albert	April 29, 1902	NYPL	Indian; suggests Grinnell as Commissioner
ALS	to Shaw, Albert	April 1 [1902]	NYPL	Indian; advocates replacing Jones
*ALS	to Shaw, Albert	[Jan. 31, 1902]	NYPL	solicits invest. in Mexican land
ALS	to Shaw, Albert	[April 5, 1902]	NYPL	Indian; new commissioner
*ALS	to Shaw, Albert	Feb. 19 [1902]	NYPL	Indian; Mexican land; "Redman"
*ALS	to Shaw, Albert	Jan. 24 [1902]	NYPL	Indian; opposed to Jones
TLC	to Shaw, Arnold	March 3, 1913	USC	
ALD	to Shaw, George Bernard	March 8 [1936]	USC	req. for meeting
ALS	to Shaw, George Bernard	March 8 [1936]	USC	req. for meeting
ApcS	to Shaw, Mary	[1891?]	USC	invite to theatre meeting
TLC	to Shearer, Thomas R.	Nov. 23, 1911	USC	
TLD	to Sheffield, [Rena Cary?]	Mon. Jan. 13 [1936?]	USC	

TLC	to Sheldon, A. E.	Dec. 6, 1913	USC	re: illegitimacy articles
TLC	to Shenk, Casper	Feb. 10, 1914	USC	
TLS	to Shepard, Edward M.	Dec. 1, 1904	Columbia	invitation to Progre and Poverty dinner
TLC	to Shepardson, Francis W.	March 3, 1913	USC	re: lectures
TLC	to Shepardson, Francis W.	n.d.	USC	
ALS	to Sherman, Philip	Aug. 8 [1922]	Brown	
TLS	to Sherman, Philip	Jan. 25 [1920]	Brown	
ALS	to Sherman, Philip	Feb. 11 [1922]	Brown	
ALS	to Sherman, Philip	March 7 [1922]	Brown	
ALS	to Sherman, Philip	March 9 [1922]	Brown	
TLS	to Sherman, Philip	Oct. 26 [1920]	Brown	
ALS	to Sherman, Philip	Feb. 1 [1922]	Brown	
*ALS	to Sherman, Philip	July 23 [1916?]	Brown	re: Crane
TLS	to Sherman, Philip	Jan. 13 [1922]	Brown	
TLS	to Sherman, Philip	Jan. 23 [1922]	Brown	
TLS	to Sherman, Philip	April 29 [1919]	Brown	describes lectures
ALS	to Sherman, Stuart Pratt	April 21 [1921]	U of Ill	Pulitzer; Main Stre
ALS	to Sherman, Stuart Pratt	May 20 [1924]	U of Ill	
ALS	to Sherman, Stuart Pratt	Dec. 23 [1925]	U of Ill	re: Greenwich Village "smut"
ALS	to Sherman, Stuart Pratt	Dec. 14 [1925]	U of Ill	HG textbook = Boy Life
ALS	to Sherman, Stuart Pratt	April 11 [1921]	U of Ill	Acad; S. nominated
ALS	to Sherman, Stuart Pratt	May 19 [1925]	U of Ill	Acad; Hergesheime
TLS	to Sherman, Stuart Pratt	Nov. 13, 1924	U of Ill	Town Hall Club circular
ALS	to Sherman, Stuart Pratt	Sept. 22 [1923]	U of Ill	
ALS	to Sherman, Stuart Pratt	Sept. 21 [1920]	U of Ill	Acad; ans. quest. re: election
TLS	to Sherman, Stuart Pratt	Dec. 2 [1925]	U of Ill	welcomes S. to Century Club
ALS	to Sherman, Stuart Pratt	April 24 [1925]	U of Ill	Acad
TLS	to Sherman, Stuart Pratt	April 14, 1921	U of Ill	Pulitzer; left cold by novels
ALS	to Sherman, Stuart Pratt	April 26 [1924]	U of Ill	
ALS	to Sherman, Stuart Pratt	Sept. 18 [1924]	U of Ill	supports S's nomina tion to Century Club
ALS	to Sherman, Stuart Pratt	Sept. 13 [1920]	U of Ill	Acad; S. nominated
TLS	to Sherman, Stuart Pratt	Nov. 5, 1917	U of Ill	Com Lit Art circula
ALS	to Sherman, Stuart Pratt	April 1 [1926]	U of Ill	Acad; re: "Book of Writers"
ALS	to Sherman, Stuart Pratt	Feb. 23 [1921]	U of Ill	Acad; welcomes S. t Acad
ALS	to Sherman, Stuart Pratt	Jan. 31 [1921]	U of Ill	Acad; election squabble
*TLS	to Sherman, Stuart Pratt	Dec. 26 [1922]	U of Ill	praises Americans

ALS	to Sherman, Stuart Pratt	July 20 [1924]	U of Ill	Acad; Hergesheimer, Robinson
ALS	to Sherman, Stuart Pratt	March 22 [1923]	U of Ill	
ALS	to Sherman, Stuart Pratt	Jan. 9 [1921]	U of Ill	Acad; election squabble
*TLS	to Sherman, Stuart Pratt	March 10 [1921]	U of Ill	Pulitzer; *Main Street*, *Lulu Bett*
*ALS	to Sherman, Stuart Pratt	Jan. 5 [1923]	U of Ill	re: Mencken
*ALS	to Sherman, Stuart Pratt	June 8 [1925]	U of Ill	Acad; re: Hergesheimer as Jew
*ALS	to Sherman, Stuart Pratt	March 16 [1921]	U of Ill	Pulitzer; evals novels
*TLS	to Sherman, Stuart Pratt	Feb. 8 [1921]	U of Ill	Pulitzer; suggested novels
*TLS	to Sherman, Stuart Pratt	Dec. 17 [1920]	U of Ill	Pulitzer; jury notification
*TLS	to Sherman, Stuart Pratt	Feb. 14 [1921]	U of Ill	Pulitzer; evals novels
TLC	to Sherry, Laura	Feb. 26, 1913	USC	Chicago Thea Soc; schedule
*ALS	to Shields, Peter J.	Dec. 10 [1917]	U Cal-Davis	resp. to praise of *Son*, MTR
AL	to Shippey, Lee	May 16 [1932;38?]	Hunt	
TLC	to Showerman, Grant	Nov. 19 [1919]	USC	
TLC	to Shubert Bros.	July 24, 1911	USC	Chicago Thea Soc; list
TLC	to Shubert, Lee	Aug. 18, 1911	USC	Chicago Thea Soc; list
TLD	to Sibley, Carroll	Dec. 24, 1939	USC	crosses; *Captain* film
TLC	to Sibley, Carroll	Dec. 24, 1939	USC	crosses; *Captain* film
TLS	to Siepert, Miss	Oct. 11, 1935	Homestead	re: LaCrosse school annual
ALC	to Sill, Louise Morgan	Jan. 3 [1903]	USC LB 120	lecture on "Red Man's Changing Heart"
ALC	to Sill, Louise Morgan	May 30 [1903]	USC LB 151	re: drama. adaptation
*ALC	to Sill, Louise Morgan	May 29 [1902]	USC LB 65-6	Indian; sign talk in *Captain*
*ALC	to Sill, Louise Morgan	May 12 [1902]	USC LB 47-52	Indian; work habits
ALC	to Sill, Louise Morgan	[March-May 1903]	USC LB 142-3	re: drama of ?
TLD	to Sills, Kenneth C. M.	Jan. 28 [1920]	USC	
ALD	to Simmons, Frank E.	Aug. 14, 1936	USC	thanks for praise of *Forty*
ALS	to Sinclair, Gregg M.	Aug. 19 [1932]	Virginia	
ALS	to Sinclair, Gregg M.	Dec. 29 [1932]	Virginia	re: Honolulu trip; Shaw
TLS	to Sinclair, Gregg M.	May 18 [1932]	Virginia	
TLS	to Sinclair, Gregg M.	Oct. 29, 1933	Virginia	
TLS	to Sinclair, Gregg M.	June 19, 1935	Virginia	
ALS	to Sinclair, Gregg M.	June 12, 1936	Virginia	
TLS	to Sinclair, Gregg M.	Oct. 13 [1932]	Virginia	

ALS	to Sinclair, Gregg M.	Sept. 13 [1935]	Virginia	
ALS	to Sinclair, Gregg M.	April 21 [1933]	Virginia	
ALS	to Sinclair, Gregg M.	Aug. 14 [1932]	Virginia	
TLS	to Sinclair, Gregg M.	Feb. 2 [1933]	Virginia	
TLS	to Sinclair, Gregg M.	Oct. 5 [1932]	Virginia	
TLS	to Sinclair, Upton	April 4, 1939	Indiana U	psychic query
TLS	to Sinclair, Upton	May 7 [1927]	Indiana U	"My fighting days are over"
*ALS	to Sinclair, Upton	March 14 [1911]	Indiana U	evals *Love's Pilgrimage*
TLS	to Sinclair, Upton	April 7, 1939	Indiana U	psychic; exchanges books; crosses
ALS	to Siverson, Hilding	Oct. 29, 1935	USC	thanks for rev.
TLC	to Skiff, Frederick J. V.	Dec. 23, 1912	USC	
ALS	to Skiff, Frederick W.	Nov. 3	U Texas	check is too much for unspec. books
ALD	to Slaten, Arthur W.	Feb. 25, 1940	USC	
ALC	to Slayton	Feb. 7 [1903]	USC LB 124	
ALC	to Slayton	Oct. 29 [1902]	USC LB 111	re: lecture contracts
ALC	to Slayton	Nov. 24 [1903]	USC LB 177	quits business
ALC	to Slayton Lecture Bureau	March 13 [1902]	USC LB 40	doesn't like circular
ALD	to Sloane, William M.	July 7	USC	Acad
TLC	to Sloane, William M.	n.d.	USC	
TLC	to Sloane, William M.	Dec. 20, 1911	USC	
TLD	to Sloane, William M.	Sept. 28	USC	Acad; slogan
TLC	to Sloane, William M.	Oct. 26, 1911	USC	
TLC	to Sloane, William M.	Oct. 4, 1921	Columbia	Acad; bldg ceremony plans
*TLC	to Sloane, William M.	Oct. 7 [1923]	USC	Acad; resp. to reques to stay away
ALS	to Sloane, William M.	Sept. 15 [1921]	Am Acad	suggests Acad admir Pulitzer prizes
*TLC	to Sloane, William M.	Sept. 26 [1923]	USC	Acad; resp. to reques to stay away
*TLC	to Sloane, William M.	Sept. 23 [1923]	USC	Acad; E. A. Robinsor
TLC	to Small, Albion W.	June 12, 1912	USC	
TLS	to Smith, Albert E.	March 20 [1920]	Miami U	cancellation of Vitagraph contract
ALS	to Smith, Albert E.	Oct. 8 [1920]	Miami U	re: release from Vitagraph contract
TLC	to Smith, Albert E.	[1920]	USC	Vitagraph contract
TLC	to Smith, Arthur P.	Nov. 10, 1911	USC	
ALS	to Smith, Francis Hopkinson		Oct. 30 [1902]	Miami U	congrats on *Fortunes of Oliver Horn*
TLC	to Smith, Henry J.	May 22, 1912	USC	
TLC	to Smith, Mrs. E. E.	April 11, 1937	USC	
ALD	to Smith, Paul Jordan	Sunday [1934?]	USC	thanks for praise of *Afternoon*

ALD	to Spaeth, [John D. E.?]	April 4 [1928]	USC	Acad; good diction
TLS	to Spafford, J. H.	March 23, 1925	Duke	Town Hall Club: admissions circular
TLD	to Spargo, John	Dec. 20, 1920	USC	refuses to sign Jewish "protest"
TLS	to Spargo, John	Dec. 23 [1920]	U Vermont	refuses to sign Jewish "protest"
ALS	to Spaulding, William A.	May 1, 1937	Hunt	
TLC	to Spoor, George K.	June 5, 1914	USC	won't trouble S. with interview
TLS	to Spotts,	May 6, 1938	Hunt	
TLC	to Stahl, John M.	Oct. 2, 1914	USC	
TLC	to Stahl, John M.	Oct. 12 [1926]	USC	declines invitation to speak
TLC	to Starr, Hermann	Aug. 5, 1925	USC	film; *Cavanagh*
TLC	to State Board of Assessors, NY	Aug. 23, 1939	Hunt	
ALS	to Stedman, Arthur	Feb. 21, 1894	Columbia	send out Miller article ("An American Tolstoi")
ALS	to Stedman, Arthur	July 5, 1894	Columbia	re: J. Miller article, Mosinee series
ALS	to Stedman, Arthur	Aug. 16, 1894	Columbia	returned from Colo; at work on unspec. article
ALS	to Stedman, Arthur	April 21, 1894	Columbia	sorry synd. sent no proof for stories
ALS	to Stedman, Arthur	n.d.	Columbia	re: serial of "sketches of prairie life"
ALS	to Stedman, Arthur	May 9, 1894	Columbia	give up synd. effort; return mss
ALS	to Stedman, Arthur	May 7, 1894	Columbia	recommends ms by Forrest Crissey
ApcS	to Stedman, Arthur	Jan. 24, 1894	Columbia	arranging meeting
ALS	to Stedman, Arthur	n.d.	Columbia	re: "ominous silence"; serial
ALS	to Stedman, Arthur	Jan. 29, 1894	Columbia	re: Bacheller synd. of logging stories
ALS	to Stedman, Arthur	Jan. 11, 1894	Columbia	wants to meet
ALS	to Stedman, Arthur	March 26, 1895	Columbia	enq. re: stories
ALS	to Stedman, Arthur	April 2, 1894	Columbia	re: synd. of Mosinee, Lumberjack, Only Blackman
ALS	to Stedman, Arthur	Feb. 14, 1894	Columbia	will write to Joaquin Miller for photos
ALS	to Stedman, Arthur	April 18, 1894	Columbia	sends Mosinee, Lumberjack, Woman in Camp

ALS	to Stedman, Arthur	Feb. 10, 1894	Columbia	re: Bach. synd: J. Miller interv, "Q of Caste"
ALS	to Stedman, Arthur	Sept. 3, 1894	Columbia	re: "Woman in the Camp"
ALS	to Stedman, Arthur	April 17, 1894	Yale	Only Blackman, Mosinee, Lumberjack, Woman
ALS	to Stedman, Arthur	March 21, 1895	Columbia	descibes remodeling homestead
ALS	to Stedman, Arthur	Dec. 7, 1894	Columbia	enq. re: status of stories, Crane
ALS	to Stedman, Arthur	Jan. 19, [1908]	Columbia	re: death of EC Stedman
AcS	to Stedman, Edmund C.	n.d.	Columbia	xmas card
ALS	to Stedman, Edmund C.	June 21, 1900	Columbia	re: Brett's permission for anthology
ALS	to Stedman, Edmund C.	May 9, 1900	Columbia	re: rights to HG's verse
ALS	to Stedman, Edmund C.	Sept. 14, 1900	Columbia	returns from western trip; Macmillan enquiry
ALS	to Stedman, Edmund C.	June 8, 1900	Columbia	re: rpt HG's verse
ALS	to Stedman, Edmund C.	July 3, 1900	Columbia	re: Brett, permission, HG's frustration
ALS	to Stedman, Edmund C.	May 20, 1900	Columbia	Macmillan won't release verse
ALS	to Stedman, Edmund C. [?]	Oct. 24, 1897	Columbia	asks if S. supports H. George campaign
ALS	to Stedman, Edmund C.	June 3 [1900]	Columbia	Macmillan now agrees to release verse
ALS	to Stedman, Edmund C.	June 12, 1900	Columbia	re: rpt HG's verse
ALS	to Stedman, Edmund C.	Jan. 8, 1902	Columbia	arranging meeting
ALS	to Stedman, Edmund C.	Sept. 15, 1900	Columbia	HG controls all rpt rights; at work on *Boy Life*
ALS	to Stedman, Edmund C.	Thurs	Columbia	enq. about S's health
ALS	to Stedman, Edmund C.	Nov. 24, [1905]	Columbia	MacDowell Club; M's failing health
ALS	to Stedman, Edmund C.	[Nov. 19, 1905]	Columbia	establishes MacDowell Club
ALS	to Stedman, Edmund C.	Sept. 26, 1889	Columbia	thanks for explaining situation
*ALS	to Stedman, Edmund C.	Feb. 5, 1894	Columbia	re: *Songs*, future work, ambition, preaching
*ALS	to Stedman, Edmund C.	Sept. 23, 1889	Penn HS	re: ambitions; sumbits mss

*ALS	to Stedman, Edmund C.	Nov. 2, [1903]	Columbia	re: publication of Booth letters
ALS	to Stedman, Edmund C.	April 18, 1903	Columbia	Zulime expecting birth of Mary Isabel
ALS	to Stedman, Edmund C.	[March 1906]	Columbia	MacDowell Club
TLS	to Stedman, Edmund C.	Dec. 1, 1904	Columbia	invitation to Progress and Poverty dinner
*ALS	to Stedman, Edmund C.	Dec. 22, 1885	Columbia	re: Burleigh; begs pardon for troubling S.
*ALS	to Stedman, Edmund C.	Dec. 16, 1885	Columbia	Burleigh introd; poetry disc
ALS	to Stedman, Edmund C.	March 1, 1907	Columbia	
*ALS	to Stedman, Edmund C.	Nov. 7 [1903]	Columbia	explains Booth letter controversy
TLS	to Stedman, Edmund C.	April 12, 1898	Columbia	Trans-Miss circular
ALS	to Stedman, Mrs. Edmund C.	[Jan. 7, 1900]	Columbia	unable to go to Bronxville
TLC	to Steed, Wickham	Feb. 16	Miami U	commends Steed's book
ALC	to Steffens, Lincoln	May 29 [1902]	USC LB 64	re: progress of HG's work
ALS	to Steffens, Lincoln	Sept. 10	Columbia	eager to read autobio.
ALD	to Steinbach, Reuben	[1931]	USC	re: dictionaries
TLC	to Stephens, Alice B.	n.d.	USC	re: illus. for *Son*
TLC	to Stephens, Alice B.	[April 1917]	USC	re: illus. for *Son*
ALS	to Stern, J. L	Dec. 22 [1904]	NYPL	re: Poverty and Progress dinner
ALS	to Sterner	Feb. 11	U Penn	sends autograph
TLC	to Stewart, Charles D.	May 8, 1912	USC	
ALS	to Stimson, John Ward	n.d.	Columbia	arranging meeting
ALS	to Stimson, John Ward	May 15, 1894	Columbia	sends Art pamphlet
ALS	to Stoddard, Charles W.	March 10, 1897	NYPL	encl. letter of introd. by Howells
ALS	to Stoddard, Charles W.	Thurs	Virginia	arranging meeting
ALS	to Stoddard, Charles W.	Jan. 4, 1898	NYU	arranging meeting
ALS	to Stoddard, Charles W.	Dec. 23	Morgan	arranging meeting
ALS	to Stoddart, Joseph M.	Aug. 17, 1892	Virginia	re: serial of "Love or Law"
ALS	to Stoddart, Joseph M.	July 20, 1894	Wis HS	wishes success for *New Science Review*
ALS	to Stoddart, Joseph M.	June 27, 1892	Harvard	re: serial, book rights
ALS	to Stoddart, Joseph M.	Jan. 25, 1895	Wis HS	re: prospectus of Trans-Atlantic Pub. Co.
ALS	to Stoddart, Joseph M.	Feb. 3, 1895	NYU	re: serials: where appear?
TLS	to Stokes, James G. P.	Jan. 20, 1905	Columbia	Progress and Poverty dinner committee

TLS	to Stokes, James G. P.	Dec. 1, 1904	Columbia	Progress and Poverty dinner invitation
TnS	to Stolper, B. J.	[March 1, 1933]	Columbia	re: dating *Maggie*
ApcS	to Stone and Kimball	1897	Virginia	
ApcS	to Stone, Herbert S.	Oct. 16 [1893]	Miami U	re: book design
ApcS	to Stone, Herbert S.	[Oct. 1895]	Miami U	arranging meeting
ApcS	to Stone, Herbert S.	[Oct. 7, 1895]	Miami U	
ApcS	to Stone, Herbert S.	[1895]	Miami U	forwarding mail
ALS	to Stone, Herbert S.	[Oct. 1893]	Miami U	re: Carpenter and *Songs*
ALS	to Stone, Herbert S.	Oct. 8, 1893	Miami U	HG revised Miller's book; wants name kept secret
ALS	to Stone, Herbert S.	Jan. 27, 1894	UNC-CH	arranges meet w/ Howells, Herne, Stedman
ALS	to Stone, Herbert S.	Feb. 23, 1894	U of Ill	re: *Idols* proof
ALS	to Stone, Herbert S.	n.d.	Yale	reissue *Folks* after *Idols*
ApcS	to Stone, Herbert S.	March 17, 1896	Virginia	
ApcS	to Stone, Herbert S.	April 28	Yale	
ALS	to Stone, Herbert S.	n.d.	Newberry	price is too low for unspec. story
ALS	to Stone, Herbert S.	June 10, 1894	U of Iowa	regrest unable to meet
ALS	to Stone, Herbert S.	Jan. 26, 1894	NYPL	re: *Idols*; rev. of *Songs*
ApcS	to Stone, Herbert S.	Feb. 16, 1894	U of Ill	
ALS	to Stone, Herbert S.	March 20, 1894	Yale	*Folks*; advertising of *Idols*
ALS	to Stone, Herbert S.	July 30, 1894	Homestead	re: advertising circular
ALS	to Stone, Herbert S.	[Dec. 16, 1893]	USC	dissatis w/ Stone [1st leaf of Newberry/ Yale ltr]
ALS	to Stone, Herbert S.	Jan. 4 [1894]	U of Iowa	illus. of *Folks*
ALS	to Stone, Herbert S.	Jan. 22, 1894	U of Ill	sends *Idols* ms; design inc; rec. Kemeys; wants *Idols* reviews
ALS	to Stone, Herbert S.	[Aug. 15, 1894?]	U of Iowa	
ALS	to Stone, Herbert S.	Feb. 9, 1894	U of Ill	corrects proof of *Idols*
ApcS	to Stone, Herbert S.	[Feb. 1894]	U of Ill	*Idols*; proof carefully
ALS	to Stone, Herbert S.	n.d.	USC	likes prospectus [photstat of New- berry ltr]
ApcS	to Stone, Herbert S.	[Oct.]	Newberry	
ALS	to Stone, Herbert S.	n.d.	Newberry	re: "Straddlebug," "Tregurtha"; "Preacher"
ALS	to Stone, Herbert S.	Feb. 11, 1895	Newberry	resigns from Attic Club
ApcS	to Stone, Herbert S.	[July 25, 1894]	U of Ill	

ALS	to Stone, Herbert S.	n.d.	Newberry	likes prospectus
ALS	to Stone, Herbert S.	n.d.	Yale	premature to use Howells introd.
ALS	to Stone, Herbert S.	Jan. 25 [1894]	NYU	*Idols*; Carpenter's illus.
ApcS	to Stone, Herbert S.	Nov. 8, 1899	Yale	
ALS	to Stone, Herbert S.	n.d.	Newberry	
*ALS	to Stone, Herbert S.	Jan. 26, 1895	U of Iowa	angry dispute over payment
ALS	to Stone, Herbert S.	Feb. 10 [1894]	Duke	req. employment for Carpenter
*ALS	to Stone, Herbert S.	Jan. 16, 1894	U of Ill	publ. arrangements for works
ALS	to Stone, Herbert S.	Dec. 19, 1893	Yale	re: *Folks* advert.
*ALS	to Stone, Herbert S.	[ca. March 1894?]	U of Ill	*Idols* design; no more controv. work
*ALS	to Stone, Herbert S.	Dec. 16, 1893	Newberry/Yale	disapp. w/ firm; w/holds *Idols*
*ALS	to Stone, Herbert S.	Jan. 3, 1894	Yale	*Folks*; more effort in selling needed
*ALS	to Stone, Herbert S.	Jan. 18, 1894	U of Ill	*Idols*; future plans
ALD	to Stone, Melville E.	Nov. 19 [1918]	USC	Q. Roosevelt memorial
TLC	to Stone, Melville E.	Nov. 19 [1918]	USC	Q. Roosevelt memorial
TLC	to Stone, Melville E.	Nov. 21 [1918]	USC	Q. Roosevelt memorial
ALS	to Stone, Melville E.	Feb. 13, 1894	U of Ill	re: employment of Carpenter
ALS	to Stone, Melville E.	Sept. 18, 1894	Newberry	discouraged w/ sales
ALS	to Stone, Melville E.	March 5, 1893	Newberry	wants to discuss publ. of work
AnS	to Strandvold, George	[Oct. 25, 1923]	Miami U	reply to req. to buy scand. story
TLS	to Stratton	Sept. 21 [1929]	Bancroft	re: school ed. of *MTR*
TLC	to Street, Julian	Feb. 16	Miami U	
ALS	to Street, Julian	March 15 [1919]	Princeton	Roosevelt Mem meeting
ALS	to Street, Julian	Oct. 17 [1919]	Princeton	re: Roosevelt Mem
TLS	to Street, Julian	Sept. 17	Princeton	Institute; nomination of Roberts
TLS	to Street, Julian	Sept. 22	Princeton	
TLS	to Street, Julian	April 22 [1919]	Princeton	Roosevelt Mem vol
ALS	to Street, Julian	Nov. 11	Princeton	
ALS	to Street, Julian	March 26 [1919]	Princeton	Roosevelt Mem vol: solicits stories
TLS	to Street, Julian	April 18 [1919]	Princeton	Roosevelt Mem vol: problems
ALS	to Street, Julian	April 12 [1929]	Princeton	

TLC	to Street, Julian	June 30	USC	
TLC	to Strong, Edward	Oct. 6, 1913	USC	
ALS	to Stuff	May 3	U of Iowa	will be glad to "write on slips"
ALS	to Stuhlman	Jan. 17, 1899	Virginia	re: purpose of his work
TLC	to Sturgess, F. W.	March 13, 1913	USC	
ALC	to Sturgis, Miss	Sept. 27, 1902	USC LB 88	re: lectures
TLC	to Sullivan, Mark	n.d.	Miami U	HG reads galleys of a Sullivan book
TLC	to Sullivan, Mark	Jan. 31 [1917]	USC	re: *Son*
TLC	to Sullivan, Mark	Jan. 3	USC	re: logbooks [incomplete]
ALC	to Sunthorpe	Jan. 10 [1902]	USC LB 29	sale of "River's Warning"
TLC	to Sutton, Vida R.	n.d.	Hunt	
TLC	to Sutton, Vida R.	Aug. 11 [1930]	USC	re: deed for Camp Neshonoc
TLD	to Sutton, Vida R.	June 9, 1930	USC	re: deed for Camp Neshonoc
TLC	to Swann, T. W.	Dec. 30, 1911	USC	
ALS	to Swift, Ivan	Dec. 5 [1912]	Knox	appreciation of S' verses
TLC	to Symonds, Gardner	Nov. 9, 1914	USC	
ALS	to Taft, Lorado	March 9, 1897	USC	
ALS	to Taft, Lorado	n.d.	USC	
ALS	to Taft, Lorado	Tue.	USC	
TL	to Taft, Lorado	Jan. 12	USC	sculpture museum
ALS	to Taft, Lorado	Dec. 27	USC	
ALS	to Taft, Lorado	Sept. 21 [1921]	USC	
ALS	to Taft, Lorado	Dec. 16, 1897	USC	
ALS	to Taft, Lorado	Sat. 25, 1900	USC	
TL	to Taft, Lorado	Oct. 28 [1932]	USC	
TLS	to Taft, Lorado	Aug. 24	USC	
TLC	to Taft, Lorado	Aug. 4	USC	
ALS	to Taft, Lorado	Nov. 6, 1896	USC	
TL	to Taft, Lorado	Sept. 16, 1935	USC	
TL	to Taft, Lorado	Sat.	USC	
ALS	to Taft, Lorado	May 14	USC	
TL	to Taft, Lorado	Mon. 25	USC	
ALS	to Taft, Lorado	Aug. 8	USC	
ALS	to Taft, Lorado	July 1 [1934]	USC	
TLS	to Taft, Lorado	Saturday	USC	
TLC	to Taft, Lorado	Feb. 18	USC	
TL	to Taft, Lorado	March 27 [1933]	USC	
ALS	to Taft, Lorado	March 9	USC	
TLS	to Taft, Lorado	May 24 [1920-1]	USC	
ALS	to Taft, Lorado	n.d.	USC	
TL	to Taft, Lorado	April 4	USC	

TL	to Taft, Lorado	Oct. 31	USC	
TLS	to Taft, Lorado	July 28	USC	Acad; req. for materials
TLS	to Taft, Lorado	Aug. 3	USC	
ALS	to Taft, Lorado	n.d.	USC	sculpture museum
TL	to Taft, Lorado	May 25	USC	Acad
ALS	to Taft, Lorado	Oct. 6, 1896	USC	re: introd to Barrie
*ALS	to Taft, Lorado	Oct. 9 [1912]	USC	re: Homestead fire
TLS	to Taft, Lorado	Sept. 21 [1934]	USC	
TL	to Taft, Lorado	Aug. 17 [1920?]	USC	
TL	to Taft, Lorado	Dec. 14	USC	Acad; req. for lecture
TLS	to Taft, Lorado	Jan. 12 [1933]	USC	
ALS	to Taft, Lorado	April 14	USC	
TLS	to Taft, Lorado	Nov. 6	USC	
ALS	to Taft, Lorado	Thur.	USC	
ALS	to Taft, Lorado	May 25	USC	
TL	to Taft, Lorado	Sun.	USC	sculpture museum
ALS	to Taft, Lorado	Sat.	USC	
TL	to Taft, Lorado	Tue. 22	USC	
TL	to Taft, Lorado	Jan. 8	USC	Acad; sculpture speaker
TL	to Taft, Lorado	Friday	USC	
ALS	to Taft, Lorado	Nov. 15, 1897	USC	
TL	to Taft, Lorado	May 18	USC	
TL	to Taft, Lorado	June 22 [1934]	USC	
ALS	to Taft, Lorado	Dec. 23	USC	
ALS	to Taft, Lorado	[Sept. 5, 1901]	USC	
ALS	to Taft, Lorado	Sat.	USC	
TLS	to Taft, Lorado	Aug. 5	USC	
ALS	to Taft, Lorado	Aug. 27	USC	
TL	to Taft, Lorado	Sept. 11, 1934	USC	
ALS	to Taft, Lorado	Feb. 9, 1898	USC	
ALS	to Taft, Lorado	June 7 [1934]	USC	
TLC	to Taft, Lorado	April 21, 1921	USC	Acad; req. for sculpture
TL	to Taft, Lorado	Oct. 3	USC	
TLS	to Taft, Lorado	March 18, 1922	USC	Mary Isabel to appear in lecture: 1st time
ALS	to Taft, Lorado	July 11	USC	
ALS	to Taft, Lorado	Jan. 9 [1930-1]	USC	
ApcS	to Taft, Lorado	July 9, 1934	USC	
TLS	to Taft, Lorado	Dec. 25	USC	Acad; req. sculpture; lecture
TpcS	to Taft, Lorado	Aug. 23, 1934	USC	
TL	to Taft, Lorado	July 2	USC	
ALS	to Taft, Lorado	April 30 [1933-4]	USC	
ALS	to Taft, Lorado	Jan. 28 [1933-4]	USC	
ALS	to Taft, Lorado	Dec. 8	Hunt	

TL	to Taft, Lorado	Sun. 25	USC	
TL	to Taft, Lorado	Oct. 8	USC	
TLS	to Taft, Lorado	Sept. 12, 1921	USC	
ALS	to Taft, Lorado	Oct. 3	USC	
ALS	to Taft, Lorado	Thur.	USC	
ALS	to Taft, Lorado	Sept. 5, 1901	USC	
TL	to Taft, Lorado	July 19	USC	
TL	to Taft, Lorado	n.d.	USC	
ALS	to Taft, Lorado	May 20	USC	
ALS	to Taft, Lorado	Jan. 7	USC	
ALS	to Taft, Lorado	Nov. 28	USC	re: logbooks
TL	to Taft, Lorado	June 24, 1936	USC	
TLS	to Taft, Lorado	Sept. 27, 1921	USC	Acad; Taft appointed to committee
TLC	to Taft, Lorado	April 8, 1914	USC	
ALS	to Taft, Lorado	Thurs. [1901]	USC	
ALS	to Taft, Lorado	Dec. 18	USC	
ALS	to Taft, Lorado	Nov. 29	USC	
ALS	to Taft, Lorado	Oct. 14	USC	
ALS	to Taft, Lorado	April 9	USC	
ALS	to Taft, Lorado	Jan. 30	USC	
TLS	to Taft, Lorado	May 8, 1921	USC	
ALS	to Taft, Lorado	Oct. 22	USC	
TLS	to Taft, Lorado	Aug. 4	USC	
ALS	to Taft, Lorado	March 17	Hunt	re: Kemeys
ALS	to Taft, Lorado	April 22 [1919?]	Hunt	re: HG's health
ALS	to Taft, Lorado	May 2 [1919?]	Hunt	re: HG's health
TL	to Taft, Lorado	June 22 [1919?]	Hunt	re: visit
ALS	to Taft, Lorado	[June 23, 1922]	Hunt	re: London visit
ALS	to Taft, Lorado	May 12	Hunt	re: Quandrangle Club; Fuller
ALS	to Taft, Lorado	May 24	Hunt	re: Quandrangle Club; Fuller
TLC	to Taft, Lorado	Nov. 14 [1933]	Hunt	re: Arts lunch
TLD	to Taft, Lorado	Nov. 14 [1933]	Hunt	re: Arts lunch
TLS	to Taft, Lorado	April 5 [1937]	Hunt	re: inscription
ans	to Taft, Lorado	Nov. 13	Hunt	re: unspec. "blast"
TL	to Taft, Lorado	Dec. 16	Hunt	re: England trip
TL	to Taft, Lorado	n.d.	Hunt	re: lighting caverns
ALS	to Taft, Lorado	n.d.	Hunt	re: Taft address at Academy
TL	to Taft, Lorado	Aug. 18 [1930]	Hunt	re: Fuller's death and letters
*ALS	to Taft, Lorado	Nov. 15, 1899	USC	re: 1st impression of Zulime's parents
TL	to Taft, Lorado	April 13	USC	
*TL	to Taft, Lorado	May 2 [1919]	USC	HG as platform humorist
*ALS	to Taft, Lorado	Aug. 14 [1929]	Hunt	re: Fuller's death

ALD	to Tait, John Leisk	July 9 [1933]	USC	
TLS	to Tarbell, Ida	Oct. 11, 1916	Allegheny	Com Lit Art: committee org.
ALS	to Tarbell, Ida	Jan. 3, 1936	Allegheny	thanks for New Year wishes
ALS	to Tarbell, Ida	Dec. [1937]	Allegheny	b-day greeting
ALS	to Tarkington, Booth	June 29, 1936	Colby	psychic; "Red Barn"; Judahs
ALS	to Tarkington, Booth	March 5, 1937	Colby	re: "Rumbin"
ALS	to Tarkington, Booth	Oct. 29, 1939	Colby	crosses; exhib; reviews are good
TLC	to Taussig, Charlotte	April 23, 1914	USC	
TLC	to Taussig, Charlotte	May 28, 1914	USC	
ALS	to Tavern Club, Board of Directors	Feb. 5, 1910	USC	
TLC	to Taylor, Alfred Reece	Aug. 6, 1939	Hunt	
TLC	to Taylor, Alfred Reece	May 29, 1938	USC	re: sale of property
TLC	to Taylor, Alfred Reece	May 29, 1930	Hunt	
TLC	to Taylor, Alfred Reece	n.d.	USC	re: sale of property
ALS	to Tewson, William Orton	Dec. 1 [1928?]	Virginia	thanks for praise of *Back-Trailers*
TLD	to Thayer, Stephen Henry	Jan. 8, 1913	USC	re: Authors Club members
TLS	to Thayer, William R.	April 23, 1921	Harvard	Acad; solicits memorabilia
ALS	to Thayer, William R.	May 24	Harvard	thanks for voting Pulitzer to *Daughter*
TLS	to Thayer, William R.	March 1917	Harvard	Com Lit Art circular
ALS	to Thayer, William R.	Nov. 22 [1919?]	Harvard	re: lectures; circular encl.
ALS	to Thayer, William R.	n.d.	Harvard	Acad; nominations
TLS	to Thayer, William R.	Sept. 1, 1919	Harvard	Com Lit Art; guest of honor invitation
TLS	to Thayer, William R.	Feb. 6, 1919	Harvard	Roosevelt mem vol circular
ALS	to Thayer, William R.	July 6, 1919	Harvard	Roosevelt Mem vol; thanks for anecdote
*ALS	to Thayer, William R.	Nov. 26 [1919]	Harvard	Roosevelt; re: T's book; HG's R article
ALS	to Thayer, William R.	April 4	Knox	thanks for praise of *Daughter*
TLS	to Thayer, William R.	June 8, 1921	Harvard	Acad; re: memorabilia
ALS	to Thayer, William R.	n.d.	Harvard	Acad
TLS	to The German National Bank	June 5, 1917	USC	
TLC	to Thoburn, Joseph B.	May 3 [1924]	USC	
TLD	to Thomas, Abel Cary	Sunday [1925]	USC	re: film adapt
TLC	to Thomas, Abel Cary	n.d.	USC	re: film adapt

ALS	to Thomas, Augustus	Sunday 19	Miami U	re: formation of MacDowell Club
ALS	to Thomas, Augustus	May 28	Miami U	
ALS	to Thomas, Augustus	March 4 [1923]	Miami U	re: T's aid w/ Mary Isabel's acting career
TLC	to Thomas, Augustus	May 28, 1914	USC	
TLC	to Thomas, Augustus	n.d.	USC	
TLC	to Thomas, Augustus	March 2 [1923]	USC	req. for agent for Mary Isabel
TLS	to Thomas, Augustus	Dec. 4, 1911	Miami U	New Theater; bad perf. of T's play
TLC	to Thomas, Augustus	April 10, 1912	USC	
TLC	to Thomas, Augustus	March 25 [1923]	USC	re: Mary Isabel's acting
ALS	to Thomas, Augustus	Oct. 5, 1897	Miami U	re: *Horse Doctor*
ALS	to Thomas, Augustus	June 12	USC	Chicago Thea Soc; list
ALS	to Thomas, Augustus	n.d.	Miami U	Institute; death of Warner
ALS	to Thomas, Augustus	Saturday	Miami U	letter of introd.
TLC	to Thomas, Augustus	Dec. 4, 1911	USC	New Theatre: bad perf. of T's play
TLC	to Thomas, Augustus	March 11, 1914	USC	re: Howells's scene for unspec. program
TLC	to Thomas, Augustus	April 8, 1914	USC	asks about film prospects
*ALS	to Thomas, Augustus	Aug. 29, 1899	Miami U	re: mss of "Miller of Boscobel"; Institute
ALS	to Thomas, Augustus	March 30	Miami U	Institute
ALS	to Thomas, Augustus	Monday 13	Miami U	Institute; suggestions for speech
TLC	to Thomas, Augustus	Sept. 15, 1914	USC	
ALS	to Thomas, Augustus	Nov. 23	Miami U	congrats for *Witching Hour*
TLC	to Thomas, Augustus	June 3, 1914	USC	
*ALS	to Thomas, Augustus	April 23, 1897	Miami U	apprec. *Hoosier Doctor*
TLC	to Thomas, Augustus	Nov. 8, 1911	USC	Chicago Thea Soc; req. for plays
ALS	to Thomas, Augustus	Dec. 30, 1909	Miami U	Institute; "Miller of Boscobel"
ALS	to Thomas, Lisle Colby	Dec. 1	Miami U	Institute
ALS	to Thomas, Lisle Colby	[Aug.] 12, 1934	UNC-CH	condolences upon death of Augustus
ALC	to Thompson	May 18 [1903]	USC LB 146	
ALS	to Thompson, Laurence	Feb. 21, 1940	Princeton	exhib; crosses exhib
TLS	to Thompson, Ralph	Aug. 7, 1939	NYPL	crosses; disagrees w/ rev in *NYT Book Rev*
TLC	to Thompson, [William B.?]	May 8	USC	

TLD	to Thoms, Frank	June 1 [1930?]	USC	re: sale of rare books
TLC	to Thorndike, Ashley	March 25 [1917]	USC	Acad; nominations
TLS	to Thorndike, Ashley	Jan. 20, [1922-3]	Columbia	re: after dinner speech
*TLS	to Thorndike, Ashley	March 29, 1917	Am Acad	Institute; nominates Wilkins, Wharton, Deland
TLS	to Thorndike, Ashley	Oct. 24	Columbia	re: contributions to "volume"
TLS	to Thorndike, Ashley	Oct. 19, [1917]	Am Acad	Institute; re: nominations
TLC	to Thorpe, James R.	Dec. 26 [1927]	USC	"Silent Eaters": most lasting work
TLS	to Tilson, Ida E.	April 20 [1926]	Homestead	re: *Trail-Makers*; family articles in *Wis St Journal*
ALS	to Tilson, Ida E.	Dec. 26	U Wis-LaCrosse	at work on *Daughter*; bought Onteora home
ALS	to Towne, Charles Hanson	Sept. 17 [1933]	NYPL	thanks for b-day greeting
ALS	to Towne, Charles Hanson	Aug. 8 [1933]	NYPL	work is nearly done
ALS	to Towne, Charles Hanson	July 22 [1933]	NYPL	thanks for unspec. review
TLC	to Townsend, James B.	Oct. 29, 1913	USC	
TLC	to Train, Arthur Cheney	March 3, 1913	USC	Authors League
TLC	to Train, Arthur Cheney	Feb. 3, 1913	USC	Authors League
TLC	to Trask, John E. D.	Jan. 13, 1913	USC	
TLC	to Trask, John E. D.	Dec. 23, 1912	USC	
ALS	to Traubel, Horace	[Dec. 9, 1897]	Congress	"Power of Henry George"
ALS	to Traubel, Horace	[Jan. 25, 1901]	Congress	comment about *Conservator*
ApcS	to Traubel, Horace	[Jan. 9, 1892]	Congress	
ALS	to Traubel, Horace	[Nov. 5, 1889]	Congress	re: banquet; single-tax
ALS	to Traubel, Horace	[Oct. 9, 1891]	Congress	praises *Conservator*
ALS	to Traubel, Horace	[Dec. 22, 1891]	Congress	hears WW is sick; rec. *Arena* article
ALS	to Traubel, Horace	Jan. 23, 1894	Congress	can't make reunion
ApcS	to Traubel, Horace	[Oct. 6, 1890]	Congress	offers single-tax lecture
ApcS	to Traubel, Horace	[Jan. 14, 1892]	Congress	
ALS	to Traubel, Horace	[May 21, 1889]	Congress	resp. to WW banquet invitation
ALS	to Traubel, Horace	Jan. 10, 1895	Congress	
ALS	to Traubel, Horace	[May 17, 1893]	Congress	
ApcS	to Traubel, Horace	[Aug. 26, 1894]	Congress	asks if T saw *Idols*
ALS	to Traubel, Horace	Aug. 15 [1912]	Congress	grants permission to publ ltrs to WW

ALS	to Traubel, Horace	Jan. 8 [1894]	Congress	revs. *In Re Walt Whitman*
ALS	to Traubel, Horace	June 28, 1894	Congress	sends Central Art leaflet; stands for "WW idea"
*ALS	to Traubel, Horace	May 24, 1901	Congress	re: WW fellowship meeting
*ALS	to Traubel, Horace	[May 24, 1891]	Congress	WW's influence bein felt
*ALS	to Traubel, Horace	Sept. 2, 1894	Congress	criticizes WW Fellowship; *Idols* under attack
*ALS	to Traubel, Horace	[July 8, 1889]	Congress	re: WW's poverty; misdirected funds
*ALS	to Traubel, Horace	Jan. 13, 1892	Congress	re: WW inscription; WW reputation is growing
ALS	to Traubel, Horace	May 28 [1902]	Congress	re: WW's influence
ALS	to Trent, William P.	Feb. 23	Columbia	re: unspec. dinner occasion at "club"
ALS	to Trent, William P.	Feb. 6	Columbia	
ALS	to Trent, William P.	Feb. 1	Columbia	
ALS	to Trent, William P.	Feb. 17	Columbia	
ALD	to Turck, Fenton B., Jr.	n.d.	USC	plans for production if Turck dies
ALD	to Turck, Fenton B., Jr.	Oct. 10 [193-]	USC	req. more cytost supply
TLD	to Turck, Fenton B.	July 5 [1927?]	USC	chides Turck for lack of focus
TLD	to Turck, Fenton B.	May 4 [1926]	USC	req. lower rate for friends
TLC	to Turck, Fenton B.	Sept. 7 [1927?]	USC	chides Turck for lack of focus
ALS	to Tweedie, Mrs.	July 1 [1924]	Bancroft	will go to "Round the World sketches"
TLC	to U.S. Forest Service	n.d.	USC	returns slides for forest ranger lectures
TLC	to U.S. Geological Service	Feb. 24, 1913	USC	re: slides for forest ranger lectures
TLD	to Ulizio, George	March 10 [1930]	USC	d. of Ohio State ltr
TLC	to Ulizio, George	June 20 [1930]	USC	d. of July 5, 1930, ltr
TLS	to Ulizio, George	April 18 [1932?]	Ohio St	
telC	to Ulizio, George	[March 1930]	USC	c. of Ohio State ltr
TLC	to Ulizio, George	[March 1930]	USC	c. of Ohio State ltr
TLS	to Ulizio, George	April 15 [1930]	Ohio St	
TLS	to Ulizio, George	July 5 [1930]	Ohio St	
tel	to Ulizio, George	[ca. March 1930]	Ohio St	
TLS	to Ulizio, George	March 22 [1930]	Ohio St	
TLS	to Ulizio, George	Dec. 26 [1929]	Ohio St	re: selling *Maggie*

TLS	to Ulizio, George	March 6, 1930	Ohio St	
TLS	to Ulizio, George	July 10 [1930]	Ohio St	
tel	to Ulizio, George	March 6, 1930	Ohio St	
ALS	to Ulizio, George	March 20 [1930]	Ohio St	
TLS	to Ulizio, George	May 10 [1930]	Ohio St	
TLS	to Ulizio, George	Nov. 21 [1930]	Ohio St	
TLS	to Ulizio, George	March 16 [1930]	Ohio St	
*TLS	to Ulizio, George	[May 25, 1930]	Ohio St	dissatisfied w/ sale of *Maggie*
*TLS	to Ulizio, George	March 10 [1930]	Ohio St	re: sale of Crane books
TLC	to Underwood, John C.	May 22, 1912	USC	
TLC	to Upham, Alfred H.	Sept. 15, 1939	Hunt	exhib at Miami U
ALS	to Van Auds	June 9	Virginia	
trL	to Van Doren, Carl	Feb. 16 [1921]	Miami U	asks for opinion of Pulitzer-worthy novel
trL	to Van Doren, Carl	May 30	Miami U	arranging meeting
trL	to Van Doren, Carl	Feb. 12, 1921	Miami U	invite to Howells Memorial meeting
trL	to Van Doren, Carl	Aug. 9 [1921]	Miami U	acquainted w/ Turck?
trL	to Van Doren, Carl	Feb. 21	Miami U	arranging meeting
trL	to Van Doren, Carl	Oct. 23	Miami U	arranging meeting
trL	to Van Doren, Carl	March 5	Miami U	
trL	to Van Doren, Carl	Nov. 18 [1921]	Miami U	has read both Van D's articles; disagrees
trL	to Van Doren, Carl	Jan 16	Miami U	not going to Bacon dinner
trL	to Van Doren, Carl	March 7	Miami U	likes *Forum* article
trL	to Van Doren, Carl	Feb. 28	Miami U	are there two Van Dorens at *Nation*?
trL	to Van Doren, Carl	March 4 [1924]	Miami U	arranging meeting
trL	to Van Doren, Carl	Oct. 27 [1928]	Miami U	will send *Trail-Makers*
trL	to Van Doren, Carl	March 26	Miami U	wants Van D. to read "Silent Eaters"
trL	to Van Doren, Carl	Nov. 22 [1924]	Miami U	welcomes Van D. to Institute
trL	to Van Doren, Carl	Oct. 29	Miami U	arranges dinner; new Middle Border book
trL	to Van Doren, Carl	March 2 [1926]	Miami U	he is no parallel to Dreiser
trL	to Van Doren, Carl	Feb. 1	Miami U	asks for names of Amer. Lit. critics
trL	to Van Doren, Carl	Dec. 3 [1921]	Miami U	notes Harpers will issue Border ed.
trL	to Van Doren, Carl	Jan 11 [1922]	Miami U	reports on revs of *Daughter*

trL	to Van Doren, Carl	March 14 [1921]	Miami U	dislikes *Main Stre*
*TLD	to Van Doren, Carl	March 2 [1926]	USC	inc; c/c w/ Dreiser and other writers
TLC	to Vanamee, Grace D.	Sat. 21	USC	exhib—Doheny
TL	to Vanamee, Grace D.	Sept. 18 [1926]	Am Acad	
TLS	to Vanamee, Grace D.	[March] 16, 1936	Am Acad	exhib; posterity
TL	to Vanamee, Grace D.	Sept. 9 [1926]	Am Acad	
TLC	to Vanamee, Grace D.	July 30	USC	Acad; suggests painting exhib.
TLS	to Vanamee, Grace D.	[March 21, 1936]	Am Acad	exhib; describes contents
TLS	to Vanamee, Grace D.	March 5, 1936	Am Acad	exhib; retrieving books for Doheny
TLS	to Vanamee, Grace D.	Feb. 1 [1937]	Am Acad	Zulime's health much improved
TLC	to Vanamee, Grace D.	n.d.	USC	c. of Jan/Feb 1940— Am Acad ltr
TLC	to Vanamee, Grace D.	March 19	USC	exhib—Doheny
ALS	to Vanamee, Grace D.	[Sept. 13, 1938]	Am Acad	revises address; crosses ms
TLS	to Vanamee, Grace D.	Feb. 23, 1938	Am Acad	wants to sell memorabilia
TL	to Vanamee, Grace D.	July 18 [1929]	Am Acad	re: *Roadside*
TLS	to Vanamee, Grace D.	Aug. 30 [1926]	Am Acad	get candidate's consent before election
TL	to Vanamee, Grace D.	[c July 15, 1929]	Am Acad	*Roadside*; good diction
TLS	to Vanamee, Grace D.	Sept. 17 [1928]	Am Acad	
TLC	to Vanamee, Grace D.	n.d.	USC	Acad; Blashfield address
TLS	to Vanamee, Grace D.	June 24 [1929]	Am Acad	re: title for *Roadsi*
ALS	to Vanamee, Grace D.	Sept. 18, 1937	Am Acad	against Lewis's nomination
ALS	to Vanamee, Grace D.	Nov. 8, 1937	Am Acad	
TLS	to Vanamee, Grace D.	Aug. 28, 1935	Am Acad	nominations; names and reasons
TLS	to Vanamee, Grace D.	Jan. 24 [1924]	Am Acad	
TLS	to Vanamee, Grace D.	[Jan/Feb 1940]	Am Acad	
TLS	to Vanamee, Grace D.	March 14, 1936	Am Acad	exhib; needs photos
TLS	to Vanamee, Grace D.	Aug. 19, 1934	Am Acad	
TLS	to Vanamee, Grace D.	[April 5, 1938]	Am Acad	Institute; porno ran distressed with members
TLS	to Vanamee, Grace D.	Sept. 1, 1938	Am Acad	sends draft of addre
TLS	to Vanamee, Grace D.	[Aug. 1920]	Am Acad	Kipling can't come
ALS	to Vanamee, Grace D.	Sept. 4 [1934]	Am Acad	
TLS	to Vanamee, Grace D.	Sept. 29, 1936	Am Acad	exhib; 5 mos successful run at Doheny

LS	to Vanamee, Grace D.	March 19 [1936]	Am Acad	exhib; photos; display
LS	to Vanamee, Grace D.	Feb. 4 [1924]	Am Acad	
LS	to Vanamee, Grace D.	Jan. 10, 1935	Am Acad	Institute; votes NO on nominations; porno rant
TLS	to Vanamee, Grace D.	Sept. 30 [1928]	Am Acad	nominations; Frost
ALS	to Vanamee, Grace D.	[ca. Sept. 4, 1926]	Am Acad	nominations: O'Neill; guard against "Lewis type"
TLS	to Vanamee, Grace D.	July 22, 1938	Am Acad	wants to do last address re: literary fashions
ALS	to Vanamee, Grace D.	Feb. 3, 1940	Am Acad	preparing for death
ALS	to Vanamee, Grace D.	Nov. 20 [1926]	Am Acad	get Huntington's opinion re: election of women
TLC	to Vanderhoof, Herbert	March 16, 1914	USC	
el	to VanVolkenberg, E. A.	Oct. 25, 1924	Harvard	re: Roosevelt
AnS	to Vesper, F. Bernard, Jr.	ca May 21, 1924	Homestead	psychic
ALS	to Von KleinSmid, Rufus B.	Nov. 8, 1936	USC	thanks for Taft sympathy message
TLS	to Von KleinSmid, Rufus B.	Sept. 6 [1936]	USC	
ALS	to Von KleinSmid, Rufus B.	April 17	USC	
ALS	to Von KleinSmid, Rufus B.	Nov. 23	USC	
TLC	to Wacker, Charles H.	March 8, 1913	USC	
ALC	to Wade	June 20 [1902]	USC LB 70	re: Richard G's health
ALC	to Wagner, Charles L.	June 24 [1902]	USC LB 75	declines lecture management
ALC	to Wagner, Charles L.	May 28 [1902]	USC LB 63	protests circular payment
ALC	to Wagner, Charles L.	Dec. 21 [1901]	USC LB 19	lecture dates
ALC	to Wagner, Charles L.	May 6 [1902]	USC LB 46	lecture outlook?
ALC	to Wagner, Charles L.	Nov. 14 [1902]	USC LB 118	
ALC	to Wagner, Charles L.	[Nov. 1-5, 1901]	USC LB 6	re: lecture management-midwest
ALC	to Wagner, Charles L.	[Nov-Dec, 1901]	USC LB 18	re: Slayton lecture management
ALC	to Wagner, Charles L.	[June-Aug, 1902]	USC LB 77	re: lectures
ALC	to Wagner, Charles L.	[Feb. 7-9, 1903]	USC LB 125	
ALS	to Wagner, Charles L.	n.d.	U Wis-Mil	re: lecture arrangements
ALS	to Wagner, Charles L.	n.d.	U Wis-Mil	
ALC	to Wagner, Charles L.	Feb. 6 [1902]	USC LB 38	re: lectures
ALC	to Wagner, Charles L.	Feb. 24, 19[1902]	USC LB 39	re: lectures
TLC	to Wagner, Franz	March 17, 1914	USC	
ALC	to Wakefield, Dr.	June 20, 1902	USC LB 71	re: Richard G's health

TLS	to Walker, Franklin	June 6 [1932?]	Bancroft	may quote from article
TLS	to Walker, Franklin	Nov. 26 [1931]	Bancroft	reply to req. for Norris info
TLS	to Walker, Franklin	July 20 [1932?]	Bancroft	grants rpt request from *Companions*
TLC	to Walker, Nellie V.	Oct. 24, 1911	USC	
TLC	to Walker, W. H.	May 31, 1913	USC	
ALS	to Wallace, Elizabeth	Nov. 8, 1895	Minn HS	$100 for 3 lectures o art
ALS	to Wallace, Elizabeth	Jan. 22, 1899	Minn HS	keep lecture prices high
ALS	to Wallace, Elizabeth	June 30 [1899?]	Minn HS	
ALS	to Wallace, Elizabeth	April 6, 1899	Minn HS	
ALS	to Wallace, Elizabeth	Jan. 26, 1895	Minn HS	re: exhib pictures
ALS	to Walls, Miss	Nov. 30 [1922]	DePauw	
TLS	to Walls, Miss	[Dec. 10, 1922]	DePauw	
TLS	to Walls, Miss	Dec. 8 [1922]	DePauw	re: lectures
ALC	to Wanchapi, S. K.	Dec. 28 [1901]	USC LB 26	re: land purchase
ALC	to Wanchapi, S. K.	Nov. 30 [1901]	USC LB 17	re: land deed
TLD	to Wann, Louis	April 10	USC	re: Julian Hawthorr —speaking tour
TLC	to Ward, [Lydia A. C.?]	July 18	USC	
ALS	to Warner, Charles Dudley	Tue.	Trinity	Institute; against Perkins as secretary
ALS	to Warner, Charles Dudley	Aug. 19, 1899	Trinity	Institute; advises delay meeting
ALS	to Warner, Charles Dudley	Sept. 7, 1897	Trinity	re: entrance into Players Club
ALS	to Warner, Charles Dudley	April 17, 1899	Trinity	Institute; HG and Thomas draft constitution
ALS	to Warner, Charles Dudley	Sun.	Trinity	arranging meeting
ALS	to Warner, Charles Dudley	Jan. 3, 1895	Trinity	wants to meet
ALS	to Warner, Charles Dudley	Jan. 20, 1900	Trinity	Institute; organization matte
ALS	to Warner, Charles Dudley	Feb. 17, 1899	Trinity	Institute; elections; constitution
ALS	to Warner, Charles Dudley	Feb. [20] 1899	Trinity	Institute; constituti (enclosed)
TLS	to Warner, Charles Dudley	April 12, 1898	Trinity	Trans-Miss circular
TLS	to Webb, Walter P.	Jan. 6	U Texas	re: lectures
ALS	to Webster, Henry K.	Dec. 8 [1911]	Newberry	Chicago Thea Soc; Robertson's eval *Jur Madness*
TLD	to Weitz, Alice C.	June 19	USC	

TLC	to Welling, J. Harry	April 3 [1917]	USC	
TLC	to Wells, Thomas B.	n.d.	USC	[incomplete]
TLC	to Wells, Thomas B.	April 2	USC	desires Harper to issue set
*ALS	to Wendell, Barrett	Dec. 12, 1891	Knox	re: praise; reform work
TLD	to Wendt, Miss	Feb. 26	USC	
ALS	to Wetmore, A.	March 24, 1937	USC	crosses
*ALS	to Wharton, Edith	July 28 [1924]	USC	thanks for visit
TLC	to Wheat, Virgina M.	Oct. 28 [1916]	USC	Authors League
TLC	to Wheeler, Edward J.	April 8, 1914	USC	re: Nat Arts Club membership
TLC	to Wheeler, Edward J.	June 8, 1912	USC	re: help in finding room for Wheeler
TLC	to Wheeler, Edward J.	March 11, 1914	USC	wants to become member of Nat Arts Club
tel	to Whigham, H.J.	Nov. 27, 1911	USC	
ALS	to Whitaker, Alma	Nov. 16, 1934	USC	
ALS	to White, Elizabeth G.	March 7 [1928]	Congress	
TLC	to White, Hervey	Dec. 23, 1912	USC	Chicago Thea Soc; declines play
TLC	to White, Hervey	Dec. 26, 1912	USC	Chicago Thea Soc; declines play
TLD	to White, Major	April 16	USC	good diction
ALD	to White, Major	Nov. 10	USC	good diction
TLS	to White, Stewart Edward	July 27	USC	crosses
TLC	to White, Stuart	March 2 [1913]	USC	
ALS	to White, William Allen	Nov. 10 [1928]	Congress	joy over Hoover's election
ALS	to White, William Allen	Aug. 25 [1929]	Congress	asks perm. to use ltr in Roadside
ALS	to White, William Allen	Oct. 10 [1932]	Congress	asks for info about Mayo clinic for Zulime
ALS	to White, William Allen	Sept. 21 [1930]	Congress	thanks for rev. of Roadside
ALS	to White, William Allen	Feb. 4 [1933]	Congress	
ALS	to White, William Allen	May 29 [1936]	Congress	
TLS	to White, William Allen	Feb. 11 [1922]	Congress	re: misplaced photos in Daughter
ALS	to White, William Allen	July 2 [1921]	Congress	Acad; book fund
TLS	to White, William Allen	Oct. 24 [1928]	Congress	
TLS	to White, William Allen	April 14 [1930]	Congress	Institute; suggest J. Hawthorne be elected
TLS	to White, William Allen	April 26 [1918]	Congress	praises W's book; world is shot in 1914
TLS	to White, William Allen	Nov. 15 [1920]	Congress	

TLS	to White, William Allen	Aug. 7, 1912	Congress	Roosevelt conventior stirs radicalism
ALS	to White, William Allen	Jan. 14 [1911]	Congress	
TLS	to White, William Allen	Oct. 25, 1910	Congress	Cliff Dwellers; purpose
ALS	to White, William Allen	Oct. 26 [1928]	Congress	praises *Masks in a Pageant*
TLS	to White, William Allen	Sept. 23 [1922]	Congress	re: W's praise; *Time* article
TLS	to White, William Allen	May 20 [1922]	Congress	*Daughter*; HG learn: of Pulitzer prize
ALS	to White, William Allen	Nov. 19 [1928]	Congress	re: Hoover—HG identifies
ALS	to White, William Allen	July 27 [1912]	Congress	Roosevelt; conventic
TLS	to White, William Allen	Feb. 24 [1918]	Congress	Institute; election of women
TLS	to White, William Allen	July 15 [1921]	Congress	Acad; thanks for boc
ALS	to White, William Allen	July 14 [1931]	Congress	
TLS	to White, William Allen	Feb. 3 [1922]	Congress	
ALS	to White, William Allen	July 18 [1930]	Congress	
TLS	to White, William Allen	March 30 [1929]	Congress	
ALS	to White, William Allen	Dec. 11 [1914]	Congress	Midland Authors Sc
ALS	to White, William Allen	July 20 [1912]	Congress	Roosevelt; abolish convention system
ALS	to White, William Allen	Feb. 10 [1933]	Congress	
TLS	to White, William Allen	Dec. 27, 1911	Congress	Institute; "western chapter"
ALS	to White, William Allen	Jan. 29 [1928]	Congress	
TLC	to White, William Allen	Dec. 27, 1911	USC	
TLS	to White, William Allen	Dec. 15 [1920]	Congress	Acad; HG now temp secretary
TLS	to White, William Allen	July 21 [1921]	Congress	Acad; re: books
TLS	to White, William Allen	Nov. 8 [1932]	Congress	thanks for rev of *Contemporaries*
*ALS	to White, William Allen	Feb. 14 [1918]	Congress	Institute; re: vote against women
ALS	to White, William Allen	March 22 [1928]	Congress	is helping with Hoover campaign
ALS	to White, William Allen	March 13 [1928]	Congress	
ALS	to White, William Allen	March 3 [1933]	Congress	
ALS	to White, [William Allen?]	Sept. 14, 1897	Virginia	re: change at Stone and Kimball
TLS	to Whiting	March 17	Virginia	Com Lit Art circular
TLC	to Whitlock, Brand	March 22	Miami U	missed meeting
TLC	to Whitlock, Brand	March 17 [1919]	USC	
TLC	to Whitlock, Brand	Dec. 27, 1911	USC	Institute; Sloane wants to meet Chicago members

TLC	to Whitlock, Brand	Feb. 16 [1917]	USC	re: unspec. translations; Mark Sullivan
ALS	to Whitlock, Brand	Feb. 25	Columbia	elected to Cliff Dwellers
ALS	to Whitlock, Brand	April 5	Columbia	enjoys W's work; renews invite to Cliff Dwellers
*ALS	to Whitman, Walt	May 28, 1889	Congress	will attend WW 70th b-day celebration
*ALS	to Whitman, Walt	Oct. 18, 1888	Congress	is lecturing on WW at Waltham
*ALS	to Whitman, Walt	[June 1889]	Congress	re: "Whitman at Seventy"; is writing plays
*ALS	to Whitman, Walt	[Jand 10-11,1889]	NYPL	has spoken with Moulton about WW
*ALS	to Whitman, Walt	Nov. 24, 1886	Congress	introduces himself to W W
*ALS	to Whitman, Walt	April 19, 1888	Congress	is lecturing on WW's work
*ALS	to Whitman, Walt	April 15, 1890	Congress	finds growing respect for WW everywhere
*ALS	to Whitman, Walt	Nov. 9, 1888	Congress	plans to review *November Boughs*
*ALS	to Whitman, Walt	[April 3, 1889?]	Congress	has heard WW is ill
*ALS	to Whitman, Walt	Nov. 16, 1888	Congress	sends review of *November Boughs*
*ALS	to Whitman, Walt	[June 1889]	Congress	sends draft of "Whitman at Seventy"
*ALS	to Whitman, Walt	Oct. 24, 1888	Congress	thanks for *November Boughs*
TLC	to Wilcox, Alice Wilson	Nov. 27 [1912]	USC	
TLC	to Wilcox, George	Oct. 30, 1911	USC	
ALS	to Wilkinson, Marguerite	July 31	Middlebury	appreciates W's Verse; visit w/ Frost
ALS	to Williams, Ben Ames	May 4 [1927]	Colby	praises *Splendour*
ALS	to Williams, Mrs.	Feb. 1899	Penn HS	cannot come to unspec. event
TLD	to Williams, Sophia	n.d.	USC	crosses
TLC	to Williams, Sophia	Feb. 11, 1939	USC	crosses
TLC	to Williams, Sophia	April 19, 1939	USC	crosses
TLC	to Williams, Sophia	Tue.	USC	crosses
TLC	to Williams, Sophia	Feb. 1, 1939	USC	crosses
TLD	to Williams, Sophia	Jan. 27, 1939	USC	crosses; other psychic books planned
TLD	to Williams, Sophia	n.d.	USC	crosses
TLC	to Williams, Sophia	Feb. 5, 1940	USC	crosses; poor sales=no royalties

TLD	to Williams, Sophia	Jan. 26, 1939	USC	crosses; royalty agreement
TLC	to Williams, Sophia	n.d.	USC	crosses
TLC	to Williams, Sophia	April 15 [1938]	USC	crosses
TLC	to Williams, Sophia	June 2, 1937	USC	crosses
TLC	to Williams, Sophia	Dec. 26, 1937	USC	crosses
TLC	to Williams, Sophia	May 17, 1938	USC	crosses
ALD	to Williams, Sophia	Dec. 24, 1937	USC	crosses
TLC	to Williams, Sophia	Jan. 27, 1939	USC	crosses; contract
TLC	to Williams, Sophia	April 19, 1939	USC	crosses
TLD	to Williams, Sophia	Jan. 17, 1939	USC	crosses; royalty agreement
TLC	to Williams, Sophia	March 12	USC	crosses
TLC	to Williams, Sophia	April 21, 1939	USC	crosses; new contract —1/3 royalties
TLD	to Williams, Sophia	n.d.	USC	crosses
TLC	to Willsie, Honore	Nov. 4 [1918]	USC	
TLC	to Wilson, Ethel L.	June 28 [1931]	USC	address to Cedar Valley Sem honor
ALS	to Wilson, Harry Leon	Sept. 8 [1904?]	Bancroft	praises "Seeker"
ALS	to Wilson, James Harrison	Feb. 22, 1897	Congress	thanks for correction of "Jomini"
*ALS	to Wilson, James Harrison	Oct. 21, 1897	Congress	dispute over quoting W's words
ALS	to Wilson, James Harrison	[May] 30, 1897	Congress	asks for person who knew McClennand & Grant
ALS	to Wilson, James Harrison	[before Feb. 22, 1897]	Congress	arranges interview
*ALS	to Wilson, James Harrison	March 8, 1897	Congress	re: difference in viewpoint of Grant
*ALS	to Wilson, James Harrison	Feb. 11, 1897	Congress	aim in *Grant* vs "Grant" in *McClures*
ALS	to Wilson, James Southall	May 19 [1925]	Virginia	likes unspec. *Review*
ALS	to Wilson, James Southall	May 11 [1925]	Virginia	interested in unspec. *Review*
ALS	to Windsor, Phineas L.	Dec. 14, 1938	U of Ill	re: disposition of mss —not at U of Ill
TLC	to Windsor, Phineas L.	Dec. 22, 1938	USC	c. of U of Ill ltr
TLS	to Windsor, Phineas L.	Dec. 22, 1938	U of Ill	exhib; disposition of mss
TLD	to Wing, Willis Kingsly	June 18, 1937	USC	crosses; article about
*ALS	to Wingate, Charles E. L.	July 23, 1891	Virginia	thanks for article re: HG
TLC	to Winter, William	March 28 [1916]	USC	pleasure to aid unspec. cause
ALS	to Winterbotham, John	Nov. 18, 1894	Rosenberg	was not able to visit
TLC	to Withers, Lucius J.	June 1, 1914	USC	Authors League

TLC	to Withers, Lucius J. [by sec'ty]	April 4, 1914	USC	Chicago Thea Soc
TLC	to Withers, Lucius J.	April 20, 1914	USC	
TLC	to Wolbert, William	Feb. 21 [1917]	USC	*Captain* title won't be changed
TLC	to Wolbert, William	Feb. 27	USC	film adapt
TLC	to Wolbert, William	Oct. 17 [1916]	USC	film adapt; *Money Magic*
TLC	to Wolbert, William	Oct. 5	USC	film adapt
TLC	to Wolbert, William	Jan. 11 [1917]	USC	film adapt; title change
TLC	to Wolbert, William	[Jan. 7, 1917]	USC	film adapt: *Captain*
*TLC	to Wolbert, William	Jan. 31 [1917]	USC	film adapt; authentic costuming: *Captain*
TLC	to Wolbert, William	Jan. 31 [1917]	USC	film adapt; wants to assist cutting
TLC	to Wolbert, William	Oct. 3	USC	film adapt
TLC	to Wood, Douglas J.	Jan. 16, 1913	USC	Chicago Thea Soc
ALC	to Woodruff, C. R.	May 23, 1902	USC LB 60	re: lectures
TLC	to Woodward, Kathleen	April 25	USC	
TLC	to Wray, Henry Russell	n.d.	USC	
TLC	to Wray, Henry Russell	Jan. 18, 1912	USC	
ALS	to Wyckoff, Walter A.	June 14 [1904]	Wis HS	congrats on marriage
ALS	to Wyer	March 24	U of Iowa	HG has no book plates
ALD	to Yarborough, Grace	Jan. 30 [1932]	USC	
ALS	to Yard, Robert Sterling	July 5 [1913]	NYPL	submits *Son*
ALS	to Yard, Robert Sterling	Feb. 16 [1914]	NYPL	
ALS	to Yard, Robert Sterling	Feb. 7 [1914]	NYPL	encloses Herne article
ALS	to Yard, Robert Sterling	April 10 [1914]	NYPL	
ALS	to Yard, Robert Sterling	March 13	NYPL	
ALS	to Yard, Robert Sterling	July 29 [1913]	NYPL	asks for "plain estimate" of *Son*
*ALS	to Yard, Robert Sterling	Aug. 14 [1913]	NYPL	asks whether he should add love story to *Son*
*ALS	to Yard, Robert Sterling	Aug. 22 [1913]	NYPL	porno rant
ALS	to Young	June 22, 1936	USC	re: praise of *Forty*
ALS	to Young, J. C.	Nov. 6	Morgan	
ALS	to Young, J. C.	Nov. 9	Morgan	
ALS	to Young, J. C.	April 29	Morgan	
ALS	to Young, J. C.	June 18	Morgan	
ALS	to Young, J. C.	Thurs. 28	Morgan	re: collecting HG books
ALS	to Young, J. C.	Sept. 15	Morgan	
ALS	to Young, J. C.	Dec. 18	Morgan	
TLC	to Zueblin, Charles	March 9, 1912	USC	
TLC	to Zueblin, Charles	May 8, 1913	USC	
TLC	to Zueblin, Charles [by sec'ty]	Dec. 9, 1911	USC	
TLC	to Zweiger, William L.	Dec. 28, 1911	USC	

Title Index

On occasion Garland republished his fiction under a different title in various collections. The original publication is indicated by *see also* references in this index.

Library Index

The following lists Garland's correspondents held in each library.

Miami U (continued)
Bjorkman, Edwin
Bradley, John
Bradshaw, John H.
Brigham, Johnson
Bush
Campbell photographer
Case, Leland
Chubb, Thomas C.
Cliff Dwellers
Coburn
Collins, James
De Ferron, Mlle.
Dear Sir
Dow, Miss
Durant
Editor, *New York Times*
Elson [William Harris?]
Fairbanks, Douglas
Farran, Don
Freeman, Mary Wilkins
Fuller, Henry B.
Godfrey, Marjory W.
Gunn
Hagedorn, Herman
Hampden, Walter
Hatfield, James Taft
Hill, Eldon
Howells, William D.
Huntington, Archer
Johns
Johnson, Robert U.
Kimball, Hannibal Ingalls
Latham, Harold
Leup, Francis E.
Lincoln, Joseph C.
Lounsberry, Thomas
McKeighan, John H.
McKeyan
Mills, Emma
Minnich, Harvey C.
Paine, Albert B.
Risser, Miss
Rose
Roz, Firmin
Schad, Robert O.
Seitz, Don C.
Smith, Albert E.
Smith, Francis Hopkinson

Steed, Wickham
Stone, Herbert S.
Strandvold, George
Street, Julian
Sullivan, Mark
Thomas, Augustus
Thomas, Lisle Colby
Van Doren, Carl
Whitlock, Brand
Whom It May Concern
Middlebury
Browne, Francis F.
Cummings, Philip
Wilkinson, Marguerite
Minn HS
Wallace, Elizabeth
Morgan
[obliterated]
Caldwell
De Vaux-Royer, Madame
Duneka, Frederick A.
Harvey, George B. M.
MacDonald
Maynard
Meyer, Annie Nathan
Munro, David A.
Overton, Grant
Stoddard, Charles W.
Young, J. C.
Mt Holyoke
Marks, Jeannette
Nat'l Arch
Hughes, Charles E.
Jones, William A.
Lane, Franklin K.
Leup, Francis
Reel, Estelle
Roosevelt, Theodore
Newberry
[incomplete note or letter]
Carlton, W. N. C.
Cram, Ralph
Dennis, Charles
French, Alice
Fuller, Henry B.
Harrison, Carter H., IV
Hutchinson, Charles L.
Lithtig, Harry H.
McCormick, Joseph Medill

Pulitzer (continued)
  Matthews, Brander
Purdue
  Ade, George
R.B.Hayes
  Howells, Joseph A.
Rochester
  Hill, David Jayne
  Hilliard
Rosenberg
  Winterbotham, John
S Dak HS
  Robinson, Doane
SE MO ST
  Lewis, Mrs.
Smith
  Branch, Anna Hempstead
  Norton, Charles P.
Southwest
  Grinnell, George Bird
  Hodge, Frederick Webb
  Lummis, Charles F.
St Mary C
  Marie, Sister Frances
Stanford
  Craig, Miss
Swarthmore
  Bangs, John Kendrick
Syracuse
  Huntington, Anna Hyatt
  Huntington, Archer M.
  Isaacs, Mrs.
  Kipling, Caroline
  Mayfield, John S.
Temple
  Caplan, Albert
Tenn-Nash
  Mims, Edwin
Trinity
  Warner, Charles Dudley
Tulane
  Cable, George W.
U Cal-Davis
  Shields, Peter J.
U Chicago
  Herrick, Robert
  Monroe, Harriet
U of AZ
  Rouland, Minnie D.

  Rouland, Orlando
U of Del
  Donaldson
  Edgett, Edwin F.
  Holt, Hamilton
U of Ill
  American Academy
  Fackenthal, F. D.
  Halman
  Holmes, C. H.
  Kimball, Hannibal Ingalls
  Sherman, Stuart Pratt
  Stone, Herbert S.
  Stone, Melville E.
  Windsor, Phineas L.
U of Iowa
  Adams, Dr.
  American Academy
  Baxter
  Blodgett
  Butler, Ellis P.
  Clemens, Cyril
  Connelly, John R.
  Dear Sir
  Editor, *Bookman*
  Gessler
  Granberg, Fred
  Harrison
  Hickok
  Higginson, Thomas W.
  Holt, Dr.
  Meyer
  Meyer, Annie Nathan
  Norris, Edward Everett
  Perkins
  Ray, Henry Russell
  Redding, Judge
  Robinson, Doane
  Stone, Herbert S.
  Stuff
  Wyer
U of KY
  Knight, Grant C.
U of Mich
  Koch, Theodore
  Manny, Frank
  Pond, Irving K.
U of OK
  Eddleman, Ora V.